The Soul of a Nation

Culture, Morality, Law, Education, Faith

Bernard J. Coughlin

Hamilton Books

A member of
The Rowman & Littlefield Publishing Group
Lanham • Boulder • New York • Toronto • Plymouth, UK

Library of Congress Control Number: 2012904942
ISBN: 978-0-7618-5893-5 (cloth : alk. paper)—ISBN: 978-0-7618-5894-2 (electronic)

Contents

Preface

I was born and grew up in Galveston, Texas; In 1942 I moved to St. Louis, Missouri to join the Society of Jesus. As a Jesuit scholastic I taught for three years at Campion High School, formerly a fine Jesuit boarding school in Wisconsin.

I have had wonderful educational opportunities: as an undergraduate at Saint Edwards University in Texas before entering the Jesuits; then as a Jesuit at Saint Louis University I took undergraduate studies in Arts and Science and graduate work in Philosophy and Theology. After ordination as a Jesuit Priest I took a masters degree in Social Work at the University of Southern California and a doctoral degree at Brandeis University in Boston.

At the graduate School of Social Service of St. Louis University I served as dean from 1964 to 1974, and then moved to Spokane, Washington where I served as President of Gonzaga University for 22 years. In 1996 I retired from the presidency and now serve as Gonzaga's first Chancellor.

They have been wonderful years, both at St. Louis University and at Gonzaga University. Many who read this may know Gonzaga only for its outstanding basketball programs. It is indeed that, but it is far more. Gonzaga has a superior faculty and an excellent student body of some 7,500; a Board of Trustees that is exceedingly talented and committed to the University and its students. During my time as President I served on Spokane's Chamber of Commerce for several years, and was the Chamber's president in 1989. Spokane is a fine city of wonderful people, quality businesses and institutions, located on the Spokane River in Eastern Washington.

As one may imagine over all those years I gave many talks to students, faculty, alumni and civic groups, and wrote a lot of essays and reports. Some time ago several of Gonzaga University's Trustees urged me to write my memoirs and reflections on our society and its education: "write for young American men and women of our time, for our alumni, parents and friends. We would like to read what you have to say, and so would they."

That is what I have attempted to do. This collection of essays treats some aspects of our society's Culture, Morality, Law, Education and Faith. Many are extended, historical and philosophical in content; others are brief and less scholarly; some are quite serious; others are more casual. They treat subjects of social, ethical and political consequence. So they consider subjects that are not without controversy. One of our Trustees suggested they be published as "Letters to Young People." My hope is that many young people, and elderly as well, will read them and find them challenging. Some of them question the political drift of our society over this past half century. I am under no illusion that the reader will agree with everything I have to say; I am sure many will question, even disagree with some things I have written.

Since World War II there have been lots of changes in the society we call America, changes in our culture and population, our laws and how we interpret them, our values, our educational structures and goals; changes in our political parties, our schools and their approaches to education, changes in the churches and their leaders' moral messages to our people. Many of these changes, of course, result from changes in the view we have of ourselves, of our philosophy of man, and of the way we understand our civil and moral law and the consequences of our beliefs about faith and God, and about our Declaration of Independence and the Constitution.

As I have written I have had in mind not only the alumni of our nation's universities but all who live influenced by our culture, laws and ideals. I thank all who read these essays, and I invite your personal response, positive or negative, to what I have written.

I wish to thank four Gonzaga University Trustees who especially encouraged me to write these essays: Walter Conn, Chairman and CEO of Charles Dunn Company of Los Angeles; Jim Jundt, Founder and President of Jundt Associates of Minneapolis, presently residing in Scottsdale, Arizona; Duff Kennedy, Founder and President of Kennedy Associates of Seattle Washington; and Don Nelles, Founder and President of Nelco in Bellevue, Washington. These friends all chaired the Gonzaga University Board of Trustees and encouraged me to take on this task. But for their encouragement the work it required would probably not have been done. I thank them for that, for their friendship, and for all they have meant to Gonzaga University over many years.

I also wish to thank Adrian Pauw, Librarian, Gonzaga University for her secondary research assistance and Barbara Kolbet for her expert secretarial services. The assistance of both has been invaluable.

Bernard J. Coughlin, S.J.

Chapter One

Culture

ROOTS OF THE CULTURE

Culture is the combined concepts, manners, thoughts, values, and beliefs that characterize a group or civilization. Cultural determinants are the education, training, laws and philosophies that influence and shape the culture.

The culture of American society has generally been understood to have sprung from Western Europe. From its very beginning, Christianity shaped Europe's concept of the human person and its destiny. St. John wrote that God made this world His home. Thus the culture often called Christian Humanism begins there: the human nature of Christ is the sacrament of salvation; Christ uses the world and human nature instrumentally in salvation history. Under the intellectual leadership of the Apostles and early theologians, the Church taught that the human being comes from God and is destined for eternal union with God. Christian Humanism historically was forged out of the best of Western thought infused with Christian revelation. Some say that it reached a kind of peak with Peter Lombard, Bonaventure, Albertus Magnus and Thomas Aquinas in the Thirteenth Century, but it continues to develop as humans gain increasing insight into knowledge, science, and divine revelation.

Christian Humanism is worlds apart from Christian fundamentalism; which is suspicious of human intelligence and achievement. Fundamentalism denigrates the human search for scientific understanding and achievements. Fundamentalist spokesman the Reverend Tim LaHaye, taking a swipe at Thomas Aquinas, condemned the Church for reintroducing and synthesizing Aristotelian thought with Christian theology. "It is an irony of history," he scolded, "that a man who was sainted by his church as a scholar was responsible for reviving an almost dead philosophy, which has become the most dangerous religion in the world today — humanism."[1]

Well, as most people know there are two brands of humanism: Christian Humanism and Secular Humanism. Secular Humanism, sometimes known as modern behaviorism, accepts the notion that human intelligence and behavior are simply neurological responses to outside stimuli. Most secular humanists hold that there are no causes, indeed no reality, outside the physical universe; and man's freedom to decide is essentially an illusion.

Other schools of psychology and anthropology criticize this narrowness of secular humanists on two scores: that it reduces the human being to an automaton, simply a robot, and that its ultimate assumption breaches the scientific spirit of inquiry itself. To say that only the physically observable is real because it alone is subject to scientific observation, is like the notorious ichthyologist who seined the oceans with nets of one-inch-square mesh and finally declared to the world that there were no creatures in the sea with a cross-section smaller than one inch. Contrary as this is to the spirit of scientific inquiry, secular humanism has exercised a powerful influence on many educators and scientists, and students who sit at their feet.

Secular Humanism holds that the world in which the robots move is purposeless; it proposes to offer a set of new beliefs, supposed to be appropriate for a scientific age; and it has profoundly influenced American thought and education. Secular Humanists recently issued a *Humanist Manifesto* which documents that brand of humanism. Among its major elements are:

- "Humanism considers the complete realization of human personality to be the end of man's life and seeks its development and fulfillment in the here and now."
- There are "no uniquely religious emotions and attitudes of the kind hitherto associated with belief in the supernatural."
- Man alone "is responsible for the realization of the world of his dreams."[2]
- "[F]aith in the prayer-hearing God, assumed to love and care for persons…is an unproved and outmoded faith."
- "We find insufficient evidence for belief in the existence of a supernatural."
- "As nontheists, we begin with humans not God, nature not deity."
- "We can discover no divine purpose or providence for the human species."
- "The total personality is a function of the biological organism."[3]

Under this secularist influence many scientists teaching in the universities, and their students teaching in the primary and secondary schools, have written off religious longing as either superstition or intellectual immaturity;

religion, they teach, serves neurotic needs, which sooner or later should be cast off. As people mature, they are able to discard the crutch and face the truths of life as adults, taking responsibility for themselves.

Henry Miller, as long ago as 1961, expressed the conventional wisdom of Secular Humanism: "Civilized peoples don't live according to moral codes or principles of any kind. We speak about them, we pay lip service to them, but nobody believes in them. Taboos after all are only hangovers, the product of diseased minds, you might say, of fearsome people who hadn't the courage to live."[4]

Recently there have been swelling waves of reactions against Secular Humanism. The reactions are from two groups. First there is the swell from the masses. You can tell the masses only so long that their thoughts, loves, values, and motivations are simply nerve responses to external stimuli, and that the transcendent religious aspirations they are aware of are simply either neuroses or moral infantilism, which they must learn to outgrow. Only so long will they believe that their lives have no meaning beyond the good life, here and now. The *Humanist Manifesto* satisfies neither search for truth nor hunger for happiness. The masses cannot express it, but they intuit what Edmund Burke keenly expressed: "We know, and it is our pride to know, that man is by his constitution a religious animal; that atheism is against, not only our reason, but our instincts; and that it cannot prevail long."[5]

The masses might be unable to cope with scientific subtleties, but they know the ache of the soul. They bear it only so long, and then gush out in some esoteric ways — maybe hopping onto a Humanist Manifesto bandwagon, or responding in a variety of other restless, often irrational ways. One has but to recall the years of pop psychiatry and cultism, obsessions with faith-cures and grotesque forms of groping at something beyond the material, as seen in the popular fascination with horror, Satanism, and the preternatural thrills that the film industry is itself obsessed with.

Theodore Roszak blames Secular Humanism for this wild reaction of the masses. He grants that the secular humanists' original intention may have been to free human life from superstitions; but if their intention was to liberate, secular humanists themselves only oppressed. "[t]he repressive role of secular humanism in modern culture," he says is "a tragic overreaction to the obscurantism and corruption of the European ecclesiastical establishment: a justified anti-clericalism that has hardened into a fanatical, anti-religious crusade."[6] It has become a form of atheistic religion that slams the door in the face of human beings as they reach for transcendent being.

As a matter of its own stubborn dogma, Secular Humanism refuses to allow the questions of the mystery of life, and of human search for personal salvation even to be raised as legitimate intellectual questions. But when these questions are not raised, said Roszak, human religious aspiration

...runs off into many dead ends and detours. It easily mistakes the sensational for the spiritual, the merely obscure for the authentically mysterious....It may reach out toward emotionally charged, born-again religions that generally weaken toward smugness, intolerance, and reactionary politics.

Someday in some greater age of both faith and intelligence, when scientists and theologians have put it all together, we may look back on the intellectuals of this age as bad shepherds. As Roszak continues: "The secular humanistic establishment is confirmed in its hostility and proceeds to scorn and scold, debunk and denigrate...But, indeed, this is like scolding starving people for eating out of garbage cans, while providing them with no more wholesome food."[7]

Secondly, there is also a swelling reaction against Secular Humanism from certain intellectuals. They are embarrassed that secularism often called behaviorism, while being scientific in a very narrow sense, grossly violates the scientific spirit of inquiry; and they are embarrassed that so many educators and educational institutions ignore as irrelevant life's most meaningful questions. They suggest that this void in our educational agenda accounts for much of the drift in society. Sociologist Peter Berger expressed it thus: "I am impressed by the intrinsic inability of secularized world views to answer the deeper questions of the human condition, questions of whence, whether and why. These seem to be ineradicable and they are answered only in the most banal way by the ersatz religions of secularism."[8]

The philosophical engine that fires Secular Humanism along is Nihilism, which holds despair and destructiveness as positive personal and social values. Nihilism involves the denial of all existence and, by extension, the total destruction of current moral values and the substitution of negative doctrine. In The Brothers Karamazov, Dostoyevsky has Ivan accept and enunciate the philosophy that "everything is permitted."[9] With that, Camus says, "the history of contemporary Nihilism really begins. .....Ivan compelled himself to do evil so as to be coherent. He would not allow himself to do good. Nihilism is not only despair and negation, but above all, the desire to despair and negate."[10]

Traditionally people have been convinced that honor and dishonor, good and evil, right and wrong, stand for something real. Now apparently there is a growing disbelief that these things are objectively real. If not real, they are inconsequential. Owen Barfield, attorney and professor of philosophy at Brandeis University, recently wrote: "Look closely, and you will find there is today a widespread presupposition, subconscious for the most part, but raised to the level of consciousness in the philosophy of a value-free science, that there is really no such thing as quality. There is the useful and the useless, the desirable and the undesirable, and that is all."[11]

I said that nihilism prizes destructiveness. It breeds violence. For some nations violence is apparently a matter of national policy. For some individuals it is apparently a matter of not the slightest guilt. Guilt has no reality in a world without quality. Nihilism breeds on a philosophy of reality and a world view that rejects a constitutional order, and looks for salvation in the destruction of society. This political view must still be alive and well. We are alarmed by the waves of senseless violence and shocked by assassinations, and by the ever-cheapening value that people seem to have for human life. But there is a logic in it: If all our actions are simply responses of the central nervous system to outside stimuli, if there is no true quality in human actions, if honor and dishonor, good and bad are dubiously real, if despair and destructiveness are somehow positive things, and if in any case there is no ultimate purposefulness beyond the here and now, then all choices are equally meaningful, or equally meaningless — throwing a bomb, or assassinating a President or Pope, as meaningful or meaningless as an act of love.

That's how absurd human life can be made to appear. And many intellectuals find that an arid, unfulfilling intellectual prospect and the emptiest form of humanism, that offers people and nations only despair. I am saddened that large segments, perhaps the majority, of children in our schools and young men and women in our universities are educated with little, if any, exposure to the most important intellectual questions of all: Is human existence absurd? Are humans free, and what is freedom? What is the reason for human dignity? What is human life and its purpose? Does it possess comprehensive, ultimate meaning?

But, as I noted above, there are hopeful stirrings abroad among intellectuals and among the masses of the people. The cry of people for more than bread is being listened to and recognized as something other than neurosis. Could it be that there is a reawakening in the land, a hunger for meaning, which conceals a longing for God? These years immediately ahead may be the beginning of a new spring in our education and our culture.

ON MULTICULTURALISM

The big word in the academy these days is multiculturalism. It doesn't mean what you may think — that educators are revising curricula so that students are better versed in the language, history and culture of other nations and regions — a laudable objective. It's a political word with several shades of meaning: that cultures are equal, one is as good as another, none are superior to others; that from an educational point of view the study of one culture is as good as another; that, therefore, universities should make no educational value judgment about cultures, and students should study whatever culture they want. Multiculturalism is a derivative of relativism.

In virtually all American colleges and universities the backbone of the curriculum historically has been the best of Western Civilization; specifically, Christian theology, philosophy, arts and sciences, and the humanities. Thus students were introduced to the likes of Homer, Sophocles, Virgil, Cicero, Plato, Aristotle, Augustine, Aquinas, Descartes, Bacon, Dante, Chaucer, Milton, Shakespeare, Michelangelo, Botticelli, Wordsworth, Jefferson, Madison. That array of stars, says the multiculturalist, should be put on the back shelf, and universities should give equal play to area-studies and other cultural programs such as: Far East and Middle East studies, Asian and African studies, women's studies, homosexuals in history, art and literature, etc. As they all represent achievements of human beings, none should be evaluated superior to any others.

A few years ago the multiculturalists won a victory at Stanford when the University de-emphasized its Western Civilization program. A few years later, Yale University followed suit. The Yale affair received considerable attention from the media. Yale was pleased to accept a $20 million gift, but reluctant to use it as the benefactor wanted, namely, for the program in Western Civilization. The University's distinguished dean, Donald Kagan, a strong believer in the educational value of studies in Western Civilization, enthusiastically supported the designated use of the gift. In a speech to the faculty and University community he said: "It is both right and necessary to place Western Civilization and the culture to which it has given rise at the center of our studies, and we fail to do so at the peril of our students, our country, and of the hopes for a democratic, liberal society emerging throughout the world today."[12] That speech and the idea of using the $20 million gift for studies in Western Civilization provoked a storm among the faculty. Kagan was criticized. "Criticized" is too mild a word — some of the faculty called him a "racist" and one made the charge that "the major export of Western Civilization is violence."[13] The multiculturalists won the day, and the gift was returned.

Multiculturalism is the logical outcome of intellectual and moral relativism; there is no true and false, no good and bad. There are no norms against which to measure anything. Its roots go back to the Enlightenment. They called it "Enlightenment" because it was supposed that once religion was removed from education and public life, the human mind would return to its pristine elegance prior to its corruption by faith. Faith, said the Enlightenment enthusiasts, was an obstruction in the path of progress. It was supposed that religion had darkened and deluded the mind and held humans back from achieving their infinite perfectibility. In pursuing its agenda the Enlightenment distorted the history of the Middle Ages, and renamed them the Dark

Ages. The Middle Ages admittedly had their dark years, but they also had unquestionable achievements: in art, architecture, human rights, science, and monumental developments in philosophy and theology, the likes of which will probably never be equaled.

It was the Enlightenment and relativism that obliterated theology from American universities. It is a long and interesting story that has frequently been documented. By the end of the 19th Century, theology, which had been the crown of the curriculum, was removed, not only from the state universities, but from many major private universities as well. The great irony of the Enlightenment is that when it threw out faith, it put dimmers on the light of the mind. There have been no greater defenders of intelligence than the great Christian intellectuals who recognized faith to be not an obscuring cloud but an illumination.

The removal of theology from the university curriculum was the beginning of the removal of a great deal more. Historian George Marsden details how once theology was gone, the universities became outright hostile toward Christianity and much of what the universities formerly represented. "On the one hand," he wrote, "it is a story of the disestablishment of religion; on the other hand it is a story of secularization." The result has been "the virtual establishment of nonbelief, or the near-exclusion of religious perspectives from dominant academic life...In other words, the free exercise of religion does not extend to the dominant intellectual centers of our culture."[14]

The champions of relativism within the universities then went to work to remove philosophy, or at least that grand historical development in philosophy that stretches back to Plato and Aristotle, Augustine and Aquinas, and so significantly influenced Western Civilization. Look now at the philosophy curricula of many private and most public universities, and you might think that philosophy began with the Enlightenment. The long and illustrious tradition of Christian philosophy, developed by towering intellectuals over more than 1,000 years, the academy today treats like dinosaurs' bones. The questions that those great Christian philosophers raised, explored, and left as a rich philosophical legacy, are casually referenced as historical curiosities rather than serious questions of study. The bias against a metaphysical world led to the ignoring of metaphysical questions and discarding of the philosophical concepts that respond to those questions. Such concepts as being, essence, nature, spirit, form, soul, potency and act are not in the vocabulary of modern philosophy. Natural law is disdained, because it is thought to be a limitation on human creativity, perfectibility and freedom; it is not understood.

With theology gone and philosophy dismembered, what would be the backbone of the university curriculum? There was nothing much left but the humanities. So, not surprisingly, presidents and deans turned to those other great achievements in Western culture: literature, art, history, and science.

"Great literature, such as Homer, Dante, Chaucer, Shakespeare, and Milton, thus became the canon for a popular cultural idealism," wrote Marsden.[15] Thus, throughout most of the 20th Century the arts, sciences and literature have been the backbone of the university curriculum.

Now, multiculturalism threatens to be the third wave to roll over the curriculum. Should that happen, higher education would truly be a shambles. The prospect of such a shambles is not far-fetched. Our culture is charmed by the proclaimed truisms of relativism: whatever man does is true; whatever man does is good; there are no norms; there is no nature; as for cultures and civilizations, study whatever suits you, one is as good as another.

If you think I exaggerate, read Carolyn Fluehr-Lobban's article in the *Chronicle of Higher Education*.[16] Fluehr-Lobban is an anthropologist, a discipline that in its early years of development came under the influence of Margaret Mead. Relativism has long dominated the field.

The theory went like this — and Mead claimed to document it from her field studies: humans, tribes and cultures are not to be compared or judged, for there is no common ground, nature or norm by which to judge them. There is no such thing as morality, only mores, customs, and practices. Carried to its logical conclusions absolute relativism leads to absurdities. Which is the point of Fluehr-Lobban's article, which begins: "Cultural relativism, long a key concept in anthropology, asserts that since each culture has its own values and practices, anthropologists should not make value judgments about cultural differences."[17] Therefore, anthropologists have not participated in international conventions on human rights. Nor have they taken a stand on such practices as female circumcision, infanticide, or killing of the aged, as practiced in some cultures. By way of rare, unexplained exceptions, they did oppose Nazi genocide and apartheid in South Africa.

For 25 years Fluehr-Lobban conducted research in the Sudan where female circumcision is common. For many of those years she felt trapped between her professional commitment to moral relativism and the feminist campaign in the West to eradicate such "barbaric" customs that enslave women. She wrote: "To align myself with Western feminists and condemn female circumcision seemed to me to be a betrayal of the value system and culture of the Sudan, which I had come to understand. But as I was asked over the years to comment on female circumcision because of my expertise in the Sudan, I came to realize how deeply I felt that the practice was harmful and wrong." In 1993 at the Human Rights Conference in Vienna, female circumcision was on the agenda. "Those discussions made me realize that there was a moral agenda larger than myself, larger than Western culture or the culture of the Northern Sudan or my discipline. I decided to join colleagues from other disciplines and cultures in speaking out against the practice."[18]

Fluehr-Lobban began applying the same thinking to other cultural practices: the Japanese wife who feels honor-bound to commit suicide because of the shame of her husband's infidelity; the "honor" killings of sisters and daughters who are accused of sexual misconduct in some Middle Eastern societies; the genocide in Brazil and Venezuela of the Yanomami people which, says Fluehr-Lobban, "may allow the clearest insight into where the line between local culture and universal morality lies." Her article concludes: "When there is a choice between defending human rights and defending cultural relativism, anthropologists should choose to protect and promote human rights. We cannot just be bystanders."[19]

What Fluehr-Lobban has demonstrated is a clear process of reasoning from natural law: that there is a universal human nature with certain rights and obligations, and that there is a universal morality that must respect human nature wherever it exists.

This is insufficient evidence from which to conclude that recognition of natural law theory is returning, or that relativism among academics is on the wane, or that multiculturalism is nothing more than a fad. But natural law has survived more deaths than the cat. And I'll bet on its continued survival.

But why, you may ask, do I spend time thinking and writing about these things?

For a very good reason. Relativism is a disease that deeply affects our thought, our morals, our culture, and, as you see, our education. Such thought and such a culture is, as John Paul II wrote in *Veritatis Splendor*, "quite congenial to an individualist ethic, wherein each individual is faced with his own truth, different from the truth of others. Taken to its extreme consequences, this individualism leads to a denial of the very idea of human nature."[20] This comes to a denial of the dependence of freedom on truth, and of truth altogether, as John Paul demonstrates and as Fluehr-Lobban learned. University education, if it is concerned with anything, is concerned with truth, which relativism and multiculturalism treat so casually. That's why thinking about these things is so very important.

ON HIGH AND LOW CULTURES

The garbage we're surrounded by has many names: "cultural pollution," "cultural rot," "moral decadence," "moral anarchy," etc. Garbage stories fill the newspapers, weeklies and television. People make a living off the garbage by appealing to the First Amendment.

The argument goes like this: "If you don't like pornography and violence, don't look at it, don't listen to it. If it offends you, don't buy it. All you have to do is hit the remote control button and change channels. But people have a right to see it and listen to it if they want." According to Robert Bork, rejected by the Senate for the Supreme Court, the garbage is so bad that communities are gagging, and communities also have their rights; in this case, the right to a decent cultural environment. The First Amendment argument is "pernicious rhetoric because it asserts a right without giving reasons." Wrote Bork: "If there is to be anything that can be called a community, the case for previously unrecognized individual freedoms must be thought through, and 'rights' cannot win every time."[21]

When industrial plants pollute water and air, communities' rights are appealed to and recognized. Well, the media are polluters, at least as damaging as steel mills. "If it offends you, don't buy it," is a bad principle says Bork, because "whether you buy it or not, you will be greatly offended by those who do." Michael Medved supports Bork's argument: "To say that if you don't like the popular culture then turn it off, is like saying, if you don't like the smog, stop breathing."[22]

If you think cleaning up the smog is a tough job, can you imagine how tough it will be to clean up the cultural pollution — presuming we have the will to clean it up? As pornography and violence become increasingly popular entertainment, "attitudes about marriage, fidelity, divorce, obligations to children, the use of force, and permissible public behavior and language will change, and with the change of attitudes will come changes in conduct."[23] Bork is convinced that the cultural degeneration will get worse. "What we probably face is an increasingly vulgar, violent, chaotic, and politicized culture...."[24]

Irving Kristol agrees with Bork, and points a finger at the culprit: "Sector after sector of American life has been ruthlessly corrupted by the liberal ethos. It is an ethos that aims simultaneously at political and social collectivism on the one hand, and moral anarchy on the other."[25] The liberal ethos is winning the day, says Bork, because individualism and egalitarianism have such a strong hold on the American psyche. Radical individualism claims that freedom is an absolute right; as a result the traditional restraints that religion, morality and law exercise as social controls have already been jettisoned. Radical individualism has convinced the public, the lawmakers, and the courts that individuals have the right to indulge and to purvey the crudest sexuality and the grossest violence, and to sell anything, however vulgar and barbaric. At the same time egalitarianism has convinced the public, the lawmakers and the courts — and large sectors of the universitariat — that no set of moral values is superior to any other, that we live in a morally and culturally relativistic world. There is no truth, there are only facts: therefore, no action, behavior, human choice or product is better than any other.

As a result, we have bought wholesale into "multiculturalism, sexual license, obscenity in the popular arts, an unwillingness to punish crime adequately and, sometimes, even to convict the obviously guilty." It is bad now, but it will get worse. Said one pornographic network operator: "This thing is a freight train."[26]

Bad culture drives out good culture, and bad money drives out good money. Take Time Warner, for example, whose music division is deep into rap music which parades such stuff as the fun of cop-killing, and the thrill of slicing women's throats. The Time Warner Board is said to be ashamed of the division's low standards and would like to get out of rap music. Yet the Board has done nothing about it. It's big money. Sometime ago Willie D., formerly of Geto boys told USA Today that he has some reservations about his startling lyrics, now that he has a month-old daughter; but "I have to put food on the table. For me it's a business. I say it to get paid." What did Willie D. say most recently to get paid? "A woman deserved to be raped and murdered because she had left her curtains open."[27] That's what daddy gets paid to sing.

While Willie D., under the protection of the First Amendment, sings of raping and murdering, to the supposed shame of the Time Warner Board, out in Salt Lake City another kind of First Amendment comedy is taking place. Notwithstanding a court order not to sing a certain song at a high school commencement because it used the words "Lord" and "God," one of the graduating seniors jumped to the stage and invited the choir and audience to sing "Friends," the lyrics of which go like this: "Friends are friends forever if the Lord's the Lord of them." Whereupon the principal silenced the crowd and had the student physically removed from the stage and not allowed to receive his diploma during the ceremony.

What kind of a First Amendment do we have that allows Willie D. to sing to national audiences about raping, slicing and murdering, but forbids graduates to sing the word "Lord" at commencement? How long will it take for the courts to forbid performances of Handel, Bach and Beethoven, and displays of some of the greatest painting in Western history? The Amendment seems to be discouraging the finer things we used to think were "good" and encouraging the grubby things we used to think were "bad."

Is it that we have built up such a tolerance for garbage because we are losing our taste for finer things? How is it that violence and gross sex are so pleasing to us? Are our cultural roots so quickly rotting? Have our intellectual and spiritual foundations so suddenly washed away?

Have we lost faith? Early on, for our first 100 years as a nation, faith clearly influenced our foundations, laws, mores and morals. But during this last 100 years, while we won two great wars, we seem, in their aftermath, to have given up care for our morality. Future civilizations will copy our technology, but, at the rate we are going, they will find little worth copying that has come from the nation's soul.

During the entire 200 plus years of our national life we have produced great technology, but few if any great metaphysicians. We have had a few recognized spiritual leaders, but even they are better classified as organizers, promoters, social reactionaries, or church statesmen. I mention metaphysicians, recognizing that most American universities no longer teach metaphysics.

"A barbarism of the spirit" is Notre Dame's Gerhart Niemeyer's characterization of our culture.[28] God is eliminated from our thoughts, because He has been eliminated from our world. Our universe, we are told, is simply a great clock, eternal and self-regulating. We see its hands, wheels, and balances, and know how they operate. We see nothing more; only the things we can touch, missing the soul of the world. We look at a tree, and see only a tree; a rose bush that year after year gives us roses, and we think nothing of it. We look into the eyes of a friend, and see only eyes. We miss the surprise and wonder that Chesterton knew when he wrote: "The wonder has a positive element of praise...and this pointed a profound emotion always present and sub-conscious; that this world of ours has some purpose; and if there is a purpose, there is a person."[29] We are unable to appreciate the wide-eyed exuberance of St. Anselm: Why, — there is, indeed, "something rather than nothing"![30]

Faith brings wonder, because it opens the door into mystery, teasing the mind, inviting to the search for infinity. When faith fades, cataracts form over the eyes of mind and soul, spiritual vision clouds. The prophet first said it, and great Christian minds have often repeated it: "Unless you believe, you will not understand."[31]

The founders understood that. They built the nation, as their lives, on faith.

The writings of John Adams abound with such phrases as "an overruling Providence"[32] and "devotion to God Almighty."[33] John Dickinson wrote: "We claim them from a higher source —from the King of kings, and Lord of all the earth."[34] Even Jefferson, Deist as he apparently was, filled his writings with such phrases as "God who is just," "a benevolent creator" who "rules the destinies of the universe," "His is an overruling providence."[35] Those were our roots? Have they so soon rotted?

The universe — just a great, mechanical self-regulating clock! And the people who inhabit it, no less mechanical — only a mass of protoplasm, intricate and complicated to be sure, but just a physical mechanism, fixed, unfree and amoral, responding determinately to the environment. We have it on the authority of those who should know, those who bear the title "professor" in prestigious universities: that the great clock of the universe, and all living things that dwell therein, are mechanical, self-regulating machines. God is beyond the pale. Such concepts as divine law, natural law, divine grace, good and evil, truth, soul, and freedom have been removed from our textbooks and classrooms.

A short time ago I received a letter from an alumnus of Gonzaga who is a distinguished professor, nationally recognized, in one of the most prestigious universities in the country. He wrote:

> I read your essay in your Presidential Report. Your belief concerning a university education is a courageous and most unusual statement. I refer to your 'I believe...' and the four following sentences on page 3. This credo deserves a wider exposure.
>
> My University, lost in the swamps of multiculturalism, should hear you. But it will not listen for some time to come. [36]

The sentences in my annual report to which he referred are these:

> I believe our universities have a responsibility in the arts, sciences, statecraft, education, business and the professions to do a job that's a cut far above the average. Excellence is required, and it begins in homes and schools. I believe that there are intellectual and moral hierarchies, that some knowledge is more important than others, some values more important than others, that not all cultures are equal in intellectual and moral achievement. Not everything is of equal value. Some things in life are more important than other things. So, curricula vary in their potential to educate. We should offer students the best, and we should expect the best of them. [37]

Now, why does this experienced educator think this "a courageous and most unusual statement"? Unusual? Courageous? It strikes me as sad that his university "will not listen for some time to come" to a statement such as this.

Why won't they listen? Because the roar of politicized faculty is once again sweeping over the universities. I am sure his university was represented at the January 1993 annual meeting of the Modern Language Association of America. Roger Kimball, managing editor of The New Criterion, was there and in a Wall Street Journal editorial, commented on that roar of the politicized faculty. The 32,000 member MLA is the largest and most influential scholarly organization in the country. In Kimball's view, "it has also become one of the most blatantly politicized." Kimball has attended MLA meetings for years, and has long been entertained by radical professors. In his view, the 1993 convention set a new standard, besieged as it was by "57 varieties of Marxism, feminism, homosexualism, anti-dead-white-European-male-ism, all dispensed in a smug academic double-speak." [38]

The public imagines that MLA scholars annually convene to discuss the latest scholarship on the likes of Chaucer, Milton, Shakespeare and Browning. But "the real action, and crowds," says Kimball, "were at panels devoted to 'Cultural Studies' — a fancy term for radical political sermonizing — and other defiantly nonliterary subjects."[39] It's not that the venerable literary figures were not on the program. They were — but mainly to give legitimacy to hidden agendas. "What seemed like a class on, say, Shakespeare, is really a platform for denouncing 'Western Colonialism and Imperialism.'" All the glitzy exotic stuff was there. Sex, of course: one panel discussed "The Ins and Outs of Lesbian Sex: Bi-Morphic Representations of Desire." Another eye-catcher was "Lesbian Tongues Untied." And feminism, too: one session discussed "Status of Gender and Feminism in Queer Theory," and another: "Hermaphrodites Newly Discovered: The Politics of Gender." Kimball wryly adds that there were "many other papers of 'literary' interest."[40]

In his presidential address the MLA president encouraged teachers of literature to "subordinate literary concerns to the task of fostering radical political activism." Taking advantage of his position and this platform, he "scoffed at the idea of imparting 'reading skills,' calling instead for 'local pedagogy,' his currently favored term for political activism."[41] If that sounds like an echo from the '60s, it is.

Several weeks later and a few miles away, the Prince of Wales addressed a college audience at the College of William and Mary. His message:

> We are joint heirs to what I believe to be one of the richest languages the world has ever known, and which now dominates the world. In diplomacy and law, business and the arts, sport and academic, English rules. But it will not rule, and will have no right to do so, if we do not guard it and guide it, fight for the highest standards and see it as our shared responsibility to do so.[42]

Whew! Pretty stodgy stuff! Prince, you'll never get on the MLA program with that! Returning to Mr. Kimball's concluding comments of this year's MLA convention:

> This leaves us with two questions: Will students continue to allow themselves to be cheated of an education by teachers who are more interested in radical politics than imparting knowledge? And will parents, trustees and alumni continue to capitulate as our educational institutions are transformed into centers for political indoctrination and cultural radicalism? The spectacle of the MLA does not encourage optimism.[43]

For some folks multiculturalism means teaching and learning about cultures other than one's own. That brand of multiculturalism is a welcomed educational development for students, and all of us should become more knowledgeable of other languages, beliefs, mores and thoughtways than our own, and come to appreciate them.

But there's that other multiculturalism which is purely and simply shorthand for political agendas. It disguises someone's notion of what is politically correct. And if you're not politically correct, you're not in, and you'd best not speak your mind. As my correspondent sadly wrote: "My university, lost in the swamps of multiculturalism ... will not listen for some time to come."

Listen to what? To a truism that one would expect all university professors to profess: That there are intellectual and moral hierarchies, that some knowledge is more important than others, some values more important than others, that not all cultures are equal in intellectual and moral achievement. Knowledge development, yes; and greater understanding, appreciation of, and sensitivity to other peoples, cultures and their histories, of course. But not fads, and not political agendas masquerading as culture. True education and universities true to the cultivation of the mind and the pursuit of truth, do not become mired in sexual, racial, ethnic, national, or any other political swamps. To profess to search for truth, but to declare there is no truth, only preferences and politics — that makes of a university a lie.

M. Scott Peck, physician and psychiatrist, consumed the teachings of those learned "professors," and thought himself wise. We rarely miss what we have never possessed. After a lifetime of study and medical practice, Dr. Peck reflected on the blind spots in his education. For years, he had treated patients who were often tormented by sinful lives and evil — a thing he did not understand, for in the lexicon of moral relativism there is no evil, as there is no good. Then, finally, having come, like Solzhenitsyn, from under the rubble, he summarized his reflections:

> I had received no training on the subject. It was not a recognized field of study for a psychiatrist or, for that matter, any supposedly scientific person. I had been taught that all psychopathology could be explained in terms of known diseases or psychodynamics, and was properly labeled and encompassed in the standard Diagnostic and Statistical Manual. The fact that American psychiatry almost totally ignored even the basic reality of the human will had not yet struck me as ridiculous.[44]

"The basic reality of the human will" is still "almost totally ignored" by our learned professors. Of course. It is a metaphysical reality.

There are a few of those learned professors who suspect that there must be something more than the great mechanical clock. So, says Niemeyer, they "sit at their desks seeking to produce 'values' by a sheer effort of the unaided mind." The best they can come up with is "an emotional babble of value-idioms, none of them more than a clever guess."[45]

The future of our culture? Says Niemeyer: Great on technology, rotten in its soul: "In all possibility, of all civilizations, ours is the most glittering, most astonishing, most inventive, most organized, most wealth producing one in human experience. As a network of technology, industry, trade, management, political and private organizations, science, education, and services it appears to function with amazing vitality. But at the spiritual, moral, and intellectual core rottenness is visible and expanding."[46]

Will we settle for that? Only, I believe and hope, in the short run. Maybe for a generation or so. But we will bounce back. We were made for more. God told us what we are, to our continual surprise and astonishment. "And God said: 'Let us make man in our own image, in the likeness of ourselves.... and in the image of God he created him.'"[47]

Philosophers and theologians explain it this way: we are intellectual and free beings, made to know all being, even the Supreme Being, and to love Him. Our very metaphysical make-up destines us to possess God in knowledge and love.

"Barbarism of the spirit" we can tolerate for a while. But, in time, an in-the-image-of-God spirit will find a way to clean up the culture.

ON SOPHOCLES AND CULTURE

A short time ago, in search of a paperback for airplane reading, I picked up Sophocles' Oedipus the King and enjoyed yet again a classic that I hadn't read for years.[48]

I imagine that all that most people know about Oedipus is that he was a Greek who was involved sexually with his mother; that Sigmund Freud developed a psychological theory according to which some kids are prone to grow up envious and hateful of their fathers because they control mothers' love — reams have been written about "penis envy;" that this early childhood struggle and conflict can produce adult males whose relationships with men and women are haywire; and that this phenomenon Freud called the "Oedipus complex."

In the real Oedipus, Laius, King of Thebes, had been murdered. Oedipus married the widowed queen, Jocasta, and, now King, is called by God to avenge Laius' murder by finding the murderer and driving him out of Thebes. He accepts the challenge with a vow: "I stand forth a champion of the God and of the man who died." It is fitting that he should be the avenger of Laius' murder, says Oedipus, "since I am now the holder of his office, and have his bed and wife that once was his."[49]

Oedipus never knew his father, because his father, having learned from the Delphic Oracle that he would die a victim of his own son's hands, left the infant in the forest for the wolves. Oedipus' father was Laius. Oedipus survived the wolves of the forest, and years later, journeying along the highway, he was provoked by a stranger, and in anger killed him. The stranger was Laius. Thus, as the tragedy unfolds, Oedipus learns that not only had he killed his father, but is now married to his dead father's wife. In anguish he laments:

> Who is then now more miserable than I,
> What man on earth so hated by the gods....
> I and no other have so cursed myself.
> And I pollute the bed of him I killed
> By the hands that killed him. Was I not
> Born evil? Am I not utterly unclean?[50]

When Jocasta learned into what evil fate had trapped them, she hanged herself; and when Oedipus discovers her dead body, he gouged out his eyes with Jocasta's brooch.

Several days later, while still mulling over the power of the tragedy and the issues that Sophocles deals with, I came across the following review by Michael Medved of a 1990 film, "The Cook, the Thief, His Wife and Her Lover:"

> This is not a film for the faint-of-heart—or the delicate of stomach. It begins with a scene showing the brutal beating of a naked man while the main character gleefully urinates all over him. It ends with that same character slicing off a piece of a carefully cooked and elegantly prepared human corpse in the most vivid and horrifying scene of cannibalism ever portrayed in motion pictures. In between, we see necrophilia, sex in a toilet stall, the unspeakably bloody and sadistic mutilation of a nine-year-old boy, another victim smeared with feces, a woman whose cheek is pierced with a fork, and an edifying scene with two naked bodies writhing together ecstatically in the back of a truck filled with rotting, maggot-infested garbage.[51]

They say that art reflects the culture. Happily, not all American movies are like "The Cook, the Thief, His Wife and Her Lover," which, in Medved's assessment, is "...unrelieved ugliness, horror and depravity at every turn."[52] One doesn't have to be an avid devotee of movies to know that they dish up brutality and sex, raw and depraved. Nothing is left to the imagination, and nothing is offered to either mind or soul. Sex is presented for the sake of sex, violence for the sake of violence. The audience is carried beyond neither to some more noble thought and emotion.

Oedipus also deals with sex and violence, and Sophocles was a master in their use in drama: not being engulfed in those emotions, he carries the audience to more profound emotions and ideas in portraying human tragedy. Today's unsophisticated audience, drenched as it is with the vulgarization of sex and the goriest of violence, hardly knows that Sophocles is dealing with the great issues of life: the struggle between good and evil; the individual conscience as it confronts the authority of the state; fate and human suffering; justice and injustice; God and human destiny; sin, divine retribution and forgiveness. *Oedipus* is a classic. The classics are works of enduring excellence that deal, not with ephemeral, but with enduring themes in a refined and ennobling way.

The Greek philosophers stood in wonder before nature, trying to understand it. They asked profound questions that philosophers ever since have continued to ask. The Greek tragedians sought to dramatize those questions as they impact human lives. Art reflects culture. What profound questions, I wondered, might be dramatized by urinating on a naked man being brutally beaten? What enduring theme? What refinement? Sophocles, please!

ON OPEN AND CLOSED MINDS

A few years ago Allan Bloom's book *The Closing of the American Mind*, was the talk on many college campuses. Bloom was Professor of Social Thought at the University of Chicago. The book has received high praise from eminent scholars and a "ho-hum" response from others, for reasons that will be clear if you read on.

The central themes of the book are not new to students of social thought and American culture, but from the book's reviews I've read, those themes are shocking to most American academics. That a leading academic could think the way Bloom does is, in their view, to say the least, outdated and out of vogue. So what does Bloom say that comes as such a shock to so many American students and their professors?

As every student knows, our Declaration of Independence begins "We hold these truths to be self-evident, that all men are created equal, that they are endowed by their Creator with certain inalienable rights...."[53] Well, what surprises some about this book is that Bloom actually believes those things — that there is such a thing as "nature" and a fundamental moral order, and that there are some absolutes. He obviously thinks that Aristotle had something worthwhile to say, not only to the Greeks, but to us as well. This is shocking to many of the academic establishment who consider Aristotle an intellectual antique. But in Bloom's view, it is precisely scientism's narrowness that has most contributed to the closing of the American mind. The American mind is so open, he argues, paradoxically, that it is closed.

"There is one thing a professor can be absolutely certain of," Bloom begins his book: "almost every student entering the university believes, or says he believes, that truth is relative….they are unified only in their relativism and their allegiance to equality….it is the modern replacement for the inalienable natural rights."[54]

Whether they are theists or atheists, left or right, business or professional, today's students are schooled in one overriding value: openness. They are taught to accept everything. The only moral evil is to be discriminating and judgmental. "What right," they ask, "do I or anyone else have to say that one culture, one view of life, one opinion is better than another?" As Bloom says, "The purpose of their education is not to make them scholars but to provide them with a moral virtue — openness."[55] Everything is equal — there is no truth and so no falsehood, there is neither right nor wrong, there are just different views of the world and ways of living. They are taught one virtue: to be open and accepting of everything, because everything is relative.

Bloom demonstrates that this openness is intellectual suicide, because it closes the mind. "Openness used to be the virtue that permitted us to seek the good by using reason. It now means accepting everything and denying reason's power. The unrestrained and thoughtless pursuit of openness without recognizing the inherent political, social, or cultural problem of openness as the goal of nature has rendered openness meaningless. Cultural relativism destroys both one's own and the good."[56]

Aristotle and the Western philosophical tradition taught that there is such a thing as the human good, and that reason and free choice are with reference to intermediate goods that are seen as conducive to the human good. The task of reason is to discriminate in making choices because not all things are equally conducive to the human good. Absolute relativism and absolute equality close the mind to reason.

Our nation's Declaration and Constitution were founded on a far different kind of openness; namely, the openness of people and the law to reason as the means of finding truth and discovering the good. That form of openness accepts that all ways are not equal, that there is a truth and a good that is worth seeking, and reason can discriminate the true from the false, the good from the bad. The founders rested the regime on the philosophical tradition that goes back to Aristotle: that there is a good worth pursuing. Again, Bloom: "the awareness of the good as such and the desire to possess it are priceless, humanizing acquisitions."[57] Cultures are not all equal, and the human person is not doomed blindly to pick simply what suits his fancy at any given place and moment in history.

"Men cannot remain content with what is given them by their culture if they are to be fully human....Nature should be the standard by which we judge our own lives and the lives of peoples. That is why philosophy, not history or anthropology, is the most important human science."[58]

The founding fathers indeed believed that there were some fixed stars, which guided the founding of the Republic. Reason's reading of the moral order as visible in nature was what the United States promises. "Or, to put it otherwise, the regime established here promised untrammeled freedom to reason — not to everything indiscriminately, but to reason, the essential freedom that justifies the other freedoms, and on the basis of which, and for the sake of which, much deviance is also tolerated."[59]

Most students in American universities today are schooled in skepticism about reason. Relativism reduces them to this skepticism: If everything is equal, why break one's head? If there is no truth, so there is no ignorance. "To deny the possibility of knowing good and bad is to suppress true openness."[60] So the mind is closed to the ultimate intellectual pursuit.

Bloom's is not a book on philosophy, but on universities and teachers and how they have steeped themselves in cultural relativism, thus grossly failing their students. He speaks with eloquence of teachers, and how the real teacher knows that "his task is to assist his pupil to fulfill human nature against all the deforming forces of convention and prejudice." As a kind of midwife, the teacher assists in the cultivation of the student's mind and soul. "There is no real teacher who in practice does not believe in the existence of the soul, or in a magic that acts on it through speech."[61] The teacher's function is, above all, to set for the student "a condition of investigating *the* question, 'What is man?' in relation to his highest aspirations as opposed to his low and common needs."[62] The question that every young person asks and often agonizingly explores is "Who am I?" That question in the first place means, "What is man?"

Universities that ask every other question and give every other answer, but fail to address that question, close the mind to what students seek above all else to know.

ON FREEDOM AND EQUALITY

Recent United Nations Conferences have attempted to shake and awaken the world to attend to the massive inequalities of access to such basic needs as water and food, clothing and housing. Equality now seems to be first on the world's agenda. It is a feverish movement, a drama that is variously played out across the world: in some regions major legislation effects social change that successfully narrows the gap between the classes; in others mere palliative acts only postpone the final event; and in others still nations erupt into bloody revolution. Some Western nations do not know what course to choose, and in their hesitation swear a double allegiance, with the right hand to Adam Smith's *The Wealth of Nations*, and with the left to Karl Marx's *Capital.*

Meanwhile, analysts debate the future of capitalism. The extent to which the West will continue to be capitalistic is anyone's guess. In Moss' opinion, Great Britain has entered into communism by the back door. It is not a Russian imported Communism, not a conscious adoption of the principles of Karl Marx. He calls it communism with a small c, not a capital C, but communism nonetheless, for the end result is the same. It is his opinion that "Britain has traveled more than two-thirds of the way toward becoming a fully communist society, and that it is increasingly probable that it will either complete the journey or have to endure the most shattering social and constitutional crisis the country has known since the 17th century."[63]

In a BBC interview in London, Alexander Solzhenitsyn expressed the same fear not for Great Britain alone, but for the West. When asked how the Russian people can go forward and resolve the tensions and oppression that overwhelm them in the Soviet Union, he replied: "...the question is not how the Soviet Union will find a way out of totalitarianism but how the West will be able to avoid the same fate. How will the West be able to withstand the unprecedented force of totalitarianism? That is the problem." Later in the interview he said: "I wouldn't be surprised at the sudden and imminent fall of the West."[64]

Heilbroner thinks that capitalism is so deeply entrenched in the American social and economic system that the United States will not succumb, but that the rest of the world will turn to some form of socialism or communism. As he wrote:

> All these considerations point to the very great likelihood that communism or radical national collectivism will make substantial inroads during the coming generation or two, perhaps by conquest or subversion, but more probably by the decay of existing orders unable to handle the terrible demands of political awakening and economic reformation. On the other side of the world balance sheet, it is far from hopeful that American capitalism will add many names to its side of the book.[65]

If this is a reasonably accurate outlook, what will be the impact in America? Is the system of privileges in a Communist society more or less just than in a capitalist society? Considering justice in human relations, what commitment to equality should this nation make? How much equality can a free enterprise system stand? How much inequality can it tolerate? What forms of inequality does it require? How much freedom can be guaranteed in a society committed to equality? It is the struggle between freedom and equality.

The New Equalitarians want not only equality before the law and equality of opportunity, but equality of condition and result. They champion a movement that intimately fuses spiritual and political values into a marketable ideology. The movement's message appeals to spiritual, even redemptive, ideals that arouse revolutionary instincts and generate guilt in an affluent society. "It would be hard to exaggerate," Nisbet says, "the potential spiritual dynamic that lies in the idea of equality at the present time."[66] The messianic tone in Jenck's statement is obvious: "If we want substantial redistribution, we will not only have to politicize the question of income inequality but alter people's basic assumptions about the extent to which they are responsible for their neighbors and their neighbors for them."[67] Like many social movements, egalitarianism sweeps away all opposition that it encounters, equality before the law opening the door to economic and social equality which in turn leads to equality of result. In short, the new egalitarians propose that equality be the cornerstone of national policy.

On the other side are those who think that in a democratic society freedom, not equality, should be the cornerstone of national policy. The relationship between these two values is not easily managed. Freedom implies an absence of constraints on human behavior. Its full meaning goes beyond this negative idea of "freedom from" restrictions, to the positive idea of "freedom to" become. It implies a range of psychological and social traits that include individuality, variety and differentiation, ingenuity and creativity in art and science, economic and social life. The complete meaning of freedom embraces the notion of self-realization and human fulfillment. As the egalitarians rightly point out, for its adequate functioning freedom demands certain requisite social and economic conditions, some of which are so fundamental as to constitute basic human rights. Democratic societies have achieved a remarkable degree of political freedom; but that is not enough. It is of little practical value for the state to guarantee citizens political freedoms, if the social and economic conditions under which many people live — homeless, diseased and hungry — render impossible even the minimal human fulfillment. With the break-up of feudalism, many people found themselves for the first time freed, but as they wandered from town to town, many soon found themselves worse off than they were as serfs. Political freedom is a useless gain unless accompanied by social and economic gains. This is the reason that some modern societies have committed themselves to guaranteeing all citizens some minimal level of food, shelter, clothing and health care.

Here freedom and equality meet. A serious commitment to political freedom is a commitment to some social and economic equalizing. Are there limits to this equalizing? Advocates for equality of result seem to say "no." But even Marx seemed to think that there are limits to equality. Men, he says, "would not be different individuals if they were not unequal."[68] Riesman goes a bit further: "The idea that men are created free and equal is both true and misleading. Men are created different; they lose their social liberty and their individual autonomy if they try to become equal to each other."[69] Kristol sees the freedom-equality debate in terms of democratic as contrasted with republican government. Democracies and republics are distinguished by the confidence they place in the "common man." In a democracy "the will of the people," but in a republic "the rational consensus of the people"[70] is supreme. In a democracy where politicians may be demagogues, popular passion may rule; in a republic, where there are not supposed to be politicians, only statesmen, means are taken to subdue passion to reason. "In a republic, a fair degree of equality and prosperity are important goals, but it is liberty that is given priority as the proper end of government. In a democracy, these priorities are reversed: the status of men and women as consumers of economic goods is taken to be more significant than their status as participants in the creation of political goods."[71] Dahrendorf attempts to state the taut interrelationship of liberty and equality in the following way:

> As a stimulus, a medium, and a reward of personal self-development, social stratification is essential to human freedom. The more monolithic, the less differentiated, a society is, the more it restricts its citizens' chances of liberty; the more pluralistic and differentiated a system of social stratification is, the more easily can it do justice to the citizens' multifarious individual needs and talents. Once equality of citizenship is assured, inequality of social status is necessary to the chance of liberty.[72]

These issues raise poignant questions: What are the appropriate uses and limits of power? Who should have what and how much? How can people in a stratified society live together harmoniously? How much redistribution of resources can a free society tolerate? Can love and power coexist? In American public policy, where should the priority be: freedom or equality? What ethical principles require equalization? Can freedom for all citizens be practically realized short of equality of result? Can people be equalized economically without minimizing or destroying freedom altogether?

In speaking some years ago to the graduates at the Gonzaga University Commencement, I had in mind such social issues as power, equality, freedom and the sanctity of life, when I called upon Gonzaga's graduates to face the moral dilemmas and make the moral choices that will shape the world of tomorrow. Each age must take up the task of renewing society's moral reservoirs. As I said to the graduates:

> You have more to do than stand as sleepy sentinels over ancient values. Justice and truth and freedom and human rights are not ideals that are safely embalmed and forever permanent treasures. They are alive in you, or they do not exist at all. It is the task of each generation to recreate them in the behavior of

its people, to struggle with the dilemmas of new moral choices, and to make
the moral choices that not only affect your personal lives but shape the world
about you.[73]

The social justice movement will continue to generate intellectual discussions and political activity. It would be uncharacteristic of an intellectually
enlightened age, such as this is supposed to be, for this discussion to be
carried on without research, knowledge and creative insight from the intellectuals. Discussion of issues such as these belongs in our universities,
among students and faculty. The nature of the social issues themselves, the
urgency of the social justice and human rights movements, the mission that
the Gospels impel us to — all three lay upon universities throughout the
world an undeniable challenge.

ON ART AND ARTISTS

Art is a controversial subject, and artists frequently are controversial people,
I suppose that's because people disagree about what's beautiful and about
what's in good taste. Apparently this has always been the way with art. I am
told that people threw stones at Michelangelo's *David* as it was being transported for exhibition in the public square opposite the Palazzo Vecchio.
Nude art, they said, was shocking enough, but to behold one of God's biblical heroes nude, was, for some, outrageous. As a young man Rodin himself
witnessed public outrage against Carpeaux's *The Dance* when it was un-
veiled on the façade of the Paris Opera.[74]

Quite a few years ago, thanks to the thoughtfulness and generosity of Iris
and Bernie Cantor, Gonzaga University received a number of valued pieces
of bronze art by Rodin for our museum; and we came to learn that our new
friend, Rodin, was himself the cause of major artistic controversies. Aside
from the controversies that art engenders, many simply regard it as one of
life's superfluities, engaged in only by elites and dilettantes. People have
always asked: Who needs art, anyway? What useful purpose does it serve?
Even the Greeks railed against Pericles because he spent money to finance
Phidias' *Athena Parthenos*, money that could have been spent to finance the
war against the Persians.[75] The argument is made that as long as people need
food, clothing, clean air and water, public monies should not be spent on art.
Saint Bernard of Clairvaux complained that the churches were clothed in
gold while many of the faithful were in rags.[76] But Bernard must have been a
lone voice in that wilderness, otherwise the medieval and Renaissance cathedrals would never have been built.

But to return to the controversial nature of art and artists, new styles and traditions in art, as in other things, come from pioneers and their genius. What is stylish, decorous and tasteful is a matter of opinion and culture. Ordinary artists either go along with traditional styles and culture, or if they break step attempting to create something new, they clumsily fall on their faces. Geniuses may part from tradition, creating new visions and setting new styles, but they inevitably find themselves in a vortex of controversy.

Rodin's teachers introduced him to the artistic standards of his time — classical composition, with bodies well-formed, poised and graceful and figures with looks of intelligence, breeding and dignity; if the theme of art was noble then subjects and composition should be noble, beautiful and pleasing. Public art, moreover, should present a model of ethical conduct.

But Rodin couldn't go along with all that. He accepted the traditional purpose of art as being to educate, elevate and delight; but he rejected the notions of beauty as defined by the prevailing artistic culture, and he did not think that art should carry the heavy moral burden that tradition had placed upon it. While he accepted the artist's responsibility to seek and portray the beautiful, he rejected any artistic dogmatism that insists on one absolute rule of beauty to which all artists should aspire, and he did not pursue beauty as an end in itself. Rather he relativized beauty, often giving it a supporting rather than a leading role.

But he suffered the consequences of his rebellion. His art was suspect from the start, and *The Thinker* was brutally criticized. What was to be recognized only years later as a masterpiece was originally dubbed savage and brutal, and its maker no more than a superior technician.

But Rodin had his defenders, those who understood him and what he was struggling with: that beauty and truth are found in all conditions of life and that lasting art comes from profound insight into reality and from deeply held personal convictions about it. One does not stand before the *Burghers of Calais* and dream "How beautiful!" One rather reflects on justice and injustice, and is led to think about sacrifice and love, brutality, fate, nobility, devotion and patriotism. And one surely does not stand before *She Who Once Was The Helmet Maker's Beautiful Wife* and sigh "how beautiful." One reflects on youth and age, time, hardship, disillusionment, infirmity and death. From there one is somehow drawn into the metaphysical meaning and beauty of things.

Rodin grew up in a France and Europe that were boiling with social unrest. As a young man he had entered the seminary to study for the priesthood. He felt a spiritual unity with other human beings, and considered himself bound in brotherhood with other workers. Other great sculptors had celebrated the hero statesman and athlete, churchman and soldier. Rodin would celebrate the worker-peasant, the little man. Gabriel Mourey said

"[*The Thinker*] is… no longer the exceptional being, the hero. This is our brother in suffering… It is no longer a superhuman being, one predestined, it is simply a man of all times…"[77]

To those who knew him he was a "son of the people," who had labored for many years, misunderstood, unacclaimed, and unjustly treated. The Thinker is a kind of self-portrait. Rodin seems to have had far more faith in the average man than did his contemporaries and critics. He believed that the common man, no less than the elite, is capable of appreciating art, for he is no less sensitive and responsive to the broad range of human emotions.

Of *The Thinker* Pierre Baudin said: "His is not an illustrious name, he is not famous…. He is a strong, muscular, well-balanced, calm individual who is afraid neither of his solitude nor his nothingness. He measures the value of the victory achieved by the long past of sorrows, anguish, misery, joy, and greatness, which he must make ever more far-reaching."[78]

The word poet comes to us from the Greek, *poietes*, through the Latin, *poeta*. Its root meaning is a maker, one who creates. So every artist is a *poeta*. From his own deep and impassioned look into some aspect of reality, he is seized by a meaning and beauty that he wants to express. What he creates is a kind of extension of himself. What is it? What does it say? I suspect that great artists never answer that question. It is what it is, and the thing itself says what it is. In a sense it is the artist, being an expression of his struggles and culture, values, thoughts, aspirations and ideals. It is for each viewer to be in its presence and see what it is and hear what it says. And if it is a great work of art, it will always inspire another look.

In time Rodin prevailed. Perhaps because the common man prevailed. Perhaps because, as another poet put it, even the most common things are "charged with the grandeur of God."[79] Poets like Hopkins and Rodin find that grandeur in everything, and the rest of us are the richer for their insights.

Those who say of art, "Who needs it anyway?" might reflect on Our Lord's words: "Man does not live by bread alone."[80] The great cathedrals of Europe were built by the pride, dignity and inspiration of ordinary people — built out of joy. They had a bread that I wish we all had. How rich they were — exemplifying the oxymoron of St. Francis, "It is in giving that we receive."[81]

Yes, we need art. And we will have it whether or not we realize the need, for "out of the fullness of the heart the mouth speaks."[82] It is not a superfluity, but another avenue to truth. No less than philosophy, theology, science and history, art is an essential for a university and an education. It elevates taste and style and fosters a sense of beauty in addition to itself being a search for meaning in life's events.

Perhaps one reason we have so much shallow art and hucksters who make a living on inferior, seemingly often dreadful stuff is that our tastes are so unrefined. Lacking sustained exposure to first rate art, we settle for junk that nourishes only baser tastes. Universities have a job to do — as they develop the intellect they should also develop and refine student's tastes and sensitivities and their aesthetic sense and appreciation of beauty.

WHO, THEN, WILL TEACH THEM?

Both the academics who theorize about things and the community and civic leaders who make decisions about them, seem forever to haggle over which responsibilities belong to the family and which belong to the schools. In my view, teaching ethics courses in universities has little real effect in making students ethical in their behavior unless they have already as children been schooled in moral training by their parents. Teaching courses in our schools with the aim to convert immoral into moral practice runs the risk of the fallacy: teach ethics, and you will prevent immorality. The rush in universities to teach ethics courses is an apparent response to our cultural demand for quick fixes. Schooling in virtue should begin far earlier than the university and even well before K-12; it should begin in the family.

I came across a recent statement by Harvard's former President Derek Bok, who is even more despairing of the university's effectiveness in teaching moral behavior:

> Few educators would assert that it is possible to devise a college program which is likely to help significantly in fostering such important characteristics as honesty, integrity, generosity, or even creative imagination. Under present circumstances, therefore, it would be arrogant to claim the development of these qualities among the purposes of undergraduate education. [83]

What the university can do was perhaps suggested long ago by St. Thomas Aquinas when he wrote:

> Three things are necessary for the salvation of man: to know what he ought to believe; to know what he ought to desire; to know what he ought to do. [84]

St. Thomas was always pretty strong on intelligence — which the present generation seems pretty soft on. Before we can begin to act rightly, he thought, we must have knowledge and some moral principles on which action is based. So what can the universities do? They can provide students with some insight into a moral system and the principles underlying it; they can introduce the student to the moral dimensions and questions that life holds; and they can show students how ethical decisions are arrived at. They can teach students what, according to a system of moral principles, they *ought* to believe, what they *ought* to desire, and what they *ought* to do.

Unfortunately, most American universities today do not do even this, because there is no *ought* in their vocabularies. *Ought* implies the distinction between moral right and wrong, good and evil, sin and virtue. For most universities and their professors, truth is relative, so *ought* has been replaced by *values* and values are simply *preferences*.

But even schools and universities that recognize the absoluteness of truth, that there are some things that one ought to believe and desire and do — even those schools are limited in instilling virtuous behavior in students, unless the foundations are already well laid in the family. And what the family can do is considerable and crucial. So when the family fails, the failure can be catastrophic. So it is a great mistake to slough off from the family responsibilities that only the family can effectively perform.

Allan Bloom writes of the high responsibility of the family and of its failure to do the lofty things for children that families are supposed to do. He writes not of those tragically broken homes, but of the ordinary American family which is more or less happy. Where husband and wife love each other and get along and are concerned about the children. But, as he recently wrote, "They have nothing to give their children in the way of a vision of the world, of high models of action or profound sense of connection with others."[85] The family takes care of the children's physical and emotional needs, but rarely gets into the more intricate reaches of children's personalities. Those inner regions of the child's soul need to be nourished.

> The family requires the most delicate mixture of nature and convention, of human and divine, to subsist and perform its function. Its base is merely bodily reproduction, but its purpose is the formation of civilized human beings. In teaching a language and providing names for all things, it transmits an interpretation of the order of the whole of things. It feeds on books, in which the little polity — the family — believes, which tell about right and wrong, good and bad, and explain why they are so.[86]

If there is truth to this high-sounding statement on the family and the lofty opportunity that it has to give children a vision of the world and set them along that course, one must ask such down to earth questions as: What, then, are the books that children are feeding on? What ideals do they see exemplified, lived and held up in that "little polity?"

The American image of the successful American family is one that teaches its children how to make a good living and be economically independent. Too few families consider sharing with children a common culture, history, principles, traditions and spiritual ideals as important elements in successful family rearing. Children need to develop a sense of their heritage, of their connectedness to the present and the past. Again Bloom:

The parents must have knowledge of what has happened in the past, and prescriptions for what ought to be, in order to resist the philistinism or the wickedness of the present. The family has to be a sacred unity believing in the permanence of what it teaches if its ritual and ceremony are to express and transmit the wonder of the moral law, which it alone is capable of transmitting and which makes it special in a world devoted to the humanly, all too humanly, useful.[87]

The problem is, of course, that only a few families have the faintest notion of the wonder of the moral law and the tradition that embodies it is publicly disregarded. "And fathers and mothers have lost the idea that the highest aspiration they might have for their children is for them to be wise — as priests, prophets and philosophers are wise. Specialized competence and success are all that they can imagine."[88]

Many parents are at a loss because they themselves do not know what they believe and so have no self-confidence in telling their children. So they wish off that responsibility to the school and the university years. But it is a vain hope that parents have, for by that time in a child's life those critical years with parents — the child's best teachers — have been lost. In any case, the same moral and spiritual disorientation that hampers the family affects the schools and universities. They, too, are often hollow moral instructors, not knowing what to believe and lacking self-confidence in telling their students.

If kids face a tough time growing up, it is because the spiritual landscapes of family and school alike are so barren.

MOVE OVER, MONKEY

Is the human being qualitatively different from other animals? For most of us this used to be a philosophical and speculative question having little or no relevance to our day-to-day lives. Although it was probed in university philosophy courses, it was not grist for the public forum.

The answer to the question was assumed: Humans and brute animals are essentially and qualitatively different. As least from Aristotle on, Western philosophy had recognized a specific and so qualitative difference between the human animal and the brute animal. For centuries, indeed for millennia, Westerners probed the nature of the human being and the relation of human life to other forms of life and, relying on both philosophical and theological reasoning, concurred with the tradition that stretches back many centuries.

But today, as that philosophical tradition is unknown to most, and blurred to the eyes of even those who are familiar with it, the concurrence is weakening. So the question is now being raised, not out of speculative interest, but as a practical concern of intense public debate: Is the human animal qualitatively no different from other animals?

When I say that the Western philosophical tradition for millennia acknowledged that human and brute animals are specifically and qualitatively different, I don't mean that Western society universally and consistently acted on that philosophy. There are inconsistencies. But the public uproar that accompanied those inconsistencies only verifies the strength of the accepted tradition; the exception proved the rule.

In 18th Century America, for example, there were many who said: Yes, human beings, except for blacks, are qualitatively different from other animals. You may enslave black humans and tie them to your plough, as you do your horse. It took a civil war to bring people back to the sense of the tradition.

In this century, the Nazis said: Yes, human beings, except for Jews, are qualitatively different from other animals. You may use Jews for biological and medical research experimentation, even exterminate them if they're an inconvenience, as you do rats and jack rabbits. It took a world war to bring people back to the sense of the tradition.

Still later in this century, the United State Supreme Court said: Yes, human beings are qualitatively different from other animals — except for unborn humans, which you can scrape away, chop up and flush down the toilet, as you do a scab. That was a great aberration from the tradition. But as yet, no war has erupted to bring people back to the sense of the tradition.

And maybe there will be no war. Maybe our generation will see another tradition rise and prevail. In the late 1980's a group called Trans-Species Unlimited rejected the tradition altogether and endorsed another view. They said: Human beings are not qualitatively different from other animals. Trans-Species Unlimited is an animals' rights group which challenges the right of human beings to experiment on brute animals for scientific purposes. You may not experiment on rats, they say, because they are no different from us. Peter Singer is the organization's leading spokesman, who believes that humans and brute animals are qualitatively identical and that scientific experimentation on rats and cats is "a form of prejudice no less objectionable than prejudice about a person's race or sex."[89]

Researchers find that attitude unacceptable, because for centuries the advancements that have been made in medical and biological research have depended upon animal research experimentation.

Profound questions are being raised, which cannot be ignored, questions with profound moral significance: What is a rat and a monkey? Are they moral beings? What is a moral being? What are human beings? What is the difference between them? Are there certain things about humans that make them inherently more valuable than other animals?

Peter Singer and Trans-Species Unlimited hold that both brute and human animals are of the same species, there being no qualitative difference. They don't say whether both are mere brute animals or both are humans. In any case, they hold that both should be treated alike. I assume they hold that rats are of the same moral stature as humans. If they thought neither to be moral, I imagine they would cease giving lectures urging scientists to stop experimentation. But that still doesn't explain why they don't give lectures to the rats urging them to protest the research experimentation to which they are subjected.

Bill Bennett, former Secretary of Education in the Reagan Administration, has been stumping the importance of continuing to teach Western culture, history and philosophy in our schools and universities. More than a few of our Universities have taken their lumps for downgrading the great books of Western culture in exchange for an ephemeral diet of modern class, race and sex literature. Bennett scathes educators who blindly embrace cultural relativism, apparently convinced that one culture is as good as another, one society as good as another, one philosophy of life as good as another. Bennett believes that the Western philosophical and cultural tradition has made a unique contribution to civilization and that we junk it to our great jeopardy. Yet there seems to be something about that old "barbarian within" that would have us believe: One animal is as good as another.

Don't you believe it!

DANGEROUS TO YOUR HEALTH!

A few years ago the President of the United States spoke to a Hispanic audience in Southern California that was mourning the death of a 2-year-old girl killed in a drive-by gang shooting. Deploring this killing and the general violence in our cities, the President said that it was time to crack down and take back the streets from criminals. However, cracking down on crime, he said, is only part of the solution: We must do more than simply make ourselves safer on our streets. We need more to say yes to…Our disregard for life is seen coast to coast. Indeed there does appear to be a disregard for life in this country, and arguably the most blatant disregard for life is the annual slaughter of over some one million human lives in the womb, lives who never have the opportunity to say yes to anything.

While the President was speaking, Dr. Kevorkian was jailed for putting aged people to death. Hundreds of sympathizers rallied to his support, going on national television to proclaim that Kevorkian is right, and the law should be changed. Judge Richard Kaufman in Wayne County, Michigan, agreed with Kevorkian and declared that the state law against assisted suicide is unconstitutional. The state, he said, should allow physicians to kill; it is the "reasonable" and "rational" thing to do when a person's quality of life is so low.[90] Carried to its logical conclusions, this ruling would allow the state to decide who is fit to live and who deserves to die. Once society no longer recognizes the sacredness of human life, and God as its author, then the state will move in and act as author of life and death.

While the President was telling us to take back the streets, others, disgusted at the violence and sex that flood radio and television, were clamoring: "Take back the airways, also!" However, on November 23, a Federal Court in Washington said: "You can't take them back!" Previously the Federal Communications Commission and Congress, in an attempt to clean up television programming, had tried to enact a 24-hour ban on "indecent" material; but the court struck down that attempted ban.[91] So the FCC sought a compromise with the sex and violence industry: Suppose we allow "indecent" material from midnight to 6:00 a.m. only?[92] No way! said the industry; we want the right to air indecent material around the clock. You may have it, said the Federal Court.

The FCC defines "indecent" programs as those that contain language or material that describes "in terms patently offensive as measured by contemporary community standards...sexual or excretory activities or organs."[93] The Commission said: We don't think children should be exposed to this stuff: But a broad coalition of individuals, interest groups, broadcasters and producers objected, demanding the right to show violence and indecent sex 24 hours a day. And, what about the kids? The answer came back: That's the parents' problem. In effect, government has no control over violence and indecency; we are publicly and officially 24 hours a day over radio and television a violent and indecent society, if we want to be.

In recent years drive-by shootings have taken a back seat to mass killings in the schools. Kids in high school are carrying guns, bullets, and bombs into the schools and teachers and classmates are being killed. The television, movie, video game and rock music industries are under fire; so is the gun industry. Everybody from local school superintendents to the Congress and President are scurrying around yelling: "We have to do something!" But the best that people seem to come up with are band-aid solutions like: double locks on semi-automatics and switch controls on television sets.

At issue, of course, is the First Amendment right of free speech. Previous courts have recognized that free speech is not an absolute right. One may not scream "fire" in a public theater, just for the fun of it; bodies may be damaged. But minds and sensibilities can be damaged, too. The question of priorities is a valid question. The government and the courts have great concern for the physical environment — lakes, streams and rivers, the spotted owl, grizzly bears and snail darters — and have enacted laws and put heavy sanctions on anyone who violates those laws or endangers those properties or animal species. But when it comes to the moral environment and the human species, our public stance seems to be: that's not government's business.

I recognize some consistency in the way courts decide many of these public issues. Take the schools, for instance: religion is supposed to be excluded from the schools; anti-religion is not. A teacher may not teach Christianity; but he may mock religion, in the name of academic freedom. In fact, the state will subsidize that! The Federal Appeals Court ruling in the FCC case is consistent with the rulings in school cases: You may not pollute the lakes and streams; you may pollute the airways and classrooms.

In other areas we are very inconsistent. Take the regard for life of which the President spoke. The government requires that all cigarette packages warn pregnant women that smoking may be dangerous to their baby's health.[94] Yet the law allows the killing of babies. Can you imagine the Surgeon General proposing that Congress require a sign over every abortion clinic, "abortion is fatal to your baby's health"?

I am not sure I really understand that saying, "If they do this in the green wood, what will they do in the dry?"[95] However, it may have some applicability here. If the leaders in our society are so confused about protecting life while sensationalizing violence, and indecency, and killing the unborn and the infirmed aged, can we expect the young and marginally educated to respect life, to be peace-loving, humanizing, decent people? If the courts and legislatures, the media and entertainment industry appear to have such disregard for life, and to glamorize violence and indecency, what can we expect from our youth?

SOMETIMES FAR LESS THAN ANGELS

Christ Our Lord said, "If they have hated me, they will hate you."[96] At three o'clock on a November morning, two women and six Jesuits suffered the blows of that hatred.

They were in Central America to bring peace. Of the Jesuits, four had come from Spain; two were Salvadorians, also Salvadorians were a mother and her 16-year-old daughter, who lived in the Jesuit residence as cook and housekeeper.[97] The Jesuits were professors at the University of Central

America, teaching theology, sociology, and philosophy. They taught and preached, by word and example, the Gospel of justice and human rights, love of God and love of neighbor.

A university is a place where reason exists, if it exists at all, for a university's purpose and primary commitment is to the preeminence of thought, rationality and understanding. The Jesuits were highly educated and competent teachers who were attempting to have reasonableness prevail, even among the "death squads," in that caldron which is Central America.

But the handwriting was already on the wall in sinister forms: violent threats against the hierarchy and the Jesuits, especially against the President of the University; bombs that were detonated near the University residence; and a violent press campaign demanding the expulsion of certain Jesuits from El Salvador.

When the blow fell, it was brutish, as from a mad animal. In the middle of the night they were roused from their beds; then the assassins sprayed the eight bodies with bullets and smashed their heads. As the Jesuit Provincial for Central America reported, they were tortured before being slain, and "They were assassinated with barbarity. For example, they took out their brains."[98] "I visited the site of the brutalities when one year later, the farmers and laborers from miles around came to El Salvador to commemorate the anniversary of this tragedy.

As I read and listened to the grisly accounts of that deadly night I thought of Aristotle's definition of the human being: classified in the genus of animal, he is specifically different from the brute by reason of his rational life principle. We are indeed animals, having all the potential of brutes, but brutes with the power of rationality, because immaterial and immortal souls animate our bodies. Animals, but "a little less than the angels"[99] withal, as scripture says of us.

When Aristotle considers human behavior in general, and the virtues in particular, he points out that the brute side is for the sake of the rational side, and that human intelligence should govern and direct the animal in us. It is up to reason and rationality to reign in the passions and direct them toward just and good ends.

When brutes fight over food and mates, the only recourse nature affords them is to scrap it out, to blood and sometimes even to death. Humans have reason. When we disagree over what's right and just, we have language and ideas, intelligence and the power of conversation, and a will to seek out the good, even in an adversary. We have the power to get outside of ourselves and understand others and their points of view, and through reason to compromise and reduce conflict and find harmony. So we are called human and said to be civil, to be able to build cities and develop civilizations. Civility is something we take pride in, for it suggests the absence of brutishness, and the presence of reason, culture and refinement, courtesy and politeness in social affairs. None of these things were present in El Salvador that early morning when the death squad did its work.

A few nights later on television I watched that crowd of 100,000 people in Winceslaus Square in the center of Prague. One hundred thousand people raised their hands and voices in peaceful protest and called for the resignation of the Communist Party leader.[100] Those who were asked to resign looked down solemnly from their high positions. It was a tense scene. The crowd waved like a field of wheat on a hot summer day — the smallest torch would start the wildest flame. At the snap of a hand, iron wheels could roll over and crush that crowd.

But that didn't happen. Rationality prevailed. Though the crowd resolutely forced the leadership to look at the depths to which their country had sunk, no arms were drawn, no orders given, no threats made. On both sides, reason ruled. The confrontation was carried out sanely with words, not tanks. The world watched in uncertain hope. What a hell it would have been had either side broken from civility and set a torch to the grain.

Unlike Prague there was no civility in El Salvador. The world still watches Central America and waits, hoping that ultimately, and soon, reason will prevail over brute force. We wait in hope that the deaths of the Jesuits and their companions, along with thousands of others killed in El Salvador, will somehow be the seed for new life. We pray, as Pope John Paul II wrote to Father Peter Kolvenbach, Superior General of the Jesuits, that "their sacrifice may not be in vain, but may be the seed of brotherly love and harmony for the country of El Salvador."

DEATH FOR SALE

Carol Everett is the author of *Blood Money*, an autobiography, both grisly and shocking, of her success in the business world.[101] She is a mother of two living children, a talented, ambitious, and successful businesswoman, and, by her own account, is, or at least was, exceedingly greedy.

You may not like what you are about to read. Some will object to it. If you have a squeamish stomach, you might stop right here. But, believe me, I have greatly toned down and even eliminated the more nauseating descriptions in *Blood Money*.

I say it's grisly because Carol's business was a bloody and grisly business — abortions, and her book does not spare the reader's sensibilities. It graphically describes scenes that pro-abortionists object to. Like the interview Carol had with Sheryl:

"Do you have the money, Sheryl?"

"Yes, I do. Can the abortion be done this evening?"

"Yes, it can be done right away. Come in for the examination." After the brief examination, Carol invites Sheryl into her office. "Sheryl, you thought you were eighteen weeks pregnant, but Dr. Johnson found you to be twenty weeks when he did the pelvic examination. At this stage the cost is more, and you will have to pay another $125. Do you have the money?

"No, we could barely come up with $375." Carol insisted and Sheryl pleaded. But Carol stood her ground; she was a hardened pro: "Well, we'll just hold the $375 until tomorrow. I am sure you will come up with the additional $125." The next morning Cheryl handed over the additional $125. [102]

Then came the grisly part, removing the infant from the mother piece by piece. With some difficulty, Dr. Harvey Johnson got the baby's body out, and was searching for the head. Carol wrote from years of observation: "This largest part of the baby's body is usually the last to come out. The head must be located and crushed before it can pass through the cervix. Usually it is first deflated — by suctioning out the brain and all the other contents." When Dr. Johnson called, "Suction, please," Carol turned on the machine, and the roar of the motor startled Sheryl. "Be still, Sheryl. That's the sound of normal procedure equipment. Take another deep breath. It's almost over." Johnson handed the suction tube back to Carol and once again used forceps to probe for the head. Carol's description continued: "I saw the muscles of his right arm tighten and knew what that meant: he had located the head and was crushing it. Harvey used to joke about getting 'tennis elbow' from this technique, and his right arm was actually slightly larger than his left." [103]

A short time later Sheryl was patted on her head and sent on her way. To be sure that nothing was left inside the girl's body, Dr. Johnson counted all the body parts and sent them down the disposal. But two days later Sheryl died. The coroner's report: …hemorrhaging from a cervical tear. [104]

"What did we do wrong?" Dr. Johnson shrugged his shoulders and replied: "Carol, if you deliver enough babies, a mother will die. Women will die in childbirth. We have been very lucky to have avoided a major complication before now. Our number was just up. We can't worry about it. We have to go on. If we can make it without a story getting into the newspapers, we'll be okay." [105]

The shocking part is that this is a business. Only the wildest stretch of the imagination would call it medical practice.

And it's big business, consisting not only of the abortion clinic itself, but the all-important referral centers. Girls and women come to the clinic through referrals that have only one aim — to sell the abortion. In the case of the North Dallas Women's Clinic, where Carol worked, "Advisory Referral Centers" affiliated with the clinic were strategically located, first at Irving, Taylor and Shreveport and then, as business grew, at Tyler, the Mid-Cities, Abilene and Waco. They were non-profit referral centers advertised to offer free sexual counseling and free pregnancy testing; being non-profit, they got free advertising through public service announcements. The purpose of the ARC's was to channel business to the NDWC. "Remember," a new ARC director was instructed, "we are mainly interested in the pregnancy tests, because we can funnel the pregnant women into our clinics in either Dallas or Fort Worth. We'll pick up a lot of business that we would otherwise miss." The location of the referral centers was important. The center at Irving, Texas, for example, was "on Highway 183 near two high schools. We should see a lot of girls."[106]

Carol's forte was marketing the business, and on the side she assisted doctors in the clinic. She was very successful: "The number of abortions performed at the clinic was less than 150 when I started. The first partial month I was in charge we had 168, the biggest month NDWC had ever had. We were now going well over 300 abortions a month, soon to reach 400."[107] Forty-eight hundred a year at an average of $400 per abortion — that's $1,920,000 a year. Carol said that in her business career she had sold 35,000 abortions. At an average of $400 per abortion — that's $14,000,000.

She and her colleagues realized that those goals would never be reached if they limited their practice to first-trimester abortions. "We need to start doing second-trimester abortions. We can really increase our business if we start doing bigger ones."[108] So they moved it up to twenty weeks, terminating pregnancies in the fifth month. Business swelled, but so did the greed. "What do you think about going to twenty-four weeks?" Six months into pregnancy. "It'll increase our business — and our revenue — significantly." Dr. Johnson mulled over Carol's recommendation and decided: "Let's do it to twenty-three weeks, Carol. That'll give us a one week margin of error." That's how Sheryl Mason died. And that's how the clinic got involved in cover-ups. "We were maiming at least one woman a month."[109]

Take the case of the Arkansas woman who was thought to be twenty weeks pregnant. Once Dr. Johnson started the abortion, they discovered that the baby was too far advanced. Carol described what happened:

> Its muscle structure was so strong that its body wouldn't come apart. After almost an hour on the table, with six nurses holding the woman and pulling her away from Harvey, the baby's body finally separated from the head…After the procedure, the doctor measured the baby's foot. He tried to hide the measure-ment from me, but I saw it — the baby was about 32 weeks along, probably old enough to survive outside its mother….the baby's body was too long to go down the garbage disposal, so Harvey suggested I take it to our competitor's

trash receptacle, so that if it were found, it would be in their trash, not ours. Dutifully, I wrapped the baby in a paper drape, put it in a brown paper sack, and planted it, after dark, in the other clinic's trash.[110]

A few days ago the State of Washington executed a young man who confessed to heinous murders of several young children. The death penalty became a matter of public debate. Demonstrators favoring execution and the use of capital punishment argued: Human life is so sacred, so great a good that anyone who unjustifiably takes another's life forfeits the right to his own life. On the other side, protesters against execution and the use of capital punishment argued: Killing, even hardened criminals, only makes us like those whom we execute. If there is logic to that argument against the death penalty, what transformations must take place in those who kill, not hardened criminals, but infants in the womb, who kill, not because a life has unjustifiably been taken, but simply for money, or for convenience's sake?

Seen in this light, what makes abortion most macabre, is not that the abortionist is saved from the death penalty, and not that he goes scott free, but that the law declares that he has a right to torture and mangle to death the child in the womb, without offering any justification whatever.

That being the case, if I were a betting man, I would wager that it won't be long before the law extends this legal right of physicians to kill infants in the womb to the legal right to kill the aged. Then Dr. Kevorkian will have prevailed. A legal system that grants the right to kill the unborn without any justification whatever, will sooner or later grant the right to kill the aged, first to relieve them of their discomfort, and then maybe to remove those who are costly and an inconvenience. Then we may see Clinics for the Aged ringed with their "Advisory Referral Centers." Then these death clinics, too, will be big business.

Conscience is a strong, undeniable force that, as Shakespeare wrote, "makes cowards of us all."[111] After 35,000 abortions and abortion referrals, Carol Everett gave in to conscience and now admits that the money from those abortions was "blood money." She no longer works for the North Dallas Women's Clinic. But others have taken her place, and thus as Mary Ann Glendon wrote, "the creeping degradation of life in our law and society, brought on by *Roe v. Wade* and its progeny continues."[112]

NOTES

1. Garry Wills, *Head and Heart: American Christianities* (New York: Penguin Press, 2007), 370, http://catdir.loc.gov/catdir/toc/ecip0714/2007012631.html.
2. "Humanist Manifesto I," American Humanist Association, http://www.americanhumanist.org/Who_We_Are/About_Humanism/Humanist_Manifesto_I (accessed 12/10, 2010).

3. "Humanist Manifesto II," American Humanist Association, http://www.americanhumanist.org/Who_We_Are/About_Humanism/Humanist_Manifesto_II (accessed 12/10, 2010).

4. Henry Miller, Frank L. Kersnowski and Alice Hughes, *Conversations with Henry Miller* (Jackson: University Press of Mississippi, 1994), 58.

5. Edmund Burke and J. C. D. Clark, *Reflections on the Revolution in France* (Stanford, Calif: Stanford University Press, 2001), 255, http://www.loc.gov/catdir/description/cam021/00063732.html.

6. Theodore Roszak, "On the Contemporary Hunger for Wonders," *Michigan Quarterly Review* XIX, no. 3 (1980), 303-321 (accessed 10 Dec 2010).

7. Ibid., 59.

8. Peter Berger, "Religion in a Revolutionary Society" (Christ Church, Alexandria, Virginia, American Enterprise Institute for Public Policy Research, 4 Feb 1974, 1974) (accessed 10 Dec 2010).

9. Fyodor Dostoyevsky, Richard Pevear and Larissa Volokhonsky, *The Brothers Karamazov: A Novel in Four Parts with Epilogue* (New York: Farrar, Straus and Giroux, 2002), 263, http://www.loc.gov/catdir/bios/hol051/2002022757.html.

10. Albert Camus, *The Rebel: An Essay on Man in Revolt* (New York: Knopf, 1956), 57.

11. Owen Barfield, "Language, Evolution of Consciousness, and the Recovery of Human Meaning," *Teachers College Record* 82, no. 3 (03/01, 1981), 428, http://search.ebscohost.com/login.aspx?direct=true&db=eric&AN=EJ246370&site=ehost-live (accessed 12/10/2010).

12. D. Kagan, "An Address to the Class of 1994," *Commentary* 91, no. 1 (01, 1991), 48, http://search.ebscohost.com/login.aspx?direct=true&db=a9h&AN=9104221850&site=ehost-live (accessed 12/13/2010).

13. Jennifer Kaylin, "Bass, Yale, and Western Civ." *Yale Alumni Magazine,* Summer 1995, 1995, http://www.yalealumnimagazine.com/issues/95_07/bass.html (accessed 13 Dec 2010).

14. George M. Marsden, *The Soul of the American University: From Protestant Establishment to Established Nonbelief* (New York: Oxford University Press, 1994), 6, http://www.loc.gov/catdir/enhancements/fy0639/93025486-d.html.

15. Ibid., 191.

16. Carolyn Fluehr-Lobban, "Cultural Relativism and Universal Rights," *The Chronicle of Higher Education* 41, no. 39 (Jun 9, 1995), B1, http://proxy.foley.gonzaga.edu:2048/login?url=http://proquest.umi.com/pqdweb?did=6659629&Fmt=7&clientId=10553&RQT=309&VName=PQD.

17. Ibid., B1.

18. Ibid., B2.

19. Ibid., B2.

20. Ioannes Paulus PP. II, *Veritatis Splendor* (The Vatican, Rome, Italy: Libreria Editrice Vaticana, 1993), 53.

21. Robert H. Bork, "Hard Truths about the Culture War," *First Things*, no. 54 (06/01, 1995), 20, http://search.ebscohost.com/login.aspx?direct=true&db=rfh&AN=ATLA0000901089&site=ehost-live (accessed 12/13/2010).

22. Ibid., 20.

23. Ibid., 20.

24. Ibid., 23.

25. Irving Kristol, *Neoconservatism: The Autobiography of an Idea* (New York: Free Press, 1995), 486.

26. Bork, *Hard Truths about the Culture War*, 19.

27. *The Spokesman Review* 14 June 1995, 1995.

28. Gerhart Niemeyer, "The Recovery of 'the Sacred'?" *The Intercollegiate Review* 24, no. 2 (Spring 1989, 1989), 5.

29. G. K. Chesterton, *Orthodoxy* (San Francisco: Ignatius, 1995), 59, 66.

30. Saint Anselm Archbishop of Canterbury and Thomas Williams, *Three Philosophical Dialogues* (Indianapolis, IN: Hackett Pub, 2002), 72.

31. Alexander Jones, *The Jerusalem Bible;* (London: Darton, Longman & Todd, 1966), Isa. 7:9.

32. John Adams, "John Adams' Inaugural Address," *John Adam's Inaugural Address* (01/ 04, 2009), 1, http://search.ebscohost.com/login.aspx?direct=true&db=a9h&AN=21212438& site=ehost-live (accessed 12/13/2010).

33. John Adams, Abigail Adams and Charles Francis Adams, *Familiar Letters of John Adams and His Wife Abigail Adams, during the Revolution: With a Memoir of Mrs. Adams* (New York: Hurd and Houghton, 1876), 194.

34. Edmund Clarence Stedman and others, *A Library of American Literature from the Earliest Settlement to the Present Time* (New York: C.L. Webster, 1888), 176.

35. M. Stanton Evans, *The Theme is Freedom: Religion, Politics, and the American Tradition* (Washington, DC; Lanham, MD: Regnery Pub; Distributed to the trade by National Book Network, 1994), 239-40.

36. Anonymous, Letter to the author, 1992.

37. Bernard J. Coughlin S.J., *Report of the President* (Spokane, Washington: Gonzaga University, [1991-1992]).

38. Roger Kimball, "'Heterotextuality' and Other Literary Matters," *Wall Street Journal* Dec 31, 1992, http://proxy.foley.gonzaga.edu:2048/login?url=http://proquest.umi.com/ pqdweb?did=4314261&Fmt=7&clientId=10553&RQT=309&VName=PQD.

39. Ibid.

40. Ibid.

41. Ibid.

42. HRH The Prince of Wales, "An Address by HRH the Prince of Wales Tercentenary Celebrations of the College of William and Mary, Williamsburg, Virginia USA" (Williamsburg, Virginia, 13 Feb 1993, 1993) (accessed 13 Dec 2010).

43. Kimball, *'Heterotextuality' and Other Literary Matters*, A6.

44. M. Scott Peck, *People of the Lie: The Hope for Healing Human Evil* (New York: Simon and Schuster, 1983), 178.

45. Niemeyer, *The Recovery of 'the Sacred'?*, 4.

46. Ibid., 3.

47. Jones, *The Jerusalem Bible,* Gen. 1:26-27.

48. Sophocles, David Grene and Richmond Alexander Lattimore, *Sophocles I* (Chicago: University of Chicago Press, 1954), 205.

49. Ibid., 244, 260.

50. Ibid., 815-23.

51. Michael Medved, *Hollywood Vs. America: Popular Culture and the War on Traditional Values*, 1st ed. (New York, NY; Grand Rapids, Mich: HarperCollins; Zondervan, 1992), 19.

52. Ibid., 19.

53. "The Declaration of Independence," *Essential Documents: Declaration of Independence* (01/03, 2009), 1, http://search.ebscohost.com/login.aspx?direct=true&db=a9h& AN=21213404&site=ehost-live (accessed 12/13/2010).

54. Allan David Bloom, *The Closing of the American Mind*, 1st Touchstone ed. (New York: Simon and Schuster, 1988), 25.

55. Ibid., 26.

56. Ibid., 38.

57. Ibid., 38.

58. Ibid., 38.

59. Ibid., 39.

60. Ibid., 40.

61. Ibid., 20.

62. Ibid., 21.

63. Robert Moss, "Anglocommunism?" *Commentary* February (1977), 29.

64. Aleksandr Isaevich Solzhenitsyn, *Warning to the West*, 1st ed. (New York: Farrar, Straus and Giroux, 1976), 109, 114.

65. Robert L. Heilbroner, *The Limits of American Capitalism*, 1st ed. ed. (New York: Harper & Row, 1966), 104.

66. Robert A. Nisbet, *Twilight of Authority* (Indianapolis: Liberty Fund, 2000), 184.

67. Christopher Jencks, *Inequality; a Reassessment of the Effect of Family and Schooling in America* (New York: Basic Books, 1972), 264.

68. Karl Marx and others, *Critique of the Gotha Programme. Uniform Title: Randglossen Zum Programm Der Deutschen Arbeiterpartei. English*, 1st ed. ed. (Peking: Foreign Languages Press, 1972), 16.

69. David Riesman, Nathan Glazer and Reuel Denney, *The Lonely Crowd: A Study of the Changing American Character*, Abridged and rev. ed. / with a foreword by Todd Gitlin ed. (New Haven, CT: Yale University Press, 2001), 307.

70. Kristol, *Neoconservatism: The Autobiography of an Idea*, 250.

71. Ibid., 251.

72. Ralf Dahrendorf, *Essays in the Theory of Society* (Stanford, Calif, Stanford University Press, 1968), 202.

73. Bernard J. Coughlin S.J., "Commencement Address" (Spokane, Washington).

74. Ruth Butler, *Rodin: The Shape of Genius* (New Haven: Yale University Press, 1993), 62.

75. Plutarch and John Langhorne, *Plutarch's Lives* (Philadelphia: Crissy, 1828), 125.

76. T. Byfield and others, *A Glorious Disaster: A.D. 1100 to 1300: The Crusades: Blood, Valor, Iniquity, Reason, Faith* (Edmonton: SEARCH, the Society to Explore and Record Christian History, 2008), 84.

77. Quoted in John L. Tancock and Rodin Museum, *The Sculpture of Auguste Rodin: The Collection of the Rodin Museum, Philadelphia* (Philadelphia: Philadelphia Museum of Art, 1976), 114.

78. Ibid., 114.

79. Gerard Manley Hopkins, *Poems of Gerard Manley Hopkins* (Nevada City, Calif: H. Berliner, 1986), 45.

80. Jones, *The Jerusalem Bible*, Deut. 8:3.

81. "Francis, Prayer of St." in *The HarperCollins Encyclopedia of Catholicism*, eds. Richard P. McBrien and Harold W. Attridge, 1st ed. (New York: HarperCollins, 1995), 539.

82. Jones, *The Jerusalem Bible*, Matt. 12:34.

83. Derek Bok, "On the Purposes of Undergraduate Education," *Daedalus* 103, no. 4, American Higher Education: Toward an Uncertain Future, Volume I (Fall, 1974), 162, http://www.jstor.org/stable/20024257.

84. Aquinas Thomas Saint, Josef Pieper and Drostan MacLaren, *The Human Wisdom of St. Thomas: A Breviary of Philosophy from the Works of St. Thomas Aquinas* (San Francisco: Ignatius Press, 2002), 55.

85. Bloom, *The Closing of the American Mind*, 57.

86. Ibid., 57.

87. Ibid., 57.

88. Ibid., 58.

89. Peter Singer, *Writings on an Ethical Life*, 1st ed. (New York: Ecco Press, 2000), 24.

90. *Kevorkian v. Thompson*, No. 96-CV-73777-DT *Kevorkian v. Thompson*, 947, 1152 (UNITED STATES DISTRICT COURT FOR THE EASTERN DISTRICT OF MICHIGAN, SOUTHERN DIVISION.

91. *Action for Children's Television v. FCC*, No. 88-1916 *Action for Children's Television v. FCC*, 932, 1504 (UNITED STATES COURT OF APPEALS FOR THE DISTRICT OF COLUMBIA CIRCUIT.

92. *Action for Children's Television v. FCC*, No. 93-1092, No. 93-1100 *Action for Children's Television v. FCC*, 11, 170 (UNITED STATES COURT OF APPEALS FOR THE DISTRICT OF COLUMBIA CIRCUIT.

93. Ibid.

94. Ap, "Warnings for Cigarettes Go into Effect," *The New York Times* October 13, 1985.

95. Jones, *The Jerusalem Bible*, Luke 23:31.

96. Ibid., John 15:18

97. Victoria Burnett, "Jesuit Killings in El Salvador could Reach Trial in Spain," *The New York Times*, sec. A; Foreign Desk, November 14, 2008.

98. Scott Wallace, "Six Salvador Jesuits Tortured and Killed: Gangland-Style Murders Recall Days of Death Squads," *The Guardian (London)* November 17, 1989.

99. Jones, *The Jerusalem Bible;* Ps. 8:5.

100. Paul Koring, "100,000 in Prague Demand Reform," *The Globe and Mail (Canada)* November 21, 1989.

101. Carol Everett and Jack Shaw, *Blood Money* (Sisters, OR: Multnomah, 1992).

102. Ibid., 8-9.

103. Ibid., 11-2.

104. Ibid., 21.

105. Ibid., 18.

106. Ibid., 87.

107. Ibid., 89.

108. Ibid., 103.

109. Ibid., 106.

110. Ibid., 107-8.

111. William Shakespeare, *Hamlet*, ed. David M. Bevington (Toronto; New York: Bantam Books, 1988), 121, http://www.loc.gov/catdir/bios/random051/87024096.html.

112. United States. Congress. House. Committee on the Judiciary. Subcommittee on the Constitution, *Origins and Scope of Roe v. Wade: Hearing before the Subcommittee on the Constitution of the Committee on the Judiciary, House of Representatives, One Hundred Fourth Congress, Second Session, April 22, 1996*, Serial no. 80 (United States. Congress. House. Committee on the Judiciary) ed. (Washington: U.S. G.P.O.: For sale by the U.S. G.P.O., Supt. of Docs., Congressional Sales Office, 1996), 125.

Chapter Two

Morality

THE MORAL CRISIS

In 1968 Will Herberg wrote "What is the Moral Crisis of our Time?" It was an insightful interpretation of our national character in which he held that our moral crisis was not "the widespread violation of accepted moral standards, for which our time is held to be notorious."[1] Other ages had flaunted moral standards at least as notoriously as ours; the virus of our age infects the moral roots themselves because it denies the very existence of moral standards. Our culture teaches, he said, "the repudiation of those very moral standards themselves," and so "today there seems to be no moral code to break down."[2] Moralists, even our moralists, seldom get beyond the pleasure-pain principle. "Human problems are increasingly seen as technological problems, to be dealt with by adjustment and manipulation; the test is always how it satisfies desires or enlarges power, not conformity to a truth beyond man's control....Pleasure and power have taken over, and the bitch-goddess Success, which William James so scornfully denounced, has come unto her own."[3] At the time, because Herberg was a respected social critic, the article attracted a certain attention, and then was forgotten.

A quarter century later, Michael Novak, in London's Westminster Abbey, delivered an address titled "Awakening from Nihilism."[4] Novak's address did not mention Herberg, but his theme is reminiscent of that 1968 essay. Looking back over recent history, Novak thinks we have learned especially two things from this bloodiest of centuries: that democracy, for all its flaws, is far superior to dictatorship which ends in barbaric concentration camps, and that capitalism, for all its imperfections, is the best economic system yet devised. Socialism is morally bankrupt, he said, for it leads to serfdom. He

43

recalled what a Russian artist in St. Petersburg told him: "The next time you want to try an experiment like socialism, try it out on animals first — men it hurts too much."[5]

However, continued Novak, one monumental lesson we have yet to learn, we have ignored and seem determined not to learn, and unless we learn that lesson, "the twenty-first century will be like the twentieth: tormented, sanguinary, barbarous."[6] That lesson is this: "vulgar relativism, now widely ascendant, undermines the culture of liberty. If it triumphs, free institutions may not survive the twenty-first century."[7]

They use different words but Herberg and Novak describe the same moral phenomenon. Herberg said that our age has no moral standards. Novak said that what we have is "vulgar relativism."[8] He calls it "vulgar relativism" because it is crude, absurd and contradictory, for it claims that there are no absolutes except absolute relativism; which means that there are no absolutes except the absolute that there are no absolutes; which means that there is no truth; no moral truth, no moral standard.

This, says Novak, is the "One principle that today's intellectuals most passionately disseminate." They are certain "that there is no truth, only opinion: *my* opinion, *your* opinion." Why do they believe this? Because they think, says Novak, that freedom is such an absolute that it must recognize no responsibility, not even to truth. Intellectuals though they are, they fail to recognize that this pulls the rug out from under their own intellectualism. In Novak's words: "They abandon the defense of intellect. There being no purchase of intellect upon reality, nothing else is left but preference and will in everything. They retreat to the romance of will." It is "nihilism with a happy face."[9] The message they send to this generation of students is: "Truth is bondage. Believe what seems right to you. There are as many truths as there are individuals. Follow your feelings. Do as you please. Get in touch with yourself. Do what feels comfortable."[10] This is, as Herberg said, the very denial of moral principles, a denial of the rule of law.

Novak likens relativism to an insidious weapon. "Vulgar relativism is an invisible gas, odorless, deadly, that is now polluting every free society on earth. It is a gas that attacks the central nervous system of moral striving. The most perilous threat to the free society today is, therefore, neither political nor economic. It is the poisonous, corrupting culture of relativism."[11]

Vulgar relativism, or in Herberg's language, the denial of the very existence of moral standards, is a quick road to moral anarchy. Absent truth, freedom is blind. It is the abandonment of intelligence as the human faculty of truth. It is a crass anti-intellectual position. The human will is not determined by what human intelligence presents to it as true — it remains free, that's what human freedom and choice means. Lord Acton understood this: "Liberty," he said, "is not the freedom to do what you wish; it is the freedom to do what you ought."[12] Avery Dulles, paraphrasing John Paul II, expressed the same idea: "Freedom is a capacity to fulfill one's deepest aspirations by choosing the true and the good."[13]

Various analysts of the Soviet Union have said that it was built on "the big lie." Citizens were told that the truth was whatever the leaders of the regime decreed. It went on for seventy years. In time the lie created so much moral rot that the Soviet Union collapsed.

The loud cry in Russia today is to put the lie behind them and rediscover the truth: to regain the nation's lost moral resolve. "The moral problem is the main problem," wrote Vagan Gevorgian of the Russian Academy of Science. That theme echoes from many quarters. Speaking recently on "Russia's Spiritual Wilderness," Barbara Von der Heydt said: "Whether or not the nation can build a new edifice based on democratic principles and a market economy will depend on whether it rests on a foundation of morality." The president of the Christian Legal Center in Russia wrote: "Neither social nor economic renewal can take place without spiritual renewal. It is all based on one foundation." Even agnostic economist and former St. Petersburg legislator, Michael Dmitriev, professor and researcher at Harvard, agrees: "The moral crisis is profound. The economic problems are not a crisis. Give us ten years and we'll be a normal country. But the moral crisis is far more serious."[14]

"This point may rankle some Westerners," allowed Von der Heydt, "but it is repeated by Russians."[15] Some westerners were similarly rankled by Alexander Solzhenitsyn when he told his Harvard University audience that what happened to Russia was happening to the United States. The intellectual establishment has ignored Solzhenitsyn ever since. Czechoslovakia's Vaclav Havel gave his Philadelphia audience the same message. In his Independence Day address he said: "The Declaration of Independence...states that the Creator gave man the right to liberty. It seems man can realize that liberty only if he does not forget the One who endowed him with it."[16]

This was Herberg's message in 1968, and it was Novak's message in London: Free societies are rare; to survive they require virtue; they abhor a moral vacuum; but there is no morality without some notion of the true and the good; what Western nations should fear most are teachers who indoctrinate its youth with the slogans: "there is no such thing as truth," "truth is a bondage," "there are as many truths as there are individuals," "do what feels comfortable." In Novak's words, those teachers "do the work of tyrants."[17]

It is this subjectivism that sadly our Supreme Court endorsed in its Planned Parenthood v. Casey decision. William Bennett pegs the Courts wording — "...however one defines life is not only valid but constitutionally protected" — as an awful piece of relativism philosophy. Wrote Bennett:

> Here is an example of "values clarification" being written not into school textbooks, but into Supreme Court opinion. It is an open-ended validation of subjectivism; whatever and however one defines life is not only valid but constitutionally protected. If this relativism becomes the coin of the judicial realm, we are in for very bad times indeed — judicially, politically, morally. If these words are taken seriously, how can we legislate against doctor-assisted suicide? Or drug use? Or prostitution? Or virtually anything else, for that matter? [18]

One major responsibility of American universities is to understand, interpret and transmit the cultural inheritance of the West, not only its religious content from Christianity and the Judeo-Christian tradition, but the legacy of the great artists and poets, philosophers and scientists. Instead, academics and other elites, even our Supreme Court are feeding American students ideas that contradict that sacred order and its historic accomplishments.

There are many teachers of this vulgar relativism: Educators, academics, political and religious leaders, major industries including entertainment and the media, and they all transmit the same amoral message: That nothing from the past is of significant value; students who come to the University with faith and morals from their families are taught that a wise education will show how simple and inadequate are those outmoded ideas.

What Bloom called the "closed mind" Malcolm Muggeridge called the "liberal mind," which seems intent on dismantling Western civilization, deprecating its values, dethroning its God, undermining its certainties. Other cultures have been destroyed from without, ours is corrupting from within. "Not Bolshevism, which Stalin liquidated along with all the old Bolsheviks; not Nazism, which perished with Hitler in his Berlin bunker; not Fascism, which was left hanging upside down from a lamp-post along with Mussolini and his mistress — none of these, history will record, was responsible for bringing down the darkness on our civilization, but Liberalism." [19]

This absence of moral standards, identified by Herberg, Novak, Solzhenitsyn and many others, stands out clearly in the language of our Supreme Court in its decisions affecting the right to life. Many of the Courts critics have pointed out how what began with Roe in 1972 as a right to privacy, that trumped the right to life, later escalated to a right to liberty which the Court said, "is the right to define one's own concept of existence, of meaning, of the universe, and of the mystery of human life." [20] This is precisely the mind that Novak feared and warned against: "there are as many truths as individuals," so "do what feels comfortable." [21]

Criticizing the road the Court has been following, Richard Neuhaus recently pointed out the similarity of its arguments to those used by the Nazis in the 1940's. They had a Germanism for it: *Lebensunwertes Leben*, life unworthy of life. More than one account of the Third Reich has documented how Nazi doctors, once the State determined whose lives were unworthy of life, turned from curing to killing. Neuhaus acknowledges the compassion that all decent-minded people feel for the terminally ill: "Yet, the euthanasia campaign's rhetoric of compassion only thinly veils its lethal logic....Honorable intentions aside, inherent in the euthanasia campaign is a dynamic that would transform Americans Against Human Suffering into Americans Against Suffering Humans."[22]

If Alexander Solzhenitsyn stands out as a moral giant, rising above the rubble, wrote Gerhart Niemeyer, it is because: "Beyond historical upheavals and clashing power masses he rediscovered man's perennial experiences of life in nature, of personal suffering and death, of love and sacrifice." Even in the midst of the most grossly debased and degrading physical and spiritual environment, he perceived the human soul, its grandeur and its reaching. Most characters in his novels "inhabit a place like hell," yet they "manage to sustain hope, faith, love, they remain pilgrims on their way to man's ultimate destiny."[23]

Abortion, infanticide and euthanasia can be accepted only if one has no understanding of the human soul, its immortality and transcendental relation to God. Human life is unique, made "in the image of God."[24] No one chooses it. God gives it and destines it to Himself. Whatever its quality — strong or weak, free or imprisoned, babbling or coherent, exalted, humiliated or tortured — human life is received, not owned by its recipients, but held as treasure in trust. Solzhenitsyn recognized the dignity of even the most hellish human life because he understood the human soul; witness to a thousand degrading deaths, he nevertheless understood man's glory and resurrection. He knew, even in the blackest night, the imprint of God in every life, the immortality of the soul, the summon to justice and the sunrise of eternity. In Solzhenitsyn's novel *Cancer Ward*,[25] Oleg Kostoglotov received a seemingly endless series of blows, disappointments, and indignities. But confident that his life serves a higher good, Oleg is prepared to pay any price for survival. As Niemeyer describes, "[h]is existence may have been reduced to something like nothingness, but there abides still 'the whole unfathomable universe of one man', the soul that presses toward beyonds after beyonds, undaunted by the fearsome nearbys."[26]

The problem with an ego-centered approach to moral analysis is that it offers no foundation beyond humanity itself, and indeed each individual person, as the measure of humanity. This was Will Herberg's point. The Western moral tradition teaches, he said, that "Unless *some* principle, some standard, *transcending* the particular context or situation, is somehow operative *in* the context of the situation, nothing but moral chaos and capriciousness can result. No human ethic is possible that is not itself grounded in a higher law and a higher reality beyond human manipulation or control."[27] Without transcending principles, man is always trying to pick himself up by his own bootstraps.

The stakes are high. Wrote Herberg: "It is the humanity of man that is at stake. The humanity of man — our wisdom and our suffering ought to have taught us — is ultimately grounded in that which is *above* and *beyond* man, or the pride and power of man. To realize this profound truth is to realize the full depth and measure of the moral crisis of our time."[28]

ON FREEDOM AND TRUTH

Like most great leaders, Pope John Paul II has his fans and his critics. His fans see him as the faithful servant-pastor who travels the world to meet great and small, rich and poor of all creeds and colors, bringing the Word of God. His critics see him as an authoritarian who clings to traditional Catholic Church teachings on sex and abortion, priestly celibacy and the ordination of women.

If I were a betting man, I would wager that John Paul II will go down as one of the greatest Popes of modern times, and one of the great Popes in the history of the Church. Historians will cite at least three major achievements: he traveled the world, bringing the message of Christ to every continent, race, nation and creed, the high and the low, the infirm and imprisoned; secondly he understood Communism as few did and fearlessly challenged and undermined its credibility, thus greatly contributing to its downfall; thirdly, he exposed through his writings the intellectual incongruity of absolute relativism, and has cogently argued the integral connection between freedom and truth.

The first and second of these accomplishments have already been fulfilled. How successfully John Paul II will be in convincing this and succeeding generations of his view of ordered freedom remains to be seen. But I think that future generations of scholars will break their heads for some years to expound what he has written. And it is this very essential subject that I would like to explore, even if briefly.

Not surprisingly, for one who lived most of his life behind the Iron Curtain, John Paul has written much about socialism and liberalism. Neither liberals nor socialists like everything he has written. Maciej Zieba, a Dominican priest and philosopher, is one who has devoted some effort to analyzing John Paul's writings. Like John Paul, Zieba also lived and suffered under socialism, and is now trying to adjust to liberalism. He finds the adjustment jarring. Recently he wrote "The Liberalism that We Need,"[29] an essay that borrows from John Paul II's major theme about freedom ordered to truth.

As good as Western liberalism is, Zieba finds it lacking in philosophical grounding, considers it is in a state of crisis, and headed for disaster. The symptoms are obvious: family dissolution, school dropouts, children having children, kids going to schools armed with knives and guns and killing their classmates and teachers, pornography, even child pornography, violence and drive-by shootings, abortions mounting in numbers that monthly exceed the killings from the atom bomb that fell on Hiroshima — the list goes on and on.

What is it about liberalism that produces these things? Liberalism, says Zieba, is not connected to reality, it recognizes no principles, it believes in no truth. One value alone it accepts: freedom. It holds that truth is absolutely relativistic: all things, all peoples and cultures are equally good and true. There are no judgments to be made in a pluralistic world where freedom is the only value, and truth is simply the exercise of freedom; no appeal is to be made to any truth beyond freedom itself. Zieba likens this concept of freedom to a roulette game in which the player always wins. "Such freedom" he says, "might be compared with placing a bet on any number in a game of roulette in which it is entirely up to me to decide whether black or white wins. I may tell myself that I am winning all the time, but what does 'win' mean in this context. If there is no truth apart from my choosing, if there is no absolute truth, absolute freedom is both sad and empty."[30]

Zieba borrows from John Paul II. The Pope has often said that "Man is made for freedom."[31] But freedom must be ordered. Freedom, unordered, is simply a fight for power. The Pope didn't invent the idea that freedom, to be true freedom, must be ordered to truth. That idea has been around a long time. "If there is no truth, then, everything which I say could come true….the idea of absolute truth opposes a relativism which negates the existence of truth….such an attitude leads to the right of the clenched fist and not the right of truth." That indeed sounds like John Paul, but it is British political philosopher Karl Popper writing in mid-century in "The Open Society."[32] The ordering of freedom to truth is not a Catholic or even a theological concept but part of a long tradition in Western political philosophy. Popper was reasoning with his colleagues in Great Britain, with the hope of heading off a blind post-WWII rush toward a radical liberalism that was rushing headlong toward absolute relativism.

When Popper mentioned "truth" his British audiences responded pretty much the way American audiences in those days were also beginning to respond: "Truth? Sez who? So, who's going to tell me what's true, and what I may and may not do?" Both British and American liberals were soon singing from the same sheet of music: "Be free to do what you want; there is no right or wrong; your doing it makes it true." Says Zieba: "It's like a roulette game in which the wagerer always wins. Choose red, and red is the winner; choose black, and you still win!"[33]

But no truly thinking person believes that truth and freedom are like that. You can't always win simply by choosing whatever you want. If freedom were blind — if it were undirected by intelligence and intelligence not ordered to truth — then human choices would necessarily be unintelligible. To be intelligible and purposeful, freedom requires direction. Intelligent beings are free beings, precisely so that they may attain the truth perceived as the good. This is what John Paul means where he writes that "man is made for freedom."

People under the Communist system were, indeed, fed the roulette notion of truth and freedom: Truth, they were told, is whatever the regime declared it to be. Thinking people saw it for what it was, and gave it a name, "the big lie." After 70 years not even the Russian leadership could live in the moral rot of "the big lie." Gorbachev spoke for that leadership when he said: "We've got to stop! It is a lie to say that truth is whatever we decree!"

So, what is truth? The notion of truth as developed by western philosophers is: being as related to the intellect, as known. God is the supreme reality, and so the Supreme Truth. The reality of God is absolute — that is, it depends on no other reality. All other beings depend on the Being of God, and so are said to be contingent.

The truth of a being is what it is. It functions the way that it does because it is the kind of being that it is. The purpose of intelligence as a faculty of free beings, is to understand beings, contingent or created beings and, so far as created intelligence can, the Absolute uncreated Being of God. When the mind does this successfully, without error, it is said to attain the truth. To possess the truth then is to understand the way being really is. On the other hand, when the mind observes reality incorrectly, it is in a state of falsehood.

Consistent with this view is the teaching that it is being, reality, which directs the mind, not the other way around. The mind does not determine what is true, but rather seeks to discover what is true. We are seekers of truth, so we do not own the truth but are in the service of it. Being is a gift to minds, to be observed and understood: God is the supreme gift because He is Supreme Being. Thus, Maciej Zieba observes: "When truth is viewed as something that is in our service, rather than our being in the service of truth, it is very easy for religious faith to degenerate into ideology."[34] Ideology is a debasement of the truth, for it proposes a personal political notion in order to gain something desired, regardless of its truth or authenticity.

Christ was put to death by ideologues. The chosen people had been schooled by God to believe in monotheism: "Listen, O Israel, the Lord your God is one God."[35] When Christ came claiming divinity and oneness with the Father, they didn't understand. A few were especially blessed and accepted the message, and in time found the truth. Others did not accept the message, which conflicted with the conventional wisdom. They missed many things, could not understand for example, Isaiah: "Islands, listen to me, pay attention, remotest peoples. Yahweh called before I was born, from my mother's womb He pronounced my name";[36] "Listen, O Israel, the Lord your God will give you a sign. A maiden will conceive and bear a son who will be called Immanuel, God-with-us";[37] "See, my servant...like a sapling he grew up in front of us, like a root in arid ground...there was no beauty in him, no look to attract our eyes; a thing despised and rejected by men, a man of sorrows and familiar with suffering...yet, ours were the sufferings he bore, ours the sorrows he carried."[38]

Locked in prejudices they were not free. Then came the ideology, recorded by John.

> Then the chief priests and Pharisees called a meeting. 'Here is this man working all these signs and what actions are we taking? If we let him go on in this way, everybody will believe in him, and the Romans will come and destroy the Holy Place and our nation.' One of them, Caiaphas, the high priest that year, said, You don't seem to have grasped the situation at all; you fail to see that it is better for one man to die for the people than for the whole nation to be destroyed.[39]

The chief priests and Pharisees were not the only ideologues. The Church has had its share. We are familiar with times in its history when the Church drifted away from serving the truth, appearing to own it. Recall Galileo, and the inquisitors. These are some of the things John Paul II had in mind when, recalling the Church's errors, he asked us to seek forgiveness for the Church's sins. Recently he happily said it correctly: "The Church proposes, she imposes nothing."[40] May that formulation ever guide the future Church.

Human intelligence, God knows, often errs severely. But with work and care, and humility, and especially when assisted by faith, it can attain the truth of things. And in any case, it is the best that we have to work with.

Freedom unaided by intelligence seeking the truth of things, is blind force. And truth is ignored at great cost. Gravity is truth. For one standing on a mountain path with a boulder hurtling down upon him from above, the truth of gravity is about to make itself felt, whether the fellow sees the boulder or not. The poor fellow may choose to create his own truth, but the truth of the being we call gravity will have its way. Death and decomposition of dead bodies is truth. Whether I submit to that truth or not, if I don't do something with the dead body, it will stink up the house. That's the reality. I don't cause it, I don't own it, I can't change it. I can ignore it, but I pay a price. The rock pounding my skull, the stench abrading my nostrils, say something about the rightness of ordering freedom to truth.

Freedom and truth are not at loggerheads. Truth is a gift of God. Christ said that it is the truth that makes us free. So, John Paul's formula is neither threatening nor autocratic, simply philosophic: "there can be no secure freedom that is not grounded in truth, including the truth that man is made for freedom."[41] Several generations of students have been schooled in absolute relativism where the teachers have been teaching: "Be free to do what you want." They are instructed to let the students choose their own values, since according to their teachers there is no right or wrong.

As a nation we once professed certain truths. Have we now come to such a pass that we no longer know what those words mean — "We hold these truths?" But historians of culture and civilization tell us that no society can long endure without being able to articulate the truths that it believes and to which it commits itself. It's now time to rethink our liberalism. "We hold no truths" is a proclamation unworthy the descendants of the authors of our great Declaration of Independence.

THE MORAL ANARCHY WE WANT

If you're sick of the "culture war," join the crowd. Aren't we all. But things are likely to get worse before they get better.

In a recent article titled "The Straight '90's," William Murchison of the Dallas Morning News wrote that in this war things have become so bad that maybe we are on the verge of admitting just how bad they are. If so, maybe we're in for a reaction. "A public debate over culture has been joined in the world of national journalism," he wrote. "Hard questions are being asked at last, starting with, 'What has happened to us?' and ending up somewhere in the neighborhood of 'How do we fix it?'"[42]

According to Murchison, whatever happened didn't just happen. A new order has been assaulting us for some time. "The new order has given up on any pretense at being a moral order,"[43] for moral order implies a moral law. The new order is morally lawless; it has only one rule: be free to do whatever you like. So its only controls are those that people choose to place on themselves. No absolute governs us. It's every man for himself, every woman for herself: drive-by shooting for me, and tough luck for that Tucson girl who last week was killed; abortion for me, and too bad for the baby; twenty-four hours a day of violent and indecent television, and somebody else worry about the kids. The amazing thing is, not that so many people have bought into this anarchy, but that the intellectuals and the national leadership, including an institution supposedly so wise as the American courts, have bought into it. It's the bill of rights turned on its head: all rights, no responsibilities.

Once you separate freedom from law, and law from truth, you're in a bad way. I realize that just you mention truth and people say: "Whose truth, yours or mine?" It's the response of Pilate: "What is truth?"[44] Yet apart from truth, law is will, and freedom is simply the use of power. The disregard for life, in its many forms, is simply the exercise of power. In the early pages of his encyclical, *Veritatis Splendor*,[45] John Paul II attempted to make this clear: it is not freedom that makes us free, it is the truth that makes us free. Our Lord said: "You will know the truth, and the truth will make you free."[46] That's why they speak of it as "ordered freedom." Freedom not ordered to truth is simply license; and license in personal and social life is simply an assertion of power. Raw power does not free, it enslaves — those who exercise it, and those over whom it is exercised.[47]

It used to be that human life was thought good because it was ordered to the absolute Good, truth, who is also the absolute God. It used to be that people agreed on some "plain moral facts" that governed freedom — some things are clearly right, others clearly wrong. It used to be that parents and teachers knew and agreed on those facts and taught them to children. And it used to be that government was concerned that children be taught them.

No more. "Plain moral facts" have been replaced by relativism and agnosticism — translate, freedom to do what one likes. To the "plain moral facts" of the old order, the new order says: "Sez who?" Take sex, for example. There was such a thing as marital fidelity. To which the new order says: "Sez who? I'm free to do whatever I like." Murchison goes on to illustrate the takeover of the new order: "Non-marital sex rose in social esteem to a position of near equality with the conjugal ideal....preserved by the laws and customs of the larger society."[48] In a short time "virtue" became a lost word, "conjugal fidelity" not talked about, and "chastity" snickered at. Then, in all too short a time, "Another individual perception began to grow in society's consciousness: the heterosexual relationship was merely one possibility available to, as we nowadays say, the sexually active. Why not....homosexuality?" If one wants it, why not? Says Murchison: "The gay rights movement is engaged presently in driving that conviction into our brains, as with a clawhammer."[49] It's a good bet that so called "homosexual marriages" will begin to be legal, state by state — the movement is already well under way.

Says educator Michael Josephson: "There is a hole in the moral ozone."[50] Says philosopher Alasdair MacIntyre: "We are raising a generation of 'moral stutterers.'"[51] Says Ann Landers: "Let's face it. America is sick."[52]

In the wake of Watergate, years ago, every newspaper and weekly in the country took the nation's temperature and declared that the patient was, indeed, sick. Writers and analysts zeroed in on our schools and colleges, charging them to do a better job of teaching ethics and producing ethical and morally responsible citizens.

So the primary and secondary schools heated up their teaching courses on "values clarification." Billions of dollars have been spent on that silliness which, if it has done anything, has only made things worse. Philosopher Christina Hoff Sommers expressed it as well as anyone: "'Values clarification' in the schools is a little like putting children in a chemistry lab and saying, 'Discover your own compounds, kids.' If they blow themselves up, at least they have engaged in an authentic search for the self."[53]

The colleges have been trying to make ethical citizens of "moral stutterers" by teaching applied-ethics courses. In these courses students are asked to consider what they might do in certain dilemma situations, such as: whom do you throw out of a life boat filled with seven people when you have space and food enough only for six. From "dilemma" ethics students learn nothing about virtue or basic principles of right and wrong. Summarizing what these courses did for him, one student said: "I learned there was no such thing as right or wrong, just good and bad arguments." And another: "I learned there is no such thing as morality."[54]

Some years ago Hillary Clinton said something that caught the public's attention. She spoke of "a politics of virtue," whatever that means. That lost word, like an old penny, keeps coming back. Virtue presupposes the existence of a moral standard of behavior. It implies the superiority of one thing over another, good and bad with reference to a standard. Its opposite is vice. No vice, no virtue. Was the former First Lady suggesting that government get into the virtue business? Aristotle thought that virtue was, indeed, a concern of government; so did Thomas Aquinas and a long tradition of philosophers. But most political philosophers today do not agree, and the courts will slap your hands if you talk like that. That's why the Federal Court in Washington recently said to the television industry: You can show violent and indecent materials twenty-four hours a day, if you like, because we don't know anything about vice and virtue; and even if we did, we wouldn't dare say anything about it.[55]

Someone has said that in a democracy people get what they deserve, which means they get pretty much what they want, and what they insist on. If we have a coast to coast disregard for human life, it's because that's what we want. We kill hundreds of thousands of infants in the womb every year, because we want to kill them; and the law allows it. We have indecent sex and violence on television twenty-four hours a day, because we want it. And, if we want euthanasia, the state will then be in the euthanasia business. Remember, the new order has nothing to do with truth; its one rule is: "Be free to do whatever you like." We look for someone to blame — the courts, the President, the Congress. But they just follow the polls.

Violence, indecency, abortion, euthanasia, pornography, and all the rest, are symptoms, not the sickness. They are marks of the cancer that's eating away at the culture. It's a soul-sickness: for we want the hole in the moral ozone, we like the moral anarchy. As Shakespeare said: "The fault, dear Brutus, is not in our stars, but in ourselves."[56]

Virtue, that lost word, keeps echoing off the nation's walls. It still sounds like something we should be in favor of. Be that as it may, you may be sick of the culture war. Nevertheless, you can be sure of it, the public debate over culture has only just begun.

ON "VALUES CLARIFICATION"

A lot is said in the press and on television about the rules of the game and playing by the rules. Pete Rose violated the rules of professional baseball and has been excluded from the Hall of Fame. One star National Basketball Association player broke the rules, and is now paying for it. Rules are rather necessary for keeping order. "But there's nothing sacred about the rules, so don't get too excited about them." Rules are mere conventions that society adopts so that people can live together in some measure of order and harmony. So they are expendable. In fact, the violator of the rules may be a more intelligent, far-sighted individual who prefers to live by a different and maybe wiser set of rules. No one has a corner on the best rules. Moreover, it takes courage to follow one's vision.

This, of course, is consistent with the moral relativism that the mass of our society succumbs to, and it is what we teach in our schools. Children are taught that the rules are formed within a context of moral relativism, namely, that what is praiseworthy or contemptible is a matter of cultural conditioning. So rules have no significance beyond themselves: we just happen to have a particular set of rules; there's nothing moral about them; we follow them just because the majority of the people, or the legislators in power, have adopted them. We could have another set of rules. So it's all quite a pragmatic business. If you find the rules comfortable and to your liking, no problem; if they pinch, just bear the pinch; or if you wish to try to sidestep them, be prepared to suffer the sanctions.

We teach this in our schools under the title of "values clarification." Some time ago the authors of textbooks on moral education agreed that the "old morality"[57] should be scrapped. No one should presume to indoctrinate others; what we should do is simply help students discover their own values; that's values clarification, which Sydney Simon describes as "based on the premise that none of us has the 'right' set of values to pass on to other people's children." The methods of teaching values-clarification are designed to help students get at "their own feelings, their own ideas, their own beliefs, so that the choices and decisions they make are conscious and deliberate, based on their own value system."[58]

The following conversation took place between a values-clarification teacher and her students:

Student: Does this mean that we can decide for ourselves whether to be honest on tests?

Teacher: No, it means that you can decide on the value. I personally value honesty; and although you may choose to be dishonest, I shall insist that we be honest in our tests. In other areas of your life, you may have more freedom to be dishonest.[59]

So this teacher arbitrarily sets down the rule of "no cheating in this classroom." If the student wants to cheat in some other context of his life — say intercollegiate athletics, or in another class, or in his business, or before a grand jury under oath — that's up to the student, and apparently okay with the teacher.

It must be obvious to any thinking person that this is a heck of a way to run a railroad, not to mention human lives. There must be more to ethics than this. And there is. So what's wrong? What's wrong is that the teacher doesn't know that the rules rest on a moral foundation. A sound system of ethics is more than a bunch of rules.

There are three major elements in an ethical system. Ethics, first of all, begins with the human being and some conception of what the good human life is, that is, what the human being could be if he realized his potential as a human being. This implies that there is purpose in human life and that each human being must strive to realize his/her purpose for being.

Secondly, a system of ethics implies that there are certain human behaviors which are conducive to the good human life, as such. These are the virtues. Virtue, from the Latin *virtus*, means goodness, moral excellence — the goodness of the human being as a human being. The virtues include such behaviors, or good habits, as patience, justice, temperance and honesty (as opposed to cheating). All human beings, striving to realize their potential and perfection as human beings, should strive to be honest in all classrooms and in all circumstances. But virtue makes sense only with reference to some end product, namely, the human being conceived as having a particular purpose.

Thirdly come the rules — against cheating in the classroom, or violating one's oath of office, or trading on insider information. Ethical rules of behavior for individuals, and codes of ethics for business and professional associations and governmental bodies, are directives that foster and lead to virtuous action. They make sense only as related to virtue and its exercise, and virtue makes sense only as related to the human being realizing his perfection as a human being.

Our problem today — in our philosophy, and so in our ethics, and thus in what we teach in the classroom — is that we have lost the concept of the human-being-as-he-could-be-if-he-realized-his-perfection-as-a-human-being. Having lost that, we have lost the concept of virtue. We end up with ethics without virtue. All we have left is a bunch of rules. So all the poor teacher in the classroom can say is, "pick and choose what rules suit you," since "none of us has the 'right' set of values to pass on to other people's children."[60]

When you pass on that meaningless mess to teenagers in the classroom, it's not unlikely that later in life you'll have cheating in tests and in intercollegiate athletics, insider trading on Wall Street, lying under oath — you name it — the overriding rule being "don't get caught."

Yes, sir, that's a poor way to run a railroad, and it's a very poor way to run a country. Fact is, it's a poor way to run anything.

OR, NO MORAL RULES AT ALL

Moral relativism is taking us down a bad road. It really comes down to: "If it feels good, do it!" Rules of human behavior, to be sound, must rest on some ethical base beyond "what I prefer" or "what I like." But much of modern ethics has lost its ethical base. Having lost the concept of the good human life, it has thereby lost the concept of virtue which is understandable only with reference to the good human life; as a result, all that is left of modern ethics is a collection of rules, which are meaningless because they are seen with reference to nothing beyond themselves.

And because of the perceived meaninglessness of the rules, in time they are altogether discarded as being of no significance. So ethics today, personal as well as public and professional ethics, is virtually nonexistent.

This came home to me with a thud when a book by a Kenneth Kammeyer was called to my attention. The book is entitled *Marriage and Family: A Foundation for Personal Decisions*, and I am amazed that it is used in public school social science courses. In a chapter on "Marital Sexual Life," the author deals with "Variations in Sexuality and Sexual Behavior."[61] One section of this chapter is entitled "Open Relationships," in which the author states that in recent years married couples frequently come to an agreement about outside sexual activities, which allows them "freedom to have sexual relationships with others. The label for such an agreement is *open marriage or open relationships*."[62] He points out that these agreements can be advantageous or disadvantageous to the marriage. They can be disadvantageous if either partner is insecure in the relationship, and then they are better avoided.

But in other cases, states Kammeyer, where both partners are secure, an "open relationship" may enhance the marriage relationship since "the partners do not have to focus all their attention on each other." Open relationships introduce greater freedom into the marriage because the partners allow each other to "engage in different activities with other people (of both sexes)." He believes that these marriages "should be entered into openly with the awareness and concurrence of the spouse." Of course not all couples will want an open marriage, but "if both partners find the openness comfortable, then ultimately it might be possible to move to the level of having sexual relationships outside the marriage." It is simply a matter of both spouses feeling comfortable about open sex. Kammeyer allows that it may not be for everyone because "each person must be psychologically secure. And most important, the relationship must be cooperative, not competitive. Some couples might meet these criteria, but most do not."[63]

What happens when the relationship is not all that cooperative, and one spouse is unfaithful? How should a spouse handle sexual infidelity when it does come to light? Well, there's no one answer, but there are three ways in which marriage partners generally respond.

First, "many people feel that infidelity deals a fatal blow to marriage,"[64] and that the only solution is to end the marriage and start anew.

Others respond differently by entering into "discussion and negotiation."[65] In this case the couple is likely to spend a consideration amount of time and energy in examining their own marriage relationship and what has contributed to the infidelity. They will have to consider their personal likes, dislikes and preferences; they will have to look to the future and what problems they will have to face in their relationship should they continue together. Outside counseling and therapy is frequently necessary.

The third response from an increasingly larger group of couples is to "ignore or downplay the matter." Since this is an age of greater sexual freedom, people tend to accept with greater calm and equanimity the sexual infidelity of a spouse. As Kammeyer says: "Sex is recognized as an enjoyable and pleasurable activity. Furthermore, the pleasure is often heightened by the novelty of a new partner."[66] Moreover, society offers many more opportunities to both men and women for free sex. "With such opportunities and freedoms, extramarital sex becomes easier and more tempting. By recognizing these facts of contemporary life, some people are able to accept the sexual infidelity of their spouses more easily. For those who accept these views, it may not even be appropriate to think in terms of 'infidelity.'" Since extramarital sex is now more common, it may be more prudent simply to "play it down," to "treat it casually or even ignore it." Kammeyer concludes this chapter of his book with the observation that open sex, after all, is "at least tacitly accepted as a part of contemporary life."[67]

Note that Kammeyer appeals to no moral principles of human behavior. He says merely that if they are "comfortable" in their mutual infidelity, then go for it; and since sexual "pleasure" is often heightened by "novelty" of new partners, then they might want to try it out and see how they like it. In other words: "If it feels good, do it!"

I bring up this subject as an example of how moral rules are meaningless apart from virtuous behavior and the good human life; apart from virtue and moral goodness, rules become meaningless, and ultimately, are abandoned altogether. So the best that Kammeyer can do is to catalogue how people in fact are behaving: some accept marriage fidelity; some are unfaithful and when caught in infidelity must face the consequences; some enter into "open marriages," freeing each spouse to engage in sex with other people of both sexes. This supposes that there is no moral context in the marriage relationship — no rules, no virtuous behavior, no moral goodness — beyond what makes two people "comfortable."

A generation or more of America's youth have been schooled in this kind of moral relativism. Isn't it time that we examine more critically what we are teaching our young people? Is this really the best we can do? I can't believe that people will long be content with that shallowness in the teaching of ethics.

WHY TEACH ETHICS?

The other day a student asked the question: "Can we teach ethics?" When I expressed doubt that ethics can be taught, he thought he had me cornered and fired back: "Then why do Catholic colleges require it?" This is an attempt to answer both of those questions.

A few years ago *Time* magazine ran a cover story titled "Whatever Happened to Ethics?" The authors, recognizing our nation's moral disarray, attempted to account for it by pointing the finger in every direction: to parents who fail to take responsibility for children; to the legal professionals who manipulate the law to beat the rules rather than being "guardians of the law;" to the national obsession with individual rights; to the "cult of personhood"[68] which inculcates excessive selfishness in children; to the schools which are "languishing for lack of moral nutrition;"[69] to the electronics media which preach "You only go around once in life, so get all the gusto you can;"[70] and even to the churches, which are often regarded as "narrow and self-serving."[71]

This moral disarray has been obvious for a long time. But with the recent media coverage of the misdemeanors of prominent businessmen, politicians and churchmen, various segments of society are scrambling more than ever "to shore up their corners of the ethical roof."[72] And universities, many that haven't offered ethics courses for years, are scurrying to offer more courses that deal with business ethics, engineering ethics, ethics for art dealers, doctors, financiers, you name it. These courses generally present for the students' consideration ethical issues in a casebook approach. Similar courses are also being adapted for the secondary and elementary school levels.

The question arises: What are those courses accomplishing? Are they making businessmen, engineers and financial experts more ethical, that is moral in their professional lives? Question: Can you teach moral behavior? You can talk about ethical questions, and you can seem to take greater interest in them. But does that translate into moral probity or virtuous behavior? I think it is at least highly questionable that it does. So, let's get to the basic questions: What is virtuous behavior? And why should one practice it? Why obey moral rules? Until these questions are answered to one's satisfaction, I see no reason to think that more laws, more rules by professional organizations, and more courses on ethics will motivate one to better moral behavior. Why be good? What is good? What does it do for me?

Today, as I said earlier, we are absorbed merely with rules, and have lost the connection between rules and virtue. But rules of themselves are meaningless. So, after a time we may disregard them altogether. Thus, everything that makes up the moral context is lost: human goodness, virtue and ethical norms. Left only with rules, the best we do for students in many of our schools is to say "do this" and "don't do that." Having lost the reason behind "do this" and "don't do that," many of our schools give poor, if any, moral guidance. So, whatever happened to ethics? Ethics, as understood by too many in our society, is floundering because it is unconnected from human goodness. We have lost a sense of the moral good. So, all that many of our schools do is simply catalogue human behavior — "this is what people are doing" — pretty much the way biologists catalogue the behavior of chipmunks.

John Goldthwait, philosophy professor at the State University of New York, reflected on his years of teaching ethics: "After teaching courses in ethics probably 20 times, I do not delude myself that all the students who passed those courses became moral models or abstained from immoral conduct significantly more than their peers who had no such courses."[73] Good moral behavior is not a science to be learned but an activity to be exercised. To be sure, one can study the science of moral philosophy; but that will not result in virtue. Virtue takes place primarily in the practical, not the intellectual order. It is a praxis, a practice, an exercise, as distinguished from a theory, as Aristotle taught: "Anything that we have to learn to do we learn by the actual doing of it: people become builders by building and instrumentalists by playing instruments. Similarly we become just by performing just acts, temperate by performing temperate ones, brave by performing brave ones."[74] Teaching courses in our schools with the aim to convert immoral into moral practices runs the risk of the fallacy: teach ethics, and you will prevent immorality. The rush to teach these courses, many of which merely flop around on the fringes of moral philosophy, may be another example of our cultural demand for quick fixes. As Goldthwait characterized it: "If you intend a moral result, you set up a moral device (an ethics course, a moral professorship), you press the button of the moral device, and presto! You have achieved somebody's moral conduct."[75]

What a solid, well planned course in moral philosophy can do is help students search for, examine and probe moral theories until they find a moral system that is intellectually supportable because it rests on a set of sufficiently consistent moral principles. And the student, who has seriously undertaken that task, has long abandoned any thought of quick fixes. If, in addition to this intellectual pursuit, the student also achieves some measure of moral probity or virtue, this, Goldthwait concludes, "is probably attributable to early moral training in *some* moral system, rather than to either high-level studies of theory or occupational studies of practice. No doubt what we had better count on, when we are seeking to protect society against improper medical practice or illicit trading in the marketplace, is that early moral training."[76]

In a word, courses on ethics in the marketplace are not likely to induce good moral practice in the marketplace, unless the people in the marketplace are trained in the practice of virtue. And the conventional wisdom has long said that that schooling should begin in the earliest years of life. So, "Whatever Happened to Ethics?" I suspect most of us would answer that we have left off or soft-peddled not only the teaching of morality but more catastrophically, the practice of that discipline all along the line — in home and school, church and college — and are now reaping the harvest of that neglect.

So we teach ethics that students may understand that there is such a thing as the moral good, that it is pursued and achieved through the practice of virtue, and that ethical rules are guides and aids in the practice of virtue. That knowledge, it is hoped, reinforces the moral training that students received at home and in their early years in school. It gives intellectual ground for individual and virtuous public behavior. So train your children in virtue now, and as they grow older, tell them the reasons why virtue is the right way to go — with the hope and expectation that years later in college they will have the opportunity to study a coherent ethical system that will intellectually ground their moral behavior.

SIFTED LIKE WHEAT

With the proliferation of news stories about devil worship, I one day asked Father Jim Powers if he thought people in this day and age could be so beguiled and enchanted as to worship Satan? Jim was a student of literature and a great teacher. "Oh yes," he said, "because evil has a lot of zing, and good is so bland. Just look at the movies. For every movie that portrays virtue and the good, there are ten movies that portray vice and evil. People are fascinated by evil."

Satan is certainly making headlines. A story from the *Boston Globe* was recently called to my attention. Aaron Zitner wrote: "A Satan scare is sweeping the nation. The occult is everywhere these days: Heavy metal bands have adopted demonic symbols, and religious fundamentalists often take Satanism as a fact."[77]

From her childhood in Boston, Gail MacDonough remembers satanic rituals involving "cannibalism, rape, animal sacrifice and murder, all to honor Satan." According to MacDonough, several times a year her parents and ten or so strangers would don masks and robes. "At a farm by our home, the ritual would occur. The powers of Satan would be called on. There would be a black Mass."[78]

There is even a Church of Satan, founded in 1966 by Anton LaVey,[79] a former carnival performer. Perhaps the carnival business went sour, and LaVey was enterprising enough to understand that fascination with the devil has always attracted crowds. His book *The Satanic Bible* is on the racks of many bookstores throughout the country.

Satan and Satanism, or the worship of Satan, has had a long history. Whether out of sheer fear, or simply to hedge their bets, people have always been ready to strike a deal with the devil. In the legend, Faust sold his soul to the devil for twenty-four years of earthly delights, signing the contract with his own blood. As the twenty-four years rolled around, he grew weary with the emptiness of his pleasures, but still asked for one more day, and then another, and then for one more day still. Faust realized that he had struck a poor bargain, and sought to evade handing himself over to a guy who, when put to the test, had so little to offer.

Captain John Smith described the sacrifice of children that he found in Virginia shortly after landing there in 1607. In the spelling of his day he wrote of the savages:

> All things that were able to do them hurt beyond their prevention they adore with their kinde of divine worship; as the fire, water, lightning, thunder, our ordinance peeces, horses, &c. But their chiefe God they worship is the Diuell. . . In some part of the Country, they haue yearely a sacrifice of children.[80]

In his *History of the Devil*, Paul Carus accounts for devil-worship among the tribes in Brazil, thus: "It might be thought that they hold the Good Being weaker in relation to the fate of man than the Evil."[81]

That there is a devil, or Satan as he is named, is the belief of the vast majority of our population. Polls today show that 70% of the American people believe that he exists. Thirty-four percent believe him to be a personal being who directs evil forces and influences people to do wrong; 36% believe him to be an impersonal force that also, somehow, influences people to do wrong. In a 1990 Gallup Poll, 49% of the respondents said they believe that people are sometimes possessed by the devil.[82]

By and large Americans agree with Billy Graham that: Satan is real and at work in the world: "Man's rebellion and fall in no way diminishes God's love. He doesn't stop loving us because of our sinful natures. But His nature is not only loving, it is also just. And He exercises justice impartially. So while His love is extended to the sinner, His justice demands severe judgment of sin."[83]

Is belief in Satan and Satan-worship growing? And belief in God and worship of God declining? I doubt it. But Nietzsche must have thought so. The Enlightenment and Rationalism have removed faith from many people's lives. So God isn't in the picture.

This was the point of Nietzsche's parable. The man comes into the marketplace early in the morning to declare that God is dead; the people have killed him. The people simply call him mad. He concludes: "I have come too early ....This tremendous event has not yet reached the ears of man....Lightening and thunder require time....Deeds require time even after they are done, before they can be seen and heard....And yet they have done it themselves."[84] The people were not even aware how completely they had removed God from their lives.

Polls today show that people say they believe in God, but when asked about the nature of that belief, it is clear that God is not important to them. Concluded pollsters James Patterson and Peter Kim:

> In every single region of the country, when we asked how people make up their minds on issues of right and wrong, we found that they simply do not turn to God or religion to help them decide about the seminal or moral issues of the day....We have established ourselves as the authority on morality. We now choose which commandments to believe and which ones not to believe....For most Americans, God is not to be feared or, for that matter, loved.[85]

This is what Nietzsche's madman meant when he said that the people have killed God. So, says Joyce Little, we search high and low for something that might take God's place and give our lives meaning:

Something, almost anything: the cosmic consciousness of New Age, the magic and witchcraft of goddess mythology, the archetypes of Jungian psychology, Joseph Campbell's hero of a thousand faces, Carl Sagan's voyage through the Cosmos, the cults of Elvis, Marilyn, and Madonna, even in alarming numbers the demonic powers promised by Satanic cults. [86]

"Actual Devil-worship," wrote Carus, "continues until the positive power of good is recognized and man finds out by experience that the good, although its progress may be ever so slow, is always victorious in the end." [87]

And Christ said to Simon: "Satan has desired to take you and sift you like wheat. But I have prayed that your faith be strengthened, and you, once converted, may strengthen your brothers." [88] Were it not for Christ, Satan would sift all of us like wheat.

AN ANGEL OF LIGHT

Following the David Koresh incident in Waco, Texas a few years ago, students frequently asked the question: "How can people be so gullible as to follow such a delusion?" Koresh was apparently convinced that he was Jesus Christ. To his followers he held the key to the revelations of the Apocalypse.

Nietzsche asked the question: After the people have killed God, what do they do? By killing God, of course, Nietzsche meant that people had removed God from their lives. That's what modern rationalism attempts to do. The secular-humanist doctrine puts it this way: People seek God because they swallow the God-myth. They do not see that the fulfillment of human life is in their own realization here and now. They do not consider God to be part of the picture. As Harvard paleontologist, George Gaylor Simpson, expresses the doctrine:

> Although many details remain to be worked out, it is already evident that all the objective phenomena of the history of life can be explained by purely naturalistic or, in a proper sense of the sometimes abused word, materialistic factors....man is the result of a purposeless and natural process that did not have him in mind. [89]

And now — brace yourself for this — since there is no God, try Satan, advises the Rev. Peter H. Gilmore, administrator for the Church of Satan in New York. His church rejects Christianity, and God as well, and even secular humanism, since humanism subscribes to altruism which Satanism rejects. Says Gilmore:

Satanism rejects these idealistic and unnatural creeds to embrace the world as it is: a ground for endless strife and struggle, a total war wherein the strong dominate the weak and the clever dominate the strong. We Satanists are our own Gods and consider Satan to be a symbol for the carnal nature of Man unleashed, as well as the dark force which permeates all of existence and fuels the evolutionary advancement of life itself.[90]

But the average person knows garbage when he smells it. In his heart of hearts he knows that there is something bigger beyond himself. Remove God from the picture and, in his frantic search for meaning, he will turn to almost anything to make sense of his life.

So, how do you explain the Wacos and the David Koreshes? If you teach people that religion is a hoax, God a myth, and that the end of human life is man's self-realization, you can expect that there will be David Koreshes. Wacos happen neither because of religion nor the lack of it. Wacos happen because people are gullible, and few know how to think about religious matters.

And religion has many enemies. Few greater than misguided faith. Christ said of Satan, "He is the father of lies" and "there is no truth in him."[91] He also said that Satan can transform himself into an "angel of light."[92] Angels of light come in many forms. One angel of light that has appeared frequently in the history of Christianity is pietism. Pietism proposes to elevate faith, and thinks it does a service to faith by removing intelligence and reason from religion and theology. It purports to substitute pure faith for intelligence, claiming that human intelligence is a whore that diminishes faith. But once people throw out intelligence and human reason, they emote, they don't think.

Theology — *theos* + *logos* — is the study of God. It is study; the science of the study of God, having its own proper object and methods of study that are peculiar to itself, just as biology has its own object and methods of study. There is no short cut to learning biology. No amount of wishing, singing or emoting will get the job done. It's the same with the study of God, except that in the case of theology the methods and tools of learning include faith, Scripture and the tradition of faith, under the employ of human intelligence.

The Catholic theological tradition throughout the long history of the Church has been a sound one, well grounded in both faith and intelligence. From time to time pietism or Gnosticism, or what Ronald Knox called "enthusiasm,"[93] have approached theology, bypassing the tough work of intelligence. Not infrequently, when that has occurred, pietism has ended in fanaticism.

The Church has always held pietism suspect. Aware that evil spirits can appear as "angels of light," the Church is skeptical about esoteric spirituality, visionaries, and apocalyptic prophets. Apparitions of Christ, His Mother and the Saints are, of course, possible, and in rare instances are recognized by the Church. Mary may surely have appeared to those young people in Yugoslavia;[94] but the Church looks cautiously on things like that. We have every reason to believe that supernatural apparitions are rare and extraordinary, that while God is indeed active in all created beings, he normally acts through His creation as secondary causes. And in its theology the Church, acknowledging this principle, long ago accepted the formula of St. Augustine: *fides quaerens intellectum; intellectus quaerens fidem* (faith seeks to understand; understanding seeks faith).

So David Koresh and his deluded followers are to be pitied, not hated. And the rest of us should be cautious, mindful of our Lord's warning that "Satan can make himself into an angel of light."[95]

ON PUBLIC MORALITY

The issue of public morality, and the extent to which it should be a concern of the state, has long been debated. There was a time when the Church was a temporal, as well as a spiritual power, and the Pope was a monarch; and there was a time when the state was a spiritual as well as a temporal power, and the monarch was a kind of bishop. The two powers for centuries were commingled. The Church held recognized spiritual authority, but also wielded considerable political influence. It was very confusing.

With the rise of the nation-states, princes, kings and emperors challenged the temporal political power of Popes and Bishops; the sword, they said, belonged to them. So the sword was wrested from the Popes and wielded by the State alone, although often at the Church's behest. But the adage "power corrupts" works both ways. It corrupted Popes, now it corrupted kings and emperors who assumed the right to grant ecclesiastical benefices, to appoint abbots and bishops and even popes, and to summon church synods and councils.

Things had gone a full cycle: Religion was now the business of the state, and kings were the heads of churches. Henry VII and his daughter, Elizabeth I, were the true heads of the Church of England, and in the name of public morality heads rolled again.

So things were no better with kings and emperors using the Church than they were with popes and cardinals using the state. Heads were still rolling in the name of public morality. The Puritans in England didn't like it and revolted, and one more head rolled — this time the king's. Then many crossed the waters to set up a "New England" where they hoped finally to straighten out the business of church and state and public morality.

Thus, when the founders wrote the Constitution, they did their darndest to take the sword away from the Church and the Bible away from the king, or whoever would take a king's place in this new democratic experiment in "New England." The church wouldn't meddle in state affairs, and the state wouldn't meddle in church affairs.

The founders, however, were concerned that public morality not fade from public concern. To them public morality was very important; that's why they argued about it so. They recognized that civic behavior involved morality, and that morality depended on religion. In the Mayflower Compact the pilgrims had declared their purpose: "For the glories of God, and advancement of the Christian faith;"[96] and all but one of the 13 original states had a tax to support the preaching of the Gospel. The First Amendment was not intended to tie the hands of the churches but to free them so that religion would flourish, and thus generate a desirable level of public morality and behavior. But the Amendment attempted to achieve this without an established state religion, as existed in England and in other European countries.

In New England, and in the United States, it worked pretty well for a long time — some would say right up until World War II. Since then, some social critics think, it has not worked very well. We have so separated church and state, they say, that faith in a Supreme Being and the "voice of conscience" in many people is dead. This is the brunt of an article a few years ago in the *Los Angeles Times* by David Briggs: "Religion's Fading Role" — religion's role in public morality is fading because of "increased separation of church and state."[97]

The separation of church and State has had far reaching unanticipated results. The Church, religion and morality have slowly been nudged out of our society's public square; America's young people have, without realizing it, missed the influence of religion and morality. The voice of the Church and its moral influence are not being heard in the public debate.

The attack is being spearheaded by the courts, says A. James Reichley, a senior fellow at the Brookings Institution and author of *Religion in American Public Life*. "Judicial rulings keep pushing the walls separating religion and public life further apart, and an increasingly secular education system is shutting out any reference to religion."[98] As the influence of religion declines, said Reichley, other institutions, whose concern is not morality, such as television, rush in to fill the void in shaping peoples' thoughts, values and ideals.

The end result, according to William McKinney, is that public morality is a shambles.[99] How much of a shambles? To answer that question, the Dean of Hartford Seminary borrowed from baseball: "The early Protestant groups built the stadium and supplied the teams. In the federal period in the late 18th Century, they were forced to admit other teams. By the 1920's, other teams had their own stadiums, but mainline Protestant churches still supplied the umpires. What's happened in the last 30 years is the umpires are gone and nobody knows what the rules are."[100]

What many fear is that, if religion is moved completely to the sidelines where it no longer influences American society, decisions will increasingly be made on the basis of power, not faith or morality. Then our public debates will center, not on right and wrong and what's best for the Good Society, but on who can prevail.

Then we will be back where we were a long time ago, when religion was the business of the state, only it will be a very different form of religion, and the state will be a new kind of high priest presiding over a now secular religion.

ON LUXOR AND THE GODS

A few years ago I visited Luxor, Thebes and the Valley of the Kings in Egypt's upper Nile. Among the many impressive sights in that historic valley are the marvelously preserved tombs of the Egyptian pharaohs. Seemingly endless stairways lead to underground chambers where once rested the body of a pharaoh, and in some tombs also bodies of family members, along with garments, artifacts, weapons, ornaments and precious jewels.

The walls of these tombs are pure white, engraved with exquisite carvings, pictographs, and multi-colored drawings of ancestors, servants, soldiers and, in at least one memorable scene, a boat carrying the pharaoh to the heavens and the gods. In his tomb, Rameses VII is depicted standing in final judgment before the gods, his deceased ancestors and friends already among the blessed, and in the lower regions of the wall are the damned. Scenes such as these make clear that the Egyptians, even then, believed in an afterlife. These paintings, due to the exceedingly dry climate and absence of sunlight, are unbelievably well preserved though they date back to 1000-2500 B.C.

The Egyptians had many gods around whom their lives revolved. There was a sun god, a river god, a god of night, a god of storms, a god of fire, a god of fierce beasts, gods for most anything that might do harm or bring safety, protection, survival, and well-being to families and the community.[101]

Religion was important to the Egyptians. History documents the striking story of Pharaoh Amenhotep IV who, a century before Moses, embarked on a religious revolution to overthrow the polytheistic customs of Egypt in favor of a supreme god, Aton. Amenhotep changed his name to Akhenaton, "the favorite of Aton." It is questionable that he believed in a single God, but "he at least conceived Aton as the Supreme God, to whom all others were subject."[102] Akhenaton's strange religious revolution was short-lived, and the Egyptians returned to their old polytheistic ways which, as Daniel-Rops notes, took the strangest forms:

> A whole pantheon, in the guise of a menagerie, a whole fauna of deities, the falcon Horus, the goose Geb, the crocodile Sebek, the bull Apis, the hippopotamus, the vulture, the adder, besides all those gods half-human half-animal, with a woman's body and a cow's head, a lion's beard and a human face. Dominating that mythology was the far purer image of Orisis, the god who died to overcome death. [103]

Across the Mediterranean the Greeks also had gods who were very much a part of Greek life. The Greek gods were more humanized and personalized than the Egyptian gods. They married among themselves, and occasionally married humans, had their favorites and petty jealousies, beguiled their rivals and fought among themselves, and knew disappointment and exaltation. They were like super-humans who were, nevertheless, very much involved in human lives and human affairs. The Greeks now, of course, are Christian, yet their mythical gods are still very much alive in Greek culture. I asked our guide at Rhodes if school children today are required to study Greek mythology. "Oh, absolutely," he replied, "every child studies Greek mythology."

There were no national enmities or competitions among these gods. The Egyptians and Greeks, and later the Romans, tolerated each other's gods, not from any notion of human brotherhood, but because religion played a particular social role. "The Greeks recognized the gods of the Egyptians....The Romans worshiped all the gods of the Greeks...There were no wars of religion."[104] If you moved from one place to another, it was expected that you would worship the local gods.

Underlying this toleration of other nations' gods, as time went on there was the growing belief that gods, wherever worshiped, were, after all, mere myths. The Greek philosophers and politicians, followed later by the Romans, first privately, then publicly, questioned the existence of the gods. By Cicero's time neither academicians nor politicians believed in them. But the mass of the people still believed, and the politicians encouraged that belief because it served a useful social purpose. Edward Gibbon put it this way: "The various modes of worship which prevailed in the Roman world were all considered by the people as equally true, by the philosopher as equally false, and by the magistrate as equally useful."[105]

While all this was going on with the Greeks, Egyptians and Romans, the God of the Hebrews was revealing Himself. The central message of that revelation was monotheism: "Know, O Israel, the Lord your God is one God." "Listen, Israel: Yahweh our God is the one Yahweh. You shall love Yahweh your God with all your heart, with all your soul, with all your strength."[106] It was a new message. And it was to avoid the contamination of polytheism and idolatry that Moses fled Egypt and led the Jews into the desert where, in solitude, they could absorb the new message. He kept them there forty years for, according to Daniel-Rops, "this is exactly the time it takes for a generation to die out, those accustomed to the amenities of Egypt, and for another, hardened in the desert, to grow up."[107]

But monotheism had a hard go of it. The surrounding competition was great, and over and over again the Jews betrayed the message and the covenant. Living in the midst of polytheistic nations, they were continually torn between the true God and the many gods of their neighbors. Military conquest and material success were considered by the ancients to reflect the power of a nation's gods and the Hebrews envied the prosperity of the surrounding polytheistic people. Their neighbors, except during the reign of Solomon, were mightier and materially more prosperous than the Israelites. So, the Jews had a hard time walking the way to which God called them and understanding that God was calling them, not to a material kingdom, but to a kingdom of justice and fidelity. And they resented the prophets berating them for their infidelity to God's call: "The people of Judah have done what is evil in my eyes, says the Lord. They have defiled the house which bears my name by setting up in it their abominable idols."[108]

The years of exile in Babylon under the Persians are presented by the prophets as a punishment from God for this infidelity. It is also presented as a divine visitation and a blessing. For under the Persian kings they encountered a people who lived under a more agreeable form of polytheism. Zoroastrianism held that there were two primary spiritual principles, originally separated by a void that existed from all eternity. Ormazd is the bountiful spirit of light, power, purity and wisdom. He created light and darkness and the material world. Ahriman is the destructive spirit of darkness and falsehood who insinuated himself into the creation process infecting it with evil which infiltrated the human heart. Thus, the human person is constantly involved in a struggle with death and defilement. Man's obligation is to live a good life of inner purity, benevolence and goodness, combating whatever is evil in the world.[109] At death, the corpses of the deceased are exposed to vultures. After four days when vultures have picked clean the bones, the soul departs to appear before the deities who pass judgment on the life of the deceased.[110]

So, the moral tone of the Persians was a cut above the polytheism of the Jews' neighbors in Canaan, but it was polytheism, nevertheless. The exile, as predicted by Jeremiah, lasted seventy years.[111] Then Cyrus the Great decreed in 538 B.C. that the Jews should be allowed to leave Babylon and should be assisted in returning to Jerusalem.[112] Back in Jerusalem with Cyrus' help, they rebuilt the temple, although it took many years before God won his way with what the prophets called "a stiff-necked people."[113]

But monotheism did finally prevail among them, even though they lived, a small people, surrounded by polytheistic civilizations. It took many years more before the Egyptians, Greeks and Romans gave up their gods for the God of Abraham, Isaac and Jacob. Not until Christ and the Christian era did those neighbors and the entire surrounding world embrace monotheism: that there is but one God, that God is personal, that God is the supreme source of all creation, that God is the goal of our aspirations, and that the Son of God became incarnate in Jesus Christ.

But strangely, and sadly, if perhaps inevitably, that was the end of religious tolerance. Once religion left the realm of myth, the truth of the being of the divinity became an ultimate concern. Religion, then, was more than a social event. In Exodus God declared "I am Yahweh your God....you shall have no gods except me."[114] Enough of polytheistic myths! Religion became something people are ready to die for, and sadly His people went to violently unnatural extremes — to wars of religion, in the name of the all-loving God. Critics of Christianity could not let that irony pass unnoticed: "polytheism," they said, "for all its vulgar absurdities, was by nature tolerant, while monotheism, with all its sublimity, gave rise to rancor and religious fury."[115] We like to think that there will be no more wars of religion. But don't bet on it.

But to return to the Egyptians, Greeks and Romans, for whom monotheism was not an easy sell. It took years, centuries. Their initial response was recorded by St. Paul. He was speaking to the sophisticated Athenians and when he came to that part about Christ rising from the dead they "burst out laughing" and walked away with an over-the-shoulder comment, "We'll see you around sometime."[116] So it took centuries, but they came around, all of northern Africa, the Middle East and all of Europe. And not just the masses of the people; it was the intellectuals and political leaders who lead the way.

But now, after all these centuries of believing in God, under whatever form and name, a strange thing has been happening. Today's intellectuals in America and Europe in large numbers are saying: There is no God. In fact they're saying worse than that: they are not simply atheists. They are antitheists. Religion, they say, is "the bane of civilization, the chief source of man's misery, the main impediment to progress and social reform;" and they advocate "the abolition of religion as the first step in the advancement of civilization."[117] They have discarded the one true God of the Christians and Jews, not, of course, to adopt many mythical gods as did the Egyptians, Greeks and Romans; not even to embrace the dualism of the Zoroastrians; they recognize neither the one true God nor the many gods of antiquity.

They recognize only themselves as they say: man is the crown of creation, and he is evolving toward perfection; where he came from, or why he is, we do not profess to know; we only know that he is a magnificent being who continues to achieve tremendous scientific accomplishments, and the possibilities are infinite; while he has not as yet learned everything about himself and the universe, he is on the way to becoming all-knowing; at any rate, he is the supreme being of the cosmos. So, as far as religion goes, if we must adore, let us adore ourselves alone. In a sense, they have reverted to a kind of polytheism for, in their worldview, every man is his own god.

This wild turn in the road of religious history is led by a not inconsequential band of intellectuals. Theirs is a strong, if small, committed discipleship that borders on a cult. It is a cult of scientific materialism, whose primary dogma states that all reality is matter, measurable by the instruments of science. It fits nicely a narcissistic age.

The dogma is espoused by secular humanism which says: People swallow the God-myth because they are too ignorant to see that human life is fulfilled in the here and now. Harvard paleontologist, George Gaylord Simpson, put it this way:

> Although many details remain to be worked out, it is already evident that all the objective phenomena of the history of life can be explained by purely naturalistic or, in a proper sense of the sometimes abused word, materialistic factors....man is the result of a purposeless and natural process that did not have him in mind. [118]

Indeed, this is a wild turn in the road of religious history. But the masses of the people are not convinced. Like the masses of Egypt, Greece and Rome, Palestine and Persia, like people everywhere, the masses today believe in a Supreme Being who is in some way cause of their lives and destinies. The masses of the people side with Edmund Burke, who, in another time and place, took on the atheists of his day, the precursors of today's anti-theists. "We know," wrote Burke, "and what is better we feel inwardly, that religion is the basis of civil society, and the source of all good and all comfort....If our religious tenets should ever want a further elucidation, we shall not call on atheism to explain them....We know, and it is our pride to know, that man is by his constitution a religious animal; that atheism is against, not only our reason but our instincts; and that it cannot prevail long." [119]

History is on Burke's side. No matter where they have looked for Him — Luxor, Greece, Rome, Palestine, Persia, Europe, Africa, Asia or the Americas — no matter where they thought they may have found Him, peoples of all times and places have known there is God. Their restlessness without Him tells them so. The restlessness continues. And atheism, in truth, has never had a wide following, and has never long prevailed.

NOTES

1. Will Herberg, "What is the Moral Crisis of our Time?" *Intercollegiate Review* 4, no. 2-3 (1968), 63 (accessed 17 Dec 2010).
2. Ibid., 63.
3. Ibid., 67.
4. Michael Novak, "Awakening from Nihilism: The Templeton Prize Address," *First Things*, no. 45 (08/01, 1994), 18-22, http://search.ebscohost.com/login.aspx?direct=true& db=rfh&AN=ATLA0000881609&site=ehost-live (accessed 9/11/2010).
5. Ibid., 20.
6. Ibid., 20.
7. Ibid., 18.
8. Ibid., 20.
9. Ibid., 20.
10. Ibid., 21.
11. Ibid., 20-21.
12. Ibid., 21.
13. Avery Dulles, *The Prophetic Humanism of John Paul II* (New York: Fordham University, 1994), 4.
14. der Heydt von, "Russia's Spiritual Wilderness," *Policy Review*, no. 70 (Fall94, 1994), 12, http://search.ebscohost.com/login.aspx?direct=true&db=a9h&AN=9411046135& site=ehost-live (accessed 12/19/2010).
15. Ibid.
16. Vaclav Havel, "The Need for Transcendence in the Postmodern World" (Independence Hall, Philadelphia, PA, Global MindShift, 4 July 1994, 1994), http://www.global-mind-shift.com/discover/Memebase/TheNeedforTranscendenceinthePostmodernWorld.pdf (accessed 19 Dec 2010).
17. Novak, *Awakening from Nihilism: The Templeton Prize Address*, 21.
18. Mitchell S. Muncy, Richard John Neuhaus and Anatomy of a controversy, *The End of Democracy?: The Celebrated First Things Debate, with Arguments Pro and Con: And, the Anatomy of a Controversy, by Richard John Neuhaus* (Dallas: Spence Pub. Co, 1997), 66.
19. Malcolm Muggeridge, *Confessions of a Twentieth-Century Pilgrim*, 1st U.S. ed. (San Francisco: Harper & Row, 1988), 61.
20. *Planned Parenthood v. Casey,* No. 91-744 *Planned Parenthood v. Casey,* (SUPREME COURT OF THE UNITED STATES).
21. Novak, *Awakening from Nihilism: The Templeton Prize Address*, 21.
22. Richard John Neuhaus, "Dignity, Death and Dependence," *The Religion and Society Report* 5, no. 8 (August 1988, 1988).
23. Gerhart Niemeyer, "The Eternal Meaning of Solzhenitsyn," *National Review* 25 (19 January 1973, 1973), 83.
24. Jones, *The Jerusalem Bible,* Gen. 1:27.
25. Aleksandr Isaevich Solzhenitsyn, *Cancer Ward* (New York: Farrar, Straus and Giroux, 1969), 560.
26. Niemeyer, *The Eternal Meaning of Solzhenitsyn*, 84.
27. Herberg, *What is the Moral Crisis of our Time?*, 69.
28. Ibid., 69.
29. Maciej Zieba, "The Liberalism that we Need," *First Things*, no. 40 (02/01, 1994), 23-27, http://search.ebscohost.com/login.aspx?direct=true&db=rfh&AN=ATLA0000876080& site=ehost-live (accessed 9/11/2010).
30. Ibid., 25.
31. Ibid., 27.
32. Karl Raimund Popper Sir, *The Open Society and its Enemies. V. 1, the Spell of Plato*, 5th ed., rev. ed. (Princeton, NJ: Princeton University Press, 1966), 361.
33. Zieba, *The Liberalism that we Need*, 23-27.
34. Ibid., 25.

35. Jones, *The Jerusalem Bible,* Deut. 6:4.
36. Ibid., Isa. 49:1.
37. Ibid., Isa. 7:14.
38. Ibid., Isa. 53:2-6.
39. Ibid., John 11:47-49.
40. Ioannes Paulus PP. II, *Redemptoris Missio: On the Permanent Validity of the Church's Missionary Mandate* (The Vatican, Rome, Italy: Libreria Editrice Vaticana, 1990).
41. Zieba, *The Liberalism that we Need*, 27.
42. William Murchison, "The Straight '90s," *Human Life Review* (Summer 1993, 1993), 15.
43. Ibid.
44. Jones, *The Jerusalem Bible,* John 18:38.
45. Ioannes Paulus PP. II, *Veritatis Splendor.*
46. Jones, *The Jerusalem Bible,* John 8:32.
47. Richard John Neuhaus, "The Splendor of Truth: A Symposium," *First Things*, no. 39 (01/01, 1994), 14, http://search.ebscohost.com/login.aspx?direct=true&db=rfh& AN=ATLA0000875901&site=ehost-live (accessed 9/11/2010).
48. Murchison, *The Straight '90s*, 9.
49. Ibid., 9.
50. Michael S. Josephson and Wes Hanson, *The Power of Character: Prominent Americans Talk about Life, Family, Work, Values, and More*, 2nd ed. (Bloomington, Ind; Los Angeles: Unlimited Pub; Josephson Institute of Ethics, 2004), 218.
51. Christina Hoff Sommers and Frederic Tamler Sommers, *Vice & Virtue in Everyday Life: Introductory Readings in Ethics*, 5th ed. (Fort Worth, TX: Harcourt College Publishers, 2000), 672.
52. Isabel Wilkerson, "AT HOME WITH: Ann Landers; She could Sign Herself 'Open-Minded in Chicago,'" *The New York Times* June 10, 1993.
53. Christina Hoff Sommers, "Teaching the Virtues," *Public Interest*, no. 111 (Spring93, 1993), 10, http://search.ebscohost.com/login.aspx?direct=true&db=a9h&AN=9306015516& site=ehost-live (accessed 9/11/2010).
54. Ibid., 5-6.
55. *Action for Children's Television v. FCC*, 170.
56. William Shakespeare, *Julius Caesar* (NY: Harper, 1895), 44.
57. Christina Hoff Sommers, "Ethics without Virtue: Moral Education in America," *American Scholar* 53, no. 3 (Summer84, 1984), 381, http://search.ebscohost.com/lo-gin.aspx?direct=true&db=a9h&AN=5317528&site=ehost-live (accessed 9/11/2010).
58. Ibid., 382.
59. Ibid., 383.
60. Ibid., 382.
61. Kenneth C. W. Kammeyer, *Marriage and Family: A Foundation for Personal Decisions* (Boston: Allyn and Bacon, 1987), 263.
62. Ibid., 287.
63. Ibid., 288.
64. Ibid., 290.
65. Ibid., 291.
66. Ibid., 291.
67. Ibid., 292.
68. "Whatever Happened to Ethics?" *Time Magazine,* 25 May 1987, 1987, 15 (accessed 20 Dec 2010).
69. Ibid.16.
70. Ibid.17.
71. Ibid.16.
72. Ibid.17.
73. Source Unknown.
74. Aristotle and Martin Ostwald, *Nicomachean Ethics* (Indianapolis, Ind: Bobbs-Merrill, 1962), 92.
75. Source Unknown.

76. Ibid.

77. Aaron Zitner, "Many Look Back, Recall Satanism," *Boston Globe* 16 Oct 1992, 1992.

78. Ibid.

79. Blanche Barton and Anton Szandor La Vey, *The Secret Life of a Satanist: The Authorized Biography of Anton LaVey* (Los Angeles, CA: Feral House, 1992), 82, http://catdir.loc.gov/catdir/toc/fy0903/98169959.html.

80. John Smith and Edward Arber, *Works ; 1608-1631* (Birmingham: English Scholar's Library, 1884), 74-75.

81. Paul Carus, *The History of the Devil and the Idea of Evil: From the Earliest Times to the Present Day* (New York: Land's End Press, 1969), 7.

82. Frank Newport, *Americans More Likely to Believe in God than the Devil, Heaven More than Hell; Belief in the Devil has Increased since 2000,* 2007).

83. Billy Graham, *A Biblical Standard for Evangelists* (Minneapolis, MN: World Wide Publications, 1984), 44.

84. Friedrich Wilhelm Nietzsche and Walter Arnold Kaufmann, *The Gay Science; with a Prelude in Rhymes and an Appendix of Songs. Uniform Title: Fröhliche Wissenschaft. English,* 1st ed. ed. (New York: Vintage Books, 1974), 182, http://catdir.loc.gov/catdir/description/random045/73010479.html.

85. James Patterson and Peter Kim, *The Day America Told the Truth: What People really Believe about Everything that really Matters* (New York, NY, U.S.A: Plume, 1992), 200-201.

86. Joyce A. Little, "Naming Good and Evil," *First Things,* no. 23 (05/01, 1992), 29, http://search.ebscohost.com/login.aspx?direct=true&db=rfh&AN=ATLA0000851033&site=ehost-live (accessed 12/20/2010).

87. Carus, *The History of the Devil and the Idea of Evil: From the Earliest Times to the Present Day,* 14.

88. Jones, *The Jerusalem Bible,* Luke 22:31-32.

89. George Gaylord Simpson, *The Meaning of Evolution: A Study of the History of Life and of its Significance for Man,* Rev. ed. (New Haven: Yale University Press, 1974), 344.

90. Quoted in Richard John Neuhaus, "The Innovationist Edge," *First Things,* no. 27 (11/01, 1992), 64-66, http://search.ebscohost.com/login.aspx?direct=true&db=rfh&AN=ATLA0000856918&site=ehost-live.

91. Jones, *The Jerusalem Bible,* John 8:44.

92. Ibid., 2 Cor. 11:14.

93. Ronald Arbuthnott Knox, *Enthusiasm* (New York: Oxford University Press, 1961).

94. "Jugoslavia; the Virgin and the Commissars," *The Economist,* September 12, 1981, 50.

95. Jones, *The Jerusalem Bible,* 2 Cor. 11:14.

96. *Mayflower Compact,* 1620.

97. David Briggs, "Religion's Fading Role Leaves Many Adrift Morality: Increased Separation of Church and State has Silenced the 'voice of Conscience' for Many. but some Groups Vow to Continue Battle Against the Nation's Social Ills." *Los Angeles Times (Pre-1997 Full-text)* Jan 5, 1991, http://proxy.foley.gonzaga.edu:2048/login?url=http://proquest.umi.com/pqdweb?did=60991105&Fmt=7&clientId=10553&RQT=309&VName=PQD (accessed 9/11/2010).

98. Ibid.

99. Wade Clark Roof and William McKinney, *American Mainline Religion: Its Changing Shape and Future* (New Brunswick, NJ: Rutgers University Press, 1987), 37.

100. Ibid., 239-40.

101. Raymond O. Faulkner and others, *The Egyptian Book of the Dead: The Book of Going Forth by Day: Being the Papyrus of Ani (Royal Scribe of the Divine Offerings), Written and Illustrated Circa 1250 B.C.E., by Scribes and Artists Unknown, Including the Balance of Chapters of the Books of the Dead Known as the Theban Recension, Compiled from Ancient Texts, Dating Back to the Roots of Egyptian Civilization,* 2nd rev. ed. (San Francisco: Chronicle Books, 2008), 175.

102. Henri Daniel-Rops, *Israel and the Ancient World: A History of the Israelites from the Time of Abraham to the Birth of Christ* (Garden City, NY: Image Books, 1964), 104.

103. Ibid., 104.

104. Peter Gay, *The Enlightenment: An Interpretation* (New York: Norton, 1995), 167.

105. Ibid., 157.

106. Jones, *The Jerusalem Bible,* Deut. 6:2-6.

107. Daniel-Rops, *Israel and the Ancient World: A History of the Israelites from the Time of Abraham to the Birth of Christ,* 82.

108. Jones, *The Jerusalem Bible,* Jer. 7:30.

109. Mary Boyce, *Textual Sources for the Study of Zoroastrianism* (Chicago: University of Chicago Press, 1990), 51, http://catdir.loc.gov/catdir/enhancements/fy0609/90044072-b.html.

110. Ibid., 151.

111. Jones, *The Jerusalem Bible,* Jer. 25:8-12.

112. Bernard Reich, *A Brief History of Israel,* 2nd ed. (New York, NY: Facts On File/ Checkmark Books, 2008), 6, http://catdir.loc.gov/catdir/toc/ecip089/2008003838.html.

113. Jones, *The Jerusalem Bible,* Exod. 32:9-10.

114. Ibid., Exod. 20.

115. Gay, *The Enlightenment: An Interpretation,* 169.

116. Jones, *The Jerusalem Bible,* Acts 17:22-32.

117. Arther S. Trace, *Christianity and the Intellectuals,* 1st ed. (La Salle, Ill: Sherwood Sugden, 1983), 93.

118. Simpson, *The Meaning of Evolution: A Study of the History of Life and of its Significance for Man,* 344.

119. Burke and Clark, *Reflections on the Revolution in France,* 254-5.

Chapter Three

Law

A GIFT OF GOD

When in our Declaration of Independence the Founders appealed to "the laws of nature and of nature's God,"[1] they were consciously drawing on a long tradition in philosophy, theology and political theory. It was the natural law tradition. Its origins are classical Greek thought. In his *Rhetoric* Aristotle writes of "the law of nature,"[2] and quoting the Antigone of Sophocles argued that "an unjust law is not a law."[3] In his *Ethics*, Aristotle speaks of "natural" as distinguished from "legal" justice: "Of political justice," he wrote, "part is natural, part legal — natural, that which everywhere has the same force and does not exist by people's thinking this or that; legal, that which is originally indifferent...."[4]

The concept of the "rule of law," which rests on natural law theory, we also owe to Aristotle. In the *Politics* he asks whether the rule of an individual is preferable to the rule of law. He answers: "To invest the law then with authority is, it seems, to invest God and intelligence only; to invest a man is to introduce a beast, as desire is something bestial and even the best of men in authority are liable to be corrupted by anger. We may conclude then that the law is intelligence without passion *and is therefore preferable to any individual*."[5] The law's authority, therefore, is not based on the will of kings or oligarchs, or of the majority, but on "intelligence without passion," which, in turn, is based on "nature and nature's God," as the Declaration declares. This philosophy of natural law and the rule of law the Romans inherited from the Greeks, and Western Civilization received it from the Romans. Cicero wrote:

77

> True law is right reason conformable to nature, universal, unchangeable, eternal, whose commands urge us to duty, and whose prohibitions restrain us from evil ... This law cannot be contradicted by any other law, and is not liable either to derogation or abrogation.[6]

It was much later, well into the Christian era, that Augustine, Aquinas and the Christian philosophers adopted and incorporated natural law into their moral philosophy, and later still that western jurists such as Grotius, Coke, and Blackstone incorporated it into their legal philosophy. This is the legacy that the American Founders inherited.

It is called the "moral law" because unlike physical laws it addresses intelligent and free persons, and so operates by a moral, not physical necessity. It is also called a "higher law," because it is "of nature's God." Demosthenes said: "every law is a discovery, a gift of God."[7] The idea of the moral law as a discovery was taken over in the western tradition of law. The 18th Century American statesman James Otis said it neatly: "The supreme power of the state, is *jus dicere* only: — *jus dare* strictly speaking, belongs only to God."[8] Human beings and states declare and recognize natural rights (*dicere*); strictly speaking, God alone grants them (*dare*). Dr. Martin Luther King, writing from his Birmingham jail cell and referencing Thomas Aquinas, held the same doctrine: "A just law is a man-made code that squares with the moral law or the law of God."[9] This "higher law" tradition became the jurisprudential foundation of every law school in western society, including American schools of law.

At issue is whether American society has drifted away from that law inherited from our founders and written into their founding documents, and referenced by Abraham Lincoln in his Gettysburg address. Is our nation, its executive, lawmakers and courts still guided by the gift of law given us by God?

The Gonzaga School of Law sponsors the annual William O. Douglas Lecture, named after Washington State's former United States Supreme Court Justice. This lecture hosts prominent national figures from the legal profession and draws a large crowd. One year recently the guest lecturer was a law professor from one of our nation's most prestigious law schools. I was in the audience, and the auditorium was packed; the lecturer spoke on human rights, and at one point in his presentation said: "We hold these truths to be self-evident that all men are equal, that they are endowed with certain inalienable rights that among these are life, liberty and the pursuit of happiness." No one is so naïve as to suppose that this attorney inadvertently left out the words "Creator" and "created" from the Declaration of Independence. Does this law professor not acknowledge the Creator?

Robert P. George, the distinguished professor of Juris Prudence at Princeton University, recently attended a conference held by the American Constitution Society. This is an influential and distinguished group whose Board members are very prominent American professionals.

At its Conference at Princeton in 2010, the Society passed out an attractive pamphlet which reprinted the Declaration of Independence, the U.S. Constitution, and the Gettysburg address — our nation's founding documents. Dr. George was very pleased to receive this attractive booklet, until he saw that the American Constitution Society's rendition of Lincoln's Gettysburg address had eliminated the words "under God."

After studying the matter and trying to give the American Constitution Society every break that he could, Dr. George came to the conclusion that: there is no room for equivocation; the Society's decision to exclude the words "under God" from Lincoln's Gettysburg address was a cold and deliberate decision.

In a recent publication Dr. George wrote:

> The omission of the words 'under God' in a document characterized as a founding text by a liberal legal advocacy organization in the context of our contemporary debates over the role of religion in American public life and the meaning of the Constitution's provisions pertaining to religion is just too convenient. We now have positive evidence that they know exactly what they are doing, and, to achieve the result they want, they are willing to violate scholarly consensus, common sense, and the memorization of generations of school children. [10]

Yes, it is increasingly clear that leaders in our nation have removed not only from the public schools but from the public square any mention of God from our founding documents. They obviously seem to want no place for God in our national memory.

Small incidents? Well, perhaps, but not insignificant. It is not insignificant that in a little over fifty years God has been removed from the public schools and from much of the public square. Now, in this age of deconstruction, are law school professors presuming to remove the "Creator" from the Declaration of Independence? Have we so deconstructed the Declaration that we wish "God" and a "transcendent and objective moral order" removed from our law schools' creeds? If that is the mentality in hundreds of law schools and thousands of law classrooms throughout our country, our law and our law schools are in bad shape.

So what is a "transcendent and objective moral order?" At the risk of over-simplifying, I will attempt in a brief space to respond to that question. An objective order is simply an order of reality, that is, a condition or state of things that exists independent of the human mind and thought, and is discoverable by reason. A moral order is one which, when understood by intelligent and free beings, communicates an obligation, responsibility or duty to act or to refrain from acting. A transcendent order is one that exceeds human making because it is lodged in the very created beings themselves and in their interrelationships, and so owes its existence to the Creator.

Thus the Declaration says that it is "nature and nature's God" that entitles human persons to certain rights, and that those rights are "inalienable" because they are not man-made, inhering, as they do, in the very nature of human beings themselves. People may interfere with the exercise of a natural right, but the right itself endures because its source is "nature and nature's God" which transcend human factoring.

The moral order has what might be considered vertical and horizontal dimensions. First, the vertical dimension: as a result of creation, human beings exist in a moral relationship with God; He is their efficient and final cause, from their side, human persons owe the Creator gratitude, reverence and obedience. That order of moral relationships exists between God and all human beings, it transcends human invention, it is not man-made.

This vertical dimension is the *raison d'etre* of the horizontal dimensions of the moral order. Since all human persons are created by God and have Him as their final Good, as such they are equal before God and have a moral obligation to respect that equality; all have certain inalienable rights, such as life and liberty, which must be respected. Further, as they are to God as children to a Father, all human persons are to one another as brothers and sisters.

Thus, human persons exist in a two-dimensional moral order that transcends human invention: it reaches to God, and it reaches to all other human persons. That moral order is the foundation of our nation and our laws.

But, some of our citizens would remove God from this scene. Why? Perhaps because they no longer believe in God. Perhaps because, even though they believe in God, they see Him, as removed from, unconnected to and uninterested in the created universe. This latter is a deist position that accepts none other than man-made law and authority. So the question arises: Can God be removed from the moral order and that order stand? Can the horizontal dimension, our relations to one another, stand on its own? That has been attempted, and invariably humans have acted less than human. Take away human nature's relationship to God, and the reason for the horizontal relationships of equality and rights, not to mention brotherhood and love, is no longer convincing. What was a moral order immediately degenerates into an order of power.

Absent God, there is no basis for equality or rights with their consequent responsibilities. There is no sense in which people are equal, save the creaturehood and destiny that they share. On the contrary, people are in every other way exceedingly unequal: in body and mind, birth and genetics, social environment and opportunity.

Absent God, there remains but that "brutish" state, described by Hobbes, where "every man is to every man a wolf."[11] That is not a world of moral but power relationships. According to John Courtney Murray, Locke attempted to disguise Hobbes' state of power relationships in the moral language of rights, but the attempt failed. As Murray wrote:

> Significantly, Locke uses the word 'power' more frequently than the word 'right' in describing the state of nature. Moreover, what the social contract does, in effect, is simply to transfer this system of power relationships into the civil state, with the sole but significant difference that there is now added to it a 'third power' the public power of government. In the naked essence of Locke's thought, government is the arbiter of 'right,' only in the sense that it is a power to check power.[12]

Absent God, as Nietzsche was quick to point out, human life has no intrinsic value, and there is no ground for morality. He taunted the Victorians for thinking they could preserve Christian morality without God. Face up to it, he said, you no longer in fact recognize God, having removed Him from your culture and public square. Then why be concerned whether you are made in the image of God or not and whether you do or do not have an immortal soul?

That truth — remove God, and human life is thoroughly devalued — came home to roost in Nietzsche's own homeland. Nazi Germany had its cultural institutions, laws and law schools, whose students graduated from the best universities in Germany and crafted the Nazi laws. But it was an amoral state, so power meant everything. The Soviet Union likewise had its cultural institutions, universities and lawyers who graduated from the finest Soviet law schools. But the culture was professedly atheistic, and the laws, without moral ground, rested on raw power alone. Absent God, as Dostoyevsky observed, "everything is permitted."[13]

So, yes, I am apprehensive when I hear a lawyer remove the Creator from the Declaration and deconstruct it to read: We hold these truths to be self-evident; that somehow we came to be, and are all equal, and somehow or other we are endowed with certain inalienable rights!

Absent God from the law, as Murray said, and government becomes simply "a power to check power."[14] So, it is not surprising that the question is asked today with increasing frequency: Is our government becoming nothing more than a power to check power? Justice Byron White noted when the Supreme Court in the *Roe* decision withdrew its protection from fetal infants,

elevating the value of personal privacy over the value of the continued existence of the fetal infant, without demonstrating a constitutional warrant for
that choice, — that, said White, was an "exercise of raw judicial power."[15]

The continuing exercise of raw judicial power is evident in the cases that
hinge upon *Roe*. Although the people are divided over the nation's abortion
policy, the Court has not backed down. When it had an opportunity to with-
draw from the *Roe* doctrine and allow the people to debate the abortion issue
in the public square and the legislatures, the Court stiffened its back and
declared in *Casey* that it stands by the *Roe* decision, and on principle, the
principle being that "to overrule under fire" might threaten the legitimacy of
the Court. That is not a very satisfying response since the Court's legitimacy
is being challenged precisely because of the *Roe* decision and the cases that
drag along behind it. Things are getting worse rather than better, and this
would not be the first time that the Supreme Court turned away from a
previous bad decision. Nevertheless, the Court insists that it is not going "to
surrender to political pressure."[16] Many people simply laugh at that because
they see the Court in the box that it is in precisely because it surrendered to
political pressure in the first place when it made *Roe* the law of the land. So
some see *Casey* as just another exercise of raw judicial power. As Gregory
Sisk wrote: "The Court held onto the basic *Roe* formulation for the express
reason that to do otherwise would suggest that they listen to and could be
moved by moral dialogue."[17]

So, the question is seriously being asked: Are we abandoning the "rule of
law" and the moral ground on which it rests? Have we already abandoned
them? The abortion path that we have entered upon is a depressing one. At
first abortion was to be limited to the first trimester, and to the second
trimester only under certain conditions. It soon became abortion on demand,
and now partial-birth abortion, which is infanticide, pure and simple. This
has happened with the approval and sanction of our highest officials: the
legislature, the president and the Supreme Court. Abortionists now openly
acknowledge, seemingly without embarrassment, that what they do is kill
babies, a near million a year, "far out stripping any other developed nation."
Our country, J. Bottum observed, is involved in a "cultural investment of
enormous proportions."[18] "Raw Judicial power," as Justice Byron White
said.

The next step along this depressing path is already being talked about and
advocated. Infanticide is the logical consequence to the legalization of abortion and partial-birth abortion. Summarizing Australian philosopher and out-
spoken pro-abortionist Peter Singer, Bottum has pointed out that we have
already adopted infanticide "in fact if not yet in rhetoric."[19] But it's not that
big a deal, he says, for infanticide has been around a long time. The Greeks

and the Romans had it. The Chinese have it today. Peter Singer suggests that we might consider changing our laws to allow parents to kill their babies up to, say, age four or five?

How far this ethic of death has advanced into our culture may be gauged from the fact of Singer's appointment to the Ira W. DeCamp Professorship of Bioethics at Princeton University — quite a recognition of the man's philosophy by a prestigious university. That he is dead serious about his commitment to infanticide, there is no doubt. Human babies, he says, "are not persons. Hence their lives would seem to be no more worthy of protection than the life of a fetus."[20] That he is part of the broad cultural wave that would wash away the legacies of Western civilization, he leaves no doubt: "After ruling our thoughts and our decisions about life and death for nearly two thousand years, the traditional western ethic has collapsed."[21] Singer is not a Johnny-come-lately on the ethical scene. As far back as 1979, right after *Roe v. Wade*, he has been beating the drum for infanticide-on-demand:

> If the fetus does not have the same claim to life as a person, it appears that the newborn baby does not either, and the life of a newborn baby is of less value than the life of a pig, a dog, or a chimpanzee....In thinking about this matter we should put aside feelings based on the small, helpless and — sometimes — cute appearance of human infants...If we can put aside these emotionally moving but strictly irrelevant aspects of the killing of a baby, we can see that the grounds for not killing persons do not apply to newborn infants.[22]

The next step along this depressing path is physician-assisted suicide. The logic is already in place: If it is O.K. to kill infants without their consent, why is it not O.K. to kill aged people with their consent? In 1994, Oregon passed the Death with Dignity Act. The U.S. Supreme Court declined to review a challenge to the Oregon Law.[23] At least one aged woman has been put to death under the law, and as of this writing, legislation is being introduced in Oregon to provide financial assistance for assisted-suicide for the infirm poor. After infants, the infirm are the weakest in society, and the infirm poor are the weakest of the weak. Clearly all this has the trappings of power rather than morality.

At no stage along this depressing path has the legal profession raised its voice and cried: "Stop!" In fact, a few years ago the House of Delegates of the American Bar Association overwhelmingly adopted a resolution supporting a woman's constitutional right to abortion. At least one lawyer, who was also a professional theologian, raised his voice in protest. Wrote Dr. John Warwick Montgomery, at that time professor at Faith Evangelical Lutheran Seminary in Tacoma, Washington, now distinguished professor at Patrick Henry College, Virginia: "This resolution has squarely placed the A.B.A. in the company of those who value convenience and self-interest over human rights and human dignity...The unborn child, above all, deserves protection from defenders of civil liberties at a time when a callous and morally insensitive society thinks only of the social convenience of its adult members."[24] When 1500 of its members resigned in protest, the A.B.A. admitted that it had greatly damaged its credibility, and so reversed itself.

I am not aware of any action by the legal profession or the nation's law schools protesting abortion, including partial-birth abortion, or assisted suicide. I do know that individual lawyers have publicly endorsed the constitutional right of women to abort their fetuses.

So, why is "a transcendent and objective moral order" such a bugbear? For two quite opposing reasons: for some it is too secular a concept, for others it is too tainted by religion. Some consider human nature so corrupted by original sin that it is untrustworthy. They think that natural law theory relies too trustingly on human intelligence, and so is perceived as diminishing faith. They read "The wisdom of this world is foolishness to God,"[25] as a condemnation by St. Paul of philosophers and philosophical wisdom. Dean Curry, political scientist at Messiah College, summarized this evangelical position: "many of the nineteenth and early twentieth century Protestants....rejected the Reformers' embrace of natural law because, from their post-Enlightenment perspective, the epistemology of natural law looked indistinguishable from secular rationalism."[26]

On the other hand, most detractors of natural law today find it too linked to religion. The idea of a law that is not man-made but imposed from above — by "nature and nature's God" — has a hard go of it in a secularistic democratic culture which absolutely rejects a transcendent moral law. Democratic cultures are more at home with the notion of liberty as enunciated by the Supreme Court in the *Casey* decision. "At the heart of liberty," said the Court, "is the right to define one's own concept of existence, of meaning, of the universe, and of the mystery of human life."[27]

But that notion of liberty, as the Court's critics were quick to point out, is wholly irresponsible. An interdenominational group of Christian leaders loudly voiced its objection:

"This is the very antithesis of the ordered liberty affirmed by the Founders. Liberty in this debased sense is utterly disengaged from the concepts of responsibility and community, and is pitted against the laws of nature and of nature's God." "Such liberty degenerates into license for the oppression of the vulnerable while the government looks the other way, and throws into question the very possibility of the rule of law itself."[28]

John Paul II has written at length on freedom as the crown of human dignity, but he never fails to point out the dreadful consequences of unbridling freedom from truth. His 1991 Encyclical *Centesimus Annus*, points out the crux of uniting freedom and truth that secularistic democracies face:

Nowadays there is a tendency to claim that agnosticism and skeptical relativism are the philosophies and the basic attitudes that correspond to democratic forms of political life. Those who are convinced that they know the truth and firmly adhere to it are considered unreliable from a democratic point of view, since they do not accept that truth is determined by the majority or that it is subject to variation according to different political trends. [29]

While truth-by-counting-noses may seem to accord nicely with a democratic culture, society ultimately pays a great price for abandoning liberty ordered to truth and the good. As John Paul continued:

....if there is no ultimate truth to guide and direct political activity, then ideas and convictions can easily be manipulated for reasons of power. As history demonstrates, a democracy without values easily turns into open or thinly disguised totalitarianism. [30]

If, as Demosthenes said, "law is a gift of God," pursuing a career in the legal profession is more than just another way to make a living. The legal profession carries a great moral burden. Not to lead law students to the moral depths that are inherent in law is a disservice to students and society alike. It deprives students of the fullness of their education; it settles for mere technical training in civil law and procedures, setting the sights of a legal education on a low target. In time, not students alone, but society and the culture are the losers. The legal profession is soon estranged from its history, and the culture is deprived of this rich heritage, which in time slips from its consciousness; society has many legal technicians but few legal philosophers; the solid foundation that was once the law's is replaced by the unstable sands of shifting times; the body politic, bereft of any moral compass, lurches meaninglessly, following one constellation after another.

I am under no illusion that requiring that students understand the moral law and its relationship to the "rule of law," and that the law school curriculum be so constituted that jurisprudence, constitutional and international law be studied within the context of moral law, will guarantee that law schools turn out large numbers of lawyers committed to justice and a moral society, not to mention large numbers of legal philosophers. But it will provide a defensible understanding of the rule of law and its heritage, which is the soul of our nation. It will assist students in understanding their profession as more than just another commercial vender in the marketplace, as a calling to serve justice, to defend the innocent, to serve the weak and defenseless, and to build up a caring, just and moral society. And it just might produce a few more outstanding legal philosophers who will lead the way in the development of such a society.

Upon recently receiving the credentials of the U.S. Ambassador to the Holy See, John Paul II spoke on the world leadership role of the United States. Because people by the millions look to us "as a model, in their search for freedom, dignity and prosperity," our nation carries a far-reaching responsibility "for the development and destiny of peoples throughout the world." But the American experiment, said John Paul, is still working itself out, and "the continuing success of American democracy" depends on how successful "each new generation, native-born and immigrant, makes its own the moral truths on which the Founding Fathers staked the future" of our Republic. He concluded his remarks with a prayer that the United States "will experience a new birth of freedom, freedom grounded in truth and ordered to goodness."[31]

After many years of reflecting on the law, Justice Holmes held that the law is "the witness and external deposit of our moral life. Its history is the history of the moral development of the race."[32] It is my view that the legal profession and schools of law carry a major responsibility in that moral development of the race, and that that development is not realized apart from a transcendent and objective moral order.

ON OUR FIRST AMENDMENT

Of the values that permeate the Constitution, few strike deeper roots in human nature than those embodied in the First Amendment: "Congress shall make no law respecting an establishment of religion, or prohibiting the free exercise thereof...."[33] This is the Amendment at the heart of our education controversies.

The Amendment says two things that create a dilemma that the Supreme Court has wrestled with intensely for more than half a century: The state may not establish or advance religion; the state may not interfere with or inhibit religion.

In the early life of the nation there was fairly common agreement on the definition of religion. The Founding Fathers all recognized that religion embraced some form of man's relationship to God. But more recently as cultural unity among us has weakened, the Court finds difficulty in defining religion, and tends to avoid doing so. In 1961 when religion for many citizens had become a set of mere humanistic or naturalistic convictions exclusive of any reference to God, the Court said: "Among religions in this country which do not teach what would generally be considered a belief in the existence of God are Buddhism, Taoism, Ethical Culture, Secular Humanism and others."[34]

However religion is defined, the Founding Fathers ordained that the federal government would not itself establish a particular religion, but neither would it prohibit its free exercise. The government must be nonecclesiastical. The state is to be secular. There is nothing irreligious about the "secular" in itself; it merely means that government, its constitutional system and laws have a legitimate and proper function independent of the church and of man's religious nature.

But here's where things get sticky. For although our government must be secular, it must not promote a secularistic philosophy. In fact, to do that would itself be a violation of the First Amendment. The state may not "establish" secularism any more than it may "establish" any other religious belief, for within the meaning of constitutional law, secularism is a religious position. Indeed, the intent of the First Amendment was not and has never been interpreted to be the establishment of state indifferentism to religion. On the contrary, the original intent was that the federal Constitution allow the states to commit themselves to religion not as a political reality, but as a cultural value. Thus, on the one hand the state's expression of concern about religious values should in no way violate the citizen's individual freedom, but on the other the state cannot afford to ignore religion without in fact prejudicing its citizens against religion and thereby violating the Constitution. "Religion," says Dean Kolb, "is not only the anchorage and justification for the ultimate moral values of a social group, it is the source of such values."[35] When its value-springs dry up, the roots of a society shrivel, for its social institutions are cut off from meaning and purpose, moral clarity and spiritual hope.

Since the 1930's especially the values that voluntary enterprises, church-related and non church-related, contribute to the common good, have tended to become eclipsed by expanding government enterprises. One hundred years ago church-related schools and services played major roles in society; those rolls have significantly diminished today. Their voice and influence has declined. And it is missed; for church-related colleges and universities perform important public services; they also express and symbolize certain needed cultural values. At some point society must come to grips with the role of the churches in modern times and give practical answers to such questions as: What positions should the churches occupy in the social life of the American community? Should government disregard them, and so doing compete with church-related colleges and universities? Can government disregard them without fostering religious secularism? Or should government effectively and by public policy encourage their operation and their social and cultural contribution? And finally, can government encourage them without undermining the church-state separation principle?

These questions pertain to the role of the churches in the society. They require consistent answers. It is enigmatic to say that voluntarism — in the business world it's called private enterprise — is important to the national culture, and then by neglect or policy to squeeze into insignificance the role of the independent colleges and universities. And it is enigmatic to say that religious values are important to the national culture, and then by neglect or legislation to prejudice the potential for church-related colleges, universities and social services.

It is the task of all of us who have a stake in these matters, but it is especially the responsibility of the Supreme Court to unravel these enigmas. It is a perplexing task, for the First Amendment conveys what almost seems to be an inherent contradiction: the state is told not to enter into matters of religion; and more than a half century ago when the Supreme Court directed its attention to this dilemma, Justice Douglas said: "The First Amendment commands the government to have no interest in theology or ritual; it admonishes government to be interested in allowing religious freedom to flourish."[36] While its past decisions have not clearly conveyed how the Court answers this dilemma, there is an indication of its genuine concern to protect the values of religion and voluntarism and of elaborating a constitutional means of doing so.

For example, in *Cochran* in 1930 the Court allowed tax-financed textbooks for parochial school children when that was challenged under the due process clause on the ground that public funds were being diverted to a private use.[37] Similarly in *Everson* the Court allowed New Jersey to provide bus transportation for children attending sectarian schools.[38] However, in the same breath that the Court allowed this benefit it spoke of separation in absolute terms: "The First Amendment has erected a wall between Church and State. That wall must be kept high and impregnable."

A year later, then, The Court stood on the wall metaphor and ruled in *McCollum* that the state must follow a course of strict neutrality, and that use of public school classrooms for religious instruction on a released time basis was "establishment,"[39] and so not to be allowed. Mr. Justice Reed was the sole dissenter in *McCollum*. He objected to the "wall of separation" metaphor stating that "A rule of law should not be drawn from a figure of speech."[40] In his opinion the kind of aid that violates the First Amendment is "purposeful assistance directly to the church itself or to some religious group or organization doing religious work of such a character that it may fairly be said to be performing ecclesiastical functions."[41] It seemed clear to Justice Reed that the First Amendment allows the state sufficient flexibility to accommodate the religious needs of the people. Neither religious liberty nor non-establishment are absolutes. One citizen's right to religious freedom may be too readily violated by another's zeal to prevent the establishment of religion. As it turned out, Justice Reed's dissent, as we shall see, partook somewhat of the prophetic.

Four years later the Court began to swing in the other direction, away from the strict neutrality "non-establishment" emphasis of *McCollum*, toward the "free-exercise" principle and the notion of accommodation that appeared in *Zorach*. In that case the Court ruled that the public school system may cooperate with religious school authorities by arranging class in the sectarian school. The Court rested its decision on arguments like these: "the First Amendment... does not say that in every and all respects there shall be a separation of Church and State;"[42] government fittingly cooperates, said *Zorach*, with a wide variety of beliefs and creeds for the sake of the spiritual need of its citizens.

Three members of the Court dissented strongly to *Zorach* and the Court's apparent retreat from *McCollum*. The stinging language of their dissents has become famous: "the *McCollum* case has passed like a storm in a tea cup;" cooperation is only a "soft euphemism" under which government will "steal into the sacred area of religious choice;" *Zorach* after *McCollum* "will be more interesting to students of psychology and of the judicial process than to students of constitutional law."[43]

The question persisted: "What constitutes aid to religion?" *McCollum* and *Zorach* — non-establishment and free exercise — stood face to face, as it were, in confrontation. About that time Professor Howe expressed what many Constitutional scholars were thinking when he testified before a Senate Education Subcommittee: "I am satisfied that a valid line can be drawn between government support of activities that are predominantly of civil concern and those that are predominantly of religious significance."[44] And in 1963 the Court first began to forge a meaningful and acceptable test of establishment based on this distinction. In *Schempp* the Court reasoned that there are certain actions and forms of state aid which have as their purpose and primary effect the achieving of a secular objective. The freedom of religion clause forbids any action by the state the purpose and primary effect of which is to inhibit religion. The test as enunciated for the Court by Mr. Justice Clark is this: what are the purpose and primary effect of the enactment? If either is the advancement or inhibition of religion then the enactment exceeds the scope of legislative power as circumscribed by the Constitution. This is to say that to withstand the strictures of the Establishment Clause there must be a secular legislative purpose and primary effect that neither advances nor inhibits religion.[45]

As Kauper said, commenting on *Schempp*, although the Court still uses the term "neutrality," there is ample evidence that it is not presently committed to a theory of strict neutrality. It is a neutrality twice tempered by considerations stemming from the two countervailing principles of the First Amendment: neutrality is first tempered by the state's responsibility to respect religious freedom and to accommodate the religious needs and interests of citizen's; this responsibility of the state to religion, however, is itself tempered by the state's obligation not to become involved with the primarily theological and evangelical aspects of religion. The test, of course, is no rigid rule of thumb. It is a pragmatic test that involves weighing the two principles of the First Amendment.[46]

In *Board of Education v. Allen* in 1968 the Court relied on the *Schempp* formulation of the "primary purpose and effect" test and allowed New York to loan secular textbooks to students in grades seven through twelve in private church-related schools. The appellants had argued that in a church-related school the entire educational program is so permeated with religion that aid to any part of the program constitutes impermissible government support for religion. Speaking for the Court Mr. Justice White recognized the obvious public function of private education: "…in raising national levels of knowledge, competence, and experience." And the Court recognized the distinction between the secular and religious functions in the schools: "…religious schools pursue two goals, religious instruction and secular education;" they perform "the task of secular education" in addition to their "sectarian function."[47]

In 1971 the Court still more clearly and decisively hammered out the test of constitutionality. In *Tilton v. Richardson* the Court ruled on the validity of the Federal Higher Education Facilities Act which authorized federal funds to finance the construction of undergraduate academic facilities in private, church-related colleges.[48] But in a companion case (*Lemon*) on the same day the Court disallowed assistance to primary and secondary schools for instruction in secular subjects.[49] The Court has consistently distinguished aid to elementary and secondary church-related schools from aid to colleges and universities on the grounds that there are significant differences between the religious aspects of these two types of institutions.[50]

In its decision *Roemer v. Maryland* in June, 1976 by the narrowest of margins, 5 to 4, the Court upheld the right of the state of Maryland to give to church-related colleges and universities a grant to cover partial tuition for each full-time student.[51] The grant amounts to 15 percent of what Maryland spends on each student in its state college system. The funds can be used only for secular educational purposes, and cannot be given to institutions that award only seminarian or theological degrees. The court used the same test it has been using in similar cases since Schempp: government aid to church-related colleges and universities is constitutional as long as: (1) the law has a secular legislative purpose; (2) its primary purpose and effect is neither to advance nor inhibit religion; (3) it does not foster excessive government entanglement with religion.

Mr. Justice Blackmun, who wrote the majority opinion contended that

Religious institutions need not be quarantined from public benefits that are neutrally available to all.... The Court has not been blind to the fact that in aiding a religious institution to perform a secular task, the state frees the institution's resources to be put to sectarian ends.... If this were impermissible, however, a church could not be protected by the police and fire departments, or have its public sidewalk kept in repair. The Court never has held that religious activities must be discriminated against in this way. Neutrality is what is required.[52]

These are narrow and tenuous victories, but for church-related colleges they indicate the Court's recognition of the necessity of protecting those institutions whose contribution is so central to American society. If the Court is determined to continue along its recent course, and to emphasize values that are important to the life of the nation, it may keep before its attention the following three propositions apropos of the First Amendment.

First, not indifference but partiality to religion inspired the First Amendment. There are those who hold that among the most important purposes of the First Amendment was the advancement of the interests of religion. When the Bill of Rights was adopted, a number of states had established religions. At least in New England the government was not merely permitted but required to exercise its authority for the advancement of religion. The fact of establishment, at least in New England, supports the view that the intention of the religion clause was to guarantee that the federal government would not interfere with the religious liberties of individuals and groups, and would not interfere with the states in their religious establishment.[53]

Second, the purpose of the religion clause of the First Amendment was not to place religion and nonreligion on an equal footing; rather it was, in part at least, "to allow all religions and all denominations to pursue, in freedom, the common enterprise of advancing what they conceived to be the spiritual welfare of the American people."[54] It is very unlikely that the religion clause was intended as a statement of rights protecting non-belief and irreligion. Other clauses of the Amendment protect the non-believer and interests that are apart from religion — freedom of speech, freedom of the press, freedom of assembly. Because of the special importance that the founding Fathers assigned to religion, and because of the oppression that some of the colonists had experienced in its name, religion is singled out and assigned a special right, and government is assigned a special responsibility with regard to it.

Third, the First Amendment must be understood and interpreted in light of the momentous social and political changes that differentiate the late twentieth from the nineteenth century. Changes in the roles of government have affected considerably the social and cultural influence of religion and voluntarism. Both the police power of the state and its power to tax are broad powers. They are exercised quite differently today than in former times. During the nineteenth century when that government was thought best which governed least, the state assumed a laissez-faire posture not only toward church-related institutions, but toward all social and economic institutions. It was considered bad government, not to say bad morality, for the state to direct the course of social and economic life. At the same time there existed what Howe called a *de facto* establishment of religion.[55] The culture and the mores of all institutions, public and private, reflected the prevailing Protestantism. Consequently the indifference of government to church-related institutions in accommodating the religious needs and desires of the people created no cultural void. The state was equally nonaccommodating to other social and economic needs for a time at least, but these needs were adequately met without government assistance. Likewise religious and other cultural needs were met independently of state aid. The state's interest in furthering religious values, as well as its interest in advancing economic growth and social development, was thought to be best fulfilled by policies of laissez-faire; and for a time it was.

Today, things are quite different. The role of government has expanded considerably. Government today adopts policies of cooperation with economic and social institutions that are thought to preserve political and social values that nourish a democracy. It is no less important that government adopt policies based on a philosophy of cooperation with church-related educational institutions in order to maintain cultural values of religion and voluntarism that are equally vital to democracy.

The crucial question may be asked perhaps this simply: must America's commitment to the separation of church and state be likewise a commitment to a secular culture? Recent decisions indicate that the Supreme Court is at last finding a way to maintain church-state separation, and a secular state, and at the same time to allow more fertile opportunities for the flowering of religious culture and voluntarism. It seems that the Court has committed itself to the primary purpose and effect test as the ruling norm in church-state cases. That may be the key that will enable the independent sector of higher education to continue strong and contributing in American society.

A discussion on this subject should not be concluded without a word about religious freedom. Dean Drinan argued that the value of religious freedom requires greater accommodation by the state in favor of students who choose to attend church-related schools.[56] Basing his argument on *Sherbert* he says that, just as the state may not pressure a Sabbatarian to work on Saturday or be deprived of unemployment compensation, neither may it pressure a student to abandon a church-related school in favor of a secular education. To deny state aid to church-related colleges places, in effect, that kind of pressure on college students and their families. Giannella carries the argument one step further: to deny state aid to sectarian colleges and universities not only indirectly pressures that student to favor a strictly secular education, but it also places sectarian colleges and universities at "a state created disadvantage vis-à-vis secular institutions."[57]

To argue that the establishment clause requires the creation of this disadvantage is to adopt a view of nonestablishment which demands that the state throw its weight against church-related colleges and universities. For the state to adopt that posture is, in effect, to run independent higher education out of business. This has wide reverberations that are clearly contrary to all that American history and culture have stood for; and recent Supreme Court decisions do not support that posture.

"WE HOLD THESE TRUTHS"

In 1960 John Courtney Murray wrote *We Hold These Truths*, with the subtitle "Reflections on the American Proposition."[58] The proposition, of course, is "We hold these truths to be self-evident; that all men are created equal and are endowed by their Creator with certain inalienable rights...." and when written, it was widely accepted by the founders and the citizenry at large. The proposition embodied certain philosophical and moral truths that rested on natural law. Those truths are recognized to come from no particular religious faith but from "nature" and "nature's God." The proposition and the truths it contained were expressed in the Declaration and embodied in the Constitution and the Bill of Rights.

By its very nature, society requires a consensus, which is the basis of people's mature trust and civic unity. And in the beginning of the Republic, people held those truths as the basis for the political consensus among believers of all faiths. They believed that the government rests on a moral foundation, the universal moral law; that the legal order of society is based on that moral law; and that the nation, in all its aspects, is founded and continues under God.

One can readily cite the founders in support of that consensus. John Adams said: "[w]e have no government armed with the power capable of contending with human passions unbridled by morality and true religion. Our Constitution was made only for a moral and a religious people. It is wholly inadequate to the government of any other."[59] Jefferson was no bell-ringer for religion, and at least once lashed Catholics for their "monkish ignorance and superstition."[60] Yet on this issue he was of the same mind as Adams: the American experiment in government would not survive apart from its religious moorings. Reflecting on the immorality of slavery, he wrote:

Can the liberties of a nation be thought secure when we have removed their only firm basis, a conviction in the minds of the people that these liberties are of the gift of God? That they are not to be violated but with his wrath? Indeed I tremble for my country when I reflect that God is just: that his justice cannot sleep for ever ... The Almighty has no attribute which can take side with us in such a contest. [61]

But time brought significant and painful changes. So when Murray wrote in the early 1960's he spoke of a vast gulf separating the philosophy of the founders and the philosophy of the mid-20th century. He raised the question: Do we still hold these truths? Of that he was skeptical. And in the following passage he takes obvious glee in poking fun at the lord high philosophers of the universities:

There is indeed talk today about a certain revival of this great tradition, notably among more thoughtful men in the legal profession. But the talk itself is significant. One would not talk of reviving the tradition, if it were in fact vigorously alive. Perhaps the American people have not taken the advice of their advanced philosophers. Perhaps they are wiser than their philosophers. The tradition of natural law is not taught or learned in the American university....the American university long since bade a quiet goodbye to the whole notion of an American consensus, as implying that these are truths that we hold in common, and a natural law that makes known to all of us the structure of the moral universe in such wise that all of us are bound by it in a common obedience. [62]

Richard John Neuhaus in his *The Naked Public Square* covers much the same ground and comes to the same conclusion as Murray: the obliteration of natural law from our public philosophy and our universities is an accepted fact. Those learned people in our universities are no longer hostile to religion; that is neither in good taste, nor indeed necessary. "Rather than attacking religion, cultural elites quietly assume its irrelevance. It is stated with smug certitude that any public appeal to religion is an effort to turn back the clock." [63]

Yet there must be some consensus. If the public square is naked, it will not remain naked. Says Neuhaus: "When the democratically affirmed institutions that generate and transmit values are excluded, the vacuum will be filled by an agent left in control of the public square, the state. In this manner, a perverse notion of the disestablishment of religion leads to the establishment of the state as church." [64]

They may be among the "cultural elites," says Neuhaus, but they are still "Barbarians" if they think that society "can get along without some moral consensus." Barbarians are those "who in principle refuse to recognize a normative ethic or the reality of public virtue." [65]

Rather than seeing the self-evident truths as the normative and unifying basis for the consensus, "barbarians" see them as bonds to be broken and discarded. The founding fathers saw them as necessary for the civil consensus. The "barbarians" think human nature is diminished by a creator, for man, they hold, has no superior, he creates himself. The founders thought that human nature was unintelligible apart from some true end toward which it is essentially but freely ordered by the Creator, who not only does not diminish but glorifies that nature. This was the faith and the foundation of the founders.

But in the course of our history, our philosophers and our schools have drifted to other things. Now we rarely teach those truths, and seldom reflect on them. By and large, they fail to influence either our private or public lives.

Murray thought that might be the tragic beginning of the end of the Republic. That's why he wrote his book. The founders thought that our survival as a free nation depended on those truths, and that the greatest threat to them lies in the souls of those who do not believe in them. Their belief was expressed in both the Massachusetts and the Virginia Bills of Rights: "no free government, or the blessing of liberty, can be preserved to any people, but by a firm adherence to justice, moderation, temperance, frugality, and virtue, and by a frequent recurrence to fundamental principles."[66]

A literary classic is a piece that, because of its excellence, authoritative and universal character, endures through the years. *We Hold These Truths* is such an essay, as timely now as when it was written. Those truths belong to a long philosophical tradition that refuses to die. If they are indeed self-evident, then I believe that even if today's philosophers never knew them, they nevertheless will live. The threads of the tradition will never be lost, but will be picked up again and woven into a consensus, either of an American or of some other democratic government.

So, why is natural law in disfavor among many jurists and legal scholars? For many reasons, perhaps, but I single out two. First, although natural law long pre-dates Christianity, having its roots in Plato, Aristotle, Cicero and the Stoics, it was early adopted by Augustine, St. Thomas and the Scholastic philosophers and theologians, and has now long been associated with Christian philosophy. That rendered it suspect by disciples of the Enlightenment. Secondly, it is essentialist in the sense that it recognizes nature and essences with their built in finality. One cannot escape the ordering that is inherent in nature, which forces us to confront an order beyond nature. Natural law is a moral compass for human behavior. It makes demands.

This is where rationalists and secular humanists hit the panic button. Both reject Christianity and both reject intrinsic finality in nature for finality means that there is something superior to human nature, that humans do not determine their own finality, and do not create their own nature and purpose.

Finality, they think incorrectly, is a denial of human freedom. In short, nature and natural law point to God, and rationalists and secular humanists long ago wrote God off.

But irony shouldn't be lost. "We hold these truths to be self evident," the founders said. They believed that there were truths that flowed from natural law. So, in justifying their revolt, the colonists appealed to "nature and nature's God." And ever since, in the course of our national history, in great and critical moments, the American people have turned to the rights and responsibilities inherent in nature and its laws, to justify decisive actions. The Civil War and the fight over slavery come immediately to mind. As President Lincoln said, in so many words and on many occasions: I don't care what the civil law says, the Dred Scott decision is wrong and immoral because it runs afoul of what we know of the nature of human persons and their finality.

Years later, we again called upon natural law to justify the Nuremberg trials. There was no world court or state-made laws with jurisdiction to try those people who had surrounded Hitler and carried out the Nazi atrocities. Had rationalists and secular humanists acted consistent with their theories, they would have said that Hitler's people were simply carrying out legitimately established Nazi law. "No way," said world opinion, and the Allies created a court that judged them against that perennial law: nature. The Court justified itself, in effect, saying: "We hold these truths to be self-evident," that human beings have a destiny beyond that determined by states; that human nature is a seat of personal responsibility; and that freedom and responsibility are not abrogated when states pass laws, and certainly not when those laws are abhorrent to nature. So the Nazis were sent to death for violating, not Nazi law, but nature's law.

More recently, the Civil Rights Movement called upon natural law to justify the overturning of customs and laws that had ruled the land an embarrassingly long time. In that famous and brilliant letter from a Birmingham jail, Dr. Martin Luther King, Jr. appealed to that long tradition from Aristotle, Cicero, Augustine, Thomas Aquinas and the Scholastic philosophers, right up to America's founding fathers. How does one determine when a law is just or unjust? Dr. King responded: "A just law is a man-made code that squares with the moral law or the law of God. An unjust law is a code that is out of harmony with the moral law."[67] And he drove that truth home by reminding his readers of Nazi Germany: "We can never forget that everything Hitler did in Germany was 'legal' and everything the Hungarian freedom fighters did in Hungary was 'illegal.' It was 'illegal' to aid and comfort a Jew in Hitler's Germany."[68] It is to the everlasting credit of the United States Congress that it finally overturned what had been 'legal' and at long last rooted our civil rights legislation in eternal and natural law.

The Second Vatican Council in the famous Declaration on Religious Freedom[69] also called up natural law when it asserted that the right of religious freedom is the most fundamental of human rights. This right, the Council insisted, is not a matter of revelation but is, in principle, knowable by human reason. That Declaration is principally the work of John Courtney Murray, and his argument for religious freedom is founded wholly on natural law. We Hold These Truths, Murray said, is the "American proposition"[70] that binds us together as people, and holds hope for binding all nations together in union — Jew and Gentile, slave and free, rich and poor, black and white, male and female. That the Second Vatican Council should incorporate such a resolution in the teachings of the Church was a monumental achievement of American thought. And we would be foolish to turn away from it.

What this brief survey tells us is that, while it may be in disfavor from time to time, natural law won't go away. It keeps coming back. Rather we keep resurrecting it in our thinking to justify what right reason tells us should be justified. It is a perennial philosophy, because nature is perennial. It won't go away.

WHAT TRUTHS WE HOLD

For some time now I, probably like most of my fellow countryman, have heard Republicans and Democrats, friends and strangers, family, co-workers and co-religionists argue their views on abortion. Those who uphold a person's right to abort the fetus generally argue for a woman's "right to choose." Those who condemn abortion argue that no one has a right to kill an innocent child.

The founders of our great nation justified what they did in their Declaration of Independence: "We hold these Truths to be self evident, that all Men are created equal, that they are endowed by their Creator with certain inalienable Rights, that among these are Life, Liberty, and the Pursuit of Happiness." They then asked God to witness their declaration and bless it by His Providence and Protection.

But from the very beginning the founders were split down the middle on the meaning and extent of "inalienable rights." Precisely not everyone, some said, possesses the "inalienable right" to liberty. Others soundly disagreed saying: "It is a universal right of all people."

Asked his view on the matter of slavery, John C. Calhoun, former vice president of the newly formed United State of America, stated: "I hold that, in the present state of civilization, where two races of different origin, and distinguished by colour, and other physical differences, as well as intellectual, are brought together, the relation now existing in the slaveholding states between the two is, instead of an evil, a good — a positive good ... I hold, then, that there never has yet existed a wealthy and civilized society in which one portion of the community did not, in point of fact, live on the labour of the other. Broad and general as is this assertion, it is fully borne out by history."[71]

But when John Quincy Adams, former president of the United States, was asked by Alexis de Tocqueville if he thought slavery was "a great plague for the United States?," Adams flatly said, "Yes, certainly that is the root of almost all the troubles of the present and the fears for the future."[72]

The fight over the right to own a slave endured for years and Abraham Lincoln, expressing his view in 1854, said: "If A. can prove, however conclusively, that he may, of right, enslave B — why may not B. snatch the same argument, and prove equally, that he may enslave A?"[73]

Then came the Civil war, and after the war came over one-hundred years of post-war hatred and anger and finally healing. And now it appears we are in a second civil war over virtually the same issue: the inalienable right this time, to life itself. Over the right to life our nation today is seriously split down the middle. One may readily today thus paraphrase Abraham Lincoln's 1854 statement, "If A can prove, however conclusively that he may of right kill B, why may not B (or one who loves B) snatch the same argument and prove equally that he may kill A?"

A short time ago, our President Barak Obama was invited to address the 2009 graduating class of Notre Dame, and to be honored by the University. President Obama is an effective speaker; and his speech at Notre Dame was eloquently delivered. But Notre Dame is a Catholic University and the Catholic Church and Hierarchy, and Catholics in large numbers believe that abortion is killing an innocent fetus and a seriously sinful violation of the child's right to life. However, President Obama believes just as strongly that the mother has the right to kill the child in her womb. Notre Dame alumni accused their *Alma Mater* of playing politics. There was tension and considerable hostility and anger around the campus that graduation day,[74] and the hostility is spreading throughout the nation.

Seeking some road to harmony among the hostile parties, President Obama encouraged both sides — pro abortionists and anti abortionists — to seek and find, notwithstanding their opposing views, a "common ground."[75] This is not the first time that President Obama has called upon antagonists to search and find common ground.

In the nineteenth Century it was the "self evident" truth of the right of freedom or the right to enslave; in the twenty-first century it is the right to life or the right to kill the innocent. And much as people would hope to find common ground, there is no common ground to be found. The right to life is not granted by kings, rulers, or clergymen, Parliaments or Congressmen. It is the Creator's work; not to be fudged.

In disputes over civil laws — the best housing policy, the best health policy, the wisest tax laws — it is reasonable to hope for common ground. But in some matters there is no common ground. The President encouraged his audience to make "adoption more available" and to "reduce the number of women seeking abortions."[76] Friends of mine have suggested the same. But abortion always kills an infant. I can readily imagine President Lincoln hearing from the slave owners: "We will decrease the number of slaves" and "we will increase social services." But one slave is still a slave. And one fetus killed is still killing an innocent life.

It is not faith that tells us that abortion kills an innocent life. It is science. And the more we know about it the more the phrase "a woman's right to choose" is recognized as simply a euphemism for "a woman's right to kill the child in her womb."

When the founders wrote the Declaration of Independence they knew full well that they were founding their work on the law of the Creator. Madison, Jefferson, Adams, Washington, and scholars of that entire era, were grounded in natural law theory. They knew and accepted the Rule of Law. They knew that with rights came responsibilities and obligations; that when they appealed to God they were addressing the Divine Law-maker; when they asked Him to confirm and protect their work they were accepting responsibility to cooperate with His providence, and were committing future generations to the same responsibility and trust.

That is why John Adams and Abraham Lincoln opposed slavery. It violated the very ground on which the Union was built; that "All men are created equal." And that is why the legal killing of infants in their mother's womb is so abhorrent to so many of the present generation of Americans; every infant is God's child, and His gift to us as a sister and brother. And just as President Obama has so praiseworthily pledged himself to guarantee every child the right to an education, so should he first and with far greater righteousness pledge himself to guarantee every child, as far as humanly possible, the right to life. The President says: "We must find a way to live together."[77] In his campaign he promised every child the right to a college education, all while the infant in the womb is crying: "But first I have to live."

ON "INTELLECTUAL AND MORAL ILLITERATES"

A deep void in the nation's public school systems is currently the center of public attention. With mounting concern, not only religious leaders, but social scientists mull over the absence of any moral and religious value-orientation in the education of children and youth. I hear the concern expressed by parents with whom I speak, and note with increasing frequency that it occupies the agenda of educational meetings. One undertakes to criticize any aspect of the public school system with some deference, so identified is it with middle America. But no American institution, however ingrained, is beyond review.

An uncommonly difficult dilemma is at the heart of the national concern. On the one hand a pluralistic society such as ours faces the problem of accommodating many different religious views and widely divergent value-orientations. We commit ourselves to this in the commitment we make to individual freedom of conscience, belief and expression. Since our Public Schools cannot accommodate all beliefs, we do not accommodate any — this is our solution. On the other hand, the exclusion of God and a moral and religious value-orientation in the schools eliminates an element in education that is not simply an adornment, but essential both for the individual and society.

Social scientists devote considerable space in their writings to the role and importance of values, which are a kind of glue that keeps people and social institutions together. Every social group for its functioning and survival requires some commonly accepted beliefs and modes of behavior as the basis of mutual trust. Simply to get along and to have some degree of agreement on policy, they need shared values which are the basis of policy and action.

Thus it is that perhaps the most important measure both of the strength and richness of a society are the values that people share, around which they come together as a people. In a great culture those values are deeply perceived and integrated into a shared philosophy of life. A nation that is united only at the technological and industrial levels of life where people share material goods, and not at the profounder levels of thought, belief and human purpose, lacks cultural depth and profound social identity.

The importance of all this to society is obvious. The primary value-forming institutions are the family, the church and the school, where personal and social ties are close, relationships intense, and the social exchange is around life's most meaningful events. Revolutionary regimes, as soon as they come to power, move quickly to take over the control of these institutions, for they must from the start build loyalty around a new set of values and shape the citizen according to a new value-orientation. This can be done successfully and ultimately only by controlling the value-forming institutions.

To return to our dilemma — the conventional wisdom had it that, in a pluralistic society such as outs, where no religious orientation can be legislated, the dilemma was resolved in the following way: The schools are public institutions and education is a function of the State, which is wholly neutral as regards God, religion and value-formation. God and religious values are private concerns of the family and the churches. These two institutions are free to fulfill the value-forming function, unimpeded by the State. The schools, as agents of the state, are stripped of the religious value-forming function. The expectation is that two-thirds of the primary value-forming institutions, by working hard at it, can make up for the neutrality of the schools.

Our experience with this suggests that whatever merit it may have theoretically, it is not working. The modern family, with all the pressures that are on it, struggles against heavy odds to transmit from one generation to the next some rudimentary ethical and moral sense. Healthy families, with a strong sense of identity, manage to survive the negative impact of the neutral schools in a neutral state, but the average family has a hard go of it.

Furthermore, the supposed neutrality of the schools is no neutrality at all. The public schools in fact present a decided value-position with a rather firm morality of their own. Well over a hundred years ago, a Protestant theologian predicted this evolution of the so-called "neutral" schools. Dr. Archibald A. Hodge, Princeton Professor, foresaw a school system whose value-orientation would be both anti-religious and anti-social. In 1861 he wrote:

> ... a comprehensive and centralized system of national education, separated from religion as is now commonly proposed, will prove to be the most appalling enginery for the propagation of anti-Christian and atheistic unbelief, and of anti-social nihilistic ethics, individual, social and political, which this sin-rent world has ever seen... [78]
> It is capable of exact demonstration that if every party in the State has the right of excluding from the public schools whatever he does not believe to be true, then he that believes most must give way to him that believes absolutely nothing, no matter in how small a minority the atheists or the agnostics may be. It is self-evident that on this scheme, if it is consistently and persistently carried out in all parts of the country, the United States system of national popular education will be the most efficient and wide instrument for the propagation of Atheism which the world has ever seen. [79]

"...The most efficient and wide instrument for the propagation of Atheism...." Is Dr. Hodge's forecast being fulfilled in our generation? I have heard it said that "We have educated a generation of intellectual and moral illiterates." Is that what we are doing? Could it be otherwise? The student is in an environment that says, in a loud and clear voice: God and moral and religious values are unimportant! Can't we turn it around?

Our nation was founded on a different set of assumptions, from which we've drifted. After long introspection, our forefathers felt they had to justify, both to themselves and to the rest of the world, what they were about to do. It was a unique kind of revolution; it did not begin with the firing of guns. The first act of the revolutionaries was to write a philosophical statement that began with a three-fold proposition which they said was self-evident; (1) that all men are created equal; (2) that they are endowed by the Creator with certain inalienable rights; and (3) that among these are life, liberty, and the pursuit of happiness.

What the proposition meant to them and what its obvious meaning is to those who study it now, is at least this: First, that there are curtain truths that tell us something about our relationships with each other. The primary truth is that man is created by God.

The second truth is that all men stand before God as creatures equal. While there is manifest inequality in natural endowment, intelligence, sensitivity, skills, and variation in human conditions, all persons have a common Father in God, and exist in relation to each other as brothers and sisters.

The third truth is that people who exercise authority, which in some way is received from God, must be mindful that those over whom they rule have certain inalienable rights. What they were intent on making unquestionably clear is that, over and beyond civil rights which are granted by civil law and so are man-made, there is another realm of rights that are not man-made. God endows people with certain entitlements necessary for the pursuit of their destiny. A person may be unjustly captured and imprisoned, and so deprived of the exercise of his right to liberty, but the right itself is not alienated, estranged or removed.

Our national beginnings, then, were justified on the transcendental nature of man, and on the existence of a fundamental moral order between God and man, and among men. There is a Higher Being and a higher law on which all laws and codes are based. These fundamental, recognized values were taught to every child — in home, church and school. Generation after generation of Americans went over the same ground — the idea of God, creaturehood, and a higher morality that governs all people — Protestant, Catholic, Jew, Hindu, Moslem, and people of no religion at all.

In the course of our history we have drifted away from that moral awareness and commitment, which to them was so self-evident. It is no wonder — we are not allowed to teach it. Only at times of great national and international crises do we turn back to it, as we did in the struggle over slavery. The national course we were then pursuing flouted the proposition. There was a higher morality than the civil law, which in this case, as Abraham Lincoln said, was morally wrong, regardless of the Supreme Court's ruling in the Dred Scott case, and it should be changed.

We came back to it again after the Holocaust. World conscience was aroused as from a sleep: it was immoral, no matter what man-made laws order and governments decide. A higher moral order requires that human beings behave differently toward one another than Nazi law and the established government had decreed. There is no firm basis in a sociological jurisprudence for condemning the Holocaust. We reached into the deeper moral reservoirs from which we have always drawn.

But we do that only in a pinch. For several generations now students have been educated only to the civil law that is — a sociological morality. And that already weak moral standard has in recent years been battered by gross forms of existential morality according to which everyone makes up his own rules as he goes along because "nothing is really right or wrong anyhow, unless I think so." One can see, as Professor Hodge did, how that might lead not only to beliefs that are atheistic, but to an anti-social and nihilistic ethic.

One should not conclude from this analysis that deficiencies in the school system are the only cause of atheistic belief, anti-social and nihilistic behavior. But the schools are, indeed, value-forming, they are not neutral, they are not pulling their weight and they are a drag on the other social institutions. And one can question the wisdom of continuing the present educational policies.

We find ourselves, as a result of history, in the following very clearly enunciated position: Educate everyone in the State schools, But the State schools, because of church-state separation, must have no reference to God or to religious moral values. Therefore, educate everyone without reference to God or those moral values. In effect: Educate the child in the best science, mathematics, art and history; teach him to read and write, and introduce him to the literature of our culture; give him good gymnasiums, fields and swimming pools; socialize him to minorities as well as to the dominant cultural groups, and to his civic responsibilities; but don't tell the child anything about God, either as transcendent or immanent Being; don't talk to him about religion or morality or about a philosophy of life; and don't teach him ethics, other than the most superficial.

This is our public policy in education. It's time we do something about it.

ON CONTRACT AND COVENANT

The Founding Fathers were religious men. They were well versed in the Bible and God's covenant with man. They saw the New World as a kind of promised land, and they looked upon themselves as having entered into a divine covenant with God to establish a new society.

Many of them were also eminent political theorists, well versed in John Locke's theory of the "social contract." John Locke was an English empirical philosopher of the late 17th Century who wrote, as philosophers are wont to do, on political theory. Political theorists in Locke's day were searching to justify individual freedom and revolutions against autocratic rulers. It was an age when the final nails were driven into the coffin of the divine right of king's theory. Our founding fathers relied heavily on Locke in laying the cornerstones of American government.

Locke rested the right of freedom for the masses on his "state of nature" theory: Once upon a time all people were equal, enjoyed absolute freedom and were subject to no laws, rulers or governments. But out of fear of those who might burglarize the property of others, people decided to establish a government and charged it to police the group and maintain order. So the people gave up the absolute freedom that they enjoyed in the "state of nature" and entered into a "social contract." They surrendered to the government only enough freedom to guarantee that their lives and their properties would be secure. Thus government, in Locke's view, has the very limited purpose of protecting the social contract. People are otherwise free to do what they want. Individuals may accumulate and horde as much wealth as they please, there being in principle no moral limit. Hence, we have both maximum freedom and limited government. Locke pushed individual freedom so far as to reject any obligation of children to their parents.

This powerful ideology greatly influenced the democracies of all Western countries. Our founding fathers consumed Locke's theory in large drafts, incorporating it explicitly in the Declaration of Independence and in the Constitution of the United States and of the several states.

But the Lockean myth about the state of nature and the social contract completely ignored the Biblical notion of covenant, which for over 2,000 years greatly influenced Western thought. Under the covenant, people, prior to any social contracts they may engage in, are interrelated by a previous order of nature: The relation between Creator and created, God and his people. "The covenant," in Robert Bellah's words, "is not a limited relation based on self-interest, but an unlimited commitment based on loyalty and trust. It involves obligations to God and the neighbor that transcend self-interest, though it promises a deeper sense of self-fulfillment through participation in a divinely instituted order that leads to life instead of death."[80]

The Lockean myth ignored another reality that also powerfully influenced Western Culture: St. Paul's understanding of the Church as the body of Christ. In addition to the covenant that binds us in loyalty and trust to God and to one another, we all share and participate in the redemptive crucifixion and resurrection, which makes us members of the Body of Christ. We have different gifts, but a common grace unites us in community more profoundly than a community based on mere contractual obligations. Freedoms in those two communities are radically different.

These two cultures — Lockean and Biblical — have been vying with each other for allegiance of the American soul. And today Locke seems to be coming out on top. Culture profoundly influences not only economics and politics, but also the very roots of community. In recent years, Locke seems to be winning the day as elements of Biblical culture fade. This would seem lamentable to the Founders, for while they valued the idea of social contract, they recognized that it does not go far enough. Again, in Lockean culture, it is difficult to find the Church and our membership in it as part of our very identity. In Biblical culture, religion is a radical reality, central to the nature of things, part of our very being. It is the reality itself that justifies freedom and human rights. In Lockean culture religion arises, not out of the nature of reality, but by a contract, and freedom is justified by a figment. In Lockean culture, then, religion is subjective and privatized, and this subjectivity permeates American culture. It says, in effect: "As long as I'm all right with Jesus, I don't need the Church." And how do people know they are "all right with Jesus?" "If they 'feel' they are all right with Jesus."[81] Thus, religion for the Lockean is very shallowly rooted in "this is how I feel" — a far cry from the Biblical covenant and the Body of Christ. And far from the Founders' view of civil society.

People enter into contracts out of self-interest, willing to surrender to a contracting party only as much wealth, power and prestige as is required to achieve what they want from the contract. You'll give up some things, if you have to, in order to get some other things. And if you can gain without having to surrender any wealth or power, you'll surrender nothing.

We do the social contract thing all the time; political life is a matter of bargaining, in a competitive world, regulated by laws which are themselves the product of bargaining and contracting. The competing parties learn the game rather quickly, accept the challenge, and say to themselves: "I think I can win," which means, "I think I can beat the other fellow." This is the shallow moral concept that our culture teaches to many young people. It is a concept that reeks of excessive individualism and social isolationism. No wonder it is producing a generation, many of whom believe that "greed is good," and that "the constant ME is always greater than the variable U."

The scriptural view of men and women in society is quite different from the social contract view. According to sacred Scripture, men and women in society are bound together by a covenant that predates all social contracts. Before we bargain over laws and social contracts, a prior reality lays claim on us all: we are created in the image of God, everyone, with rights, obligations, and a common destiny. That reality involves two sets of relationships.

There is first the vertical relationship that each of us has to God as Creator, Redeemer, and final end. That relationship is real. We exist by the power and love of God — from Him we come, to Him we go. There is secondly the horizontal relationships that we have to one another. We do not simply happen to be here, on earth, uncaused, strangers, aliens to one another. The Supreme Being makes every single being of us to be in His image. He is not only the Supreme Being, He is the loving Father who has created every single one of us to be His child, and share His blessedness. The reality, then, is that we are brothers and sisters in God.

That covenant takes precedence in time and importance over all social-contracts, which aim to achieve justice in social relationships. Justice says: "Give me what you owe me, and I'll give you what I owe you." But it's been said, and I believe, that we will never achieve justice without love. All peoples of the earth are bound together by ties of love that are deeper, richer, more fulfilling and more demanding than the ties of justice. And if we do not respect the ties of love, we will not respect the ties of justice. Our relationships as human beings are imbedded in love from the beginning — God's love for us, which has made us daughters and sons, brothers and sisters. If we do not recognize God our Father, and our brothers and sisters, we will cheat them, if we can. The founders were quite enlightened about this, and insisted that the Republic could not stand on the idea of social contract alone.

All enduring and effective social contracts exist within the context of that prior contract that stems from our creation. And we'd best teach our kids about the priority of the covenant over the contract. For, however many wise contracts we may have made, and however many brilliant accomplishments they may register for us on life's scoreboard, at the end of the game, if those contracts made during our lifetime with our brothers and sisters are without love, it will all have been a wasted time. We have His guarantee of it: "If I have all the eloquence of men and angels, but speak without love, I am simply a gong booming.... If I have the gift of prophecy, understanding all the mysteries there are, and know everything, but am without love, then I am nothing at all."[82]

IF YOU LIVE BY THE SWORD

A few years ago Arayeh Spero, rabbi at the Civic Center Synagogue in Manhattan, published an article in *Policy Review* entitled, "Therefore Choose Life: How the Great Faiths View Abortion."[83] The article concisely documented that all the great faiths have always strongly condemned the practice of abortion as being, if not murder deserving capital punishment, at least a wrongful and criminal act deserving some lesser punishment. The article leaves the reader wondering at the wide chasm that separates this long religious tradition from the modern movement to legalize abortion in the United States and other nations.

Spero summarizes the tradition thus: "For most of their history, the great religions have all strongly disapproved of abortion in the vast majority of circumstances in which it takes place today. The exceptions that religions have often permitted...have been carefully delimited, and in no way predicated on the notion of a woman's right to do as she pleases with the fetus in her womb."[84] Historically some theologians have held that the fetus in earlier stages of development is not actually but only potentially human. In those cases abortion would not constitute murder, but would still be regarded an immoral act and a crime.

Judaism, for example, does not for the most part regard the fetus as an actual human being but as nascent life or a life form. Abortion, nevertheless, is a criminal act. There are exceptions to this even in Judaism. One of the leading interpreters of the Talmud, Rabbi Yishmael, held that the fetus is an actual person and cites Genesis 9:6, "Whoever shall spill the blood of man in man, shall his blood be spilled." Rabbi Yishmael held that "man in man"[85] is a fetus, and that feticide is murder, deserving of capital punishment.

The Catholic Church has traditionally taken a strict view of abortion, but Catholic theologians have not always held that the fetus is human from the moment of conception. Thomas Aquinas, among others, distinguished between the formed and unformed fetus; and during the Middle Ages and until the middle of the 19th Century many theologians held that the fetus was probably not human until 60 to 80 days after conception. Therefore, although the Church and its theologians have always condemned abortion absolutely and considered abortion of the formed fetus as murder, there were periods when some theologians held that abortion of the unformed fetus was not murder, but nevertheless an immoral and criminal act.

Some Church theologians, however, have considered abortion at any stage as murder, among them Pope Sixtus V in the 16th Century who held that abortion at any stage was a capital offense. This is the position that was ultimately to prevail in the Catholic Church and is held at the present time.

There are strong similarities between the Catholic and the Protestant traditions. For most of their history, and indeed up until very recent times, the leading Protestant denominations have considered abortion after animation a criminal and sinful act. John Calvin held that "the fetus, though enclosed in the womb of the mother, was already a human being, and it is almost a monstrous crime to rob it of the life which it has not yet begun to enjoy."[86] Martin Luther likewise held that the child in the womb has a soul from the moment of conception. But Luther's successor, Melanchthon, like some Catholics, also distinguished between the formed and unformed embryo. This distinction, by the way, found its way into English law. The renowned William Blackstone held in the 18th Century that "Life begins, in contemplation of law, as soon as the infant is able to stir in the mother's womb."[87] Abortion prior to quickening was a felony, and after quickening, a capital offense.

Leading 20th Century Protestant theologians have strongly condemned abortion. Karl Barth held with Luther: "The unborn child is from the very first a child. It is still developing…but it is a man and not a thing […] He who destroys germinating life kills a man."[88] German theologian Helmut Thielicke held similarly: "The fetus has its own autonomous life."[89]

Leading evangelical theologians are of a like mind. Francis A. Schaeffer, for example, has written: "[Abortion] results in the total devaluation of life. The unborn child is a human being created in the image of God, and to deny this is to deny the authority of the Bible. It is impossible to read Psalm 139 and truly believe what it says without realizing that life in the womb is human life." The founding editor of *Christianity Today*, Carl F.H. Henry, labeled "monstrous" the "ready sacrifice of fetal life as a means of sexual gratification and birth control," and named abortion "'the most horrendous injustice' of this generation."[90]

As with Christianity, so for Islam, life is a gift of God. God says in the Qur'an: "And when I have proportioned him and breathed into him of My [created] soul, then fall down to him in prostration."[91] When is that breath of human life received? Islam divides gestation into four main periods: conception, conception to formation, formation to quickening, and from quickening onward. "Abortion at each new stage brings a sanction of increasing severity, ranging from disfavor to prohibition to crime, and finally, murder...."[92]

In sum, although the great faiths differ in details as to when human life begins, under what rare and extreme circumstances abortion may be permitted, and the sanctions they level at abortionists, they all share an abhorrence for abortion, and none of them holds that a person has a right to abort a fetus at any stage of its development simply as a means of birth control.

A short time after Rabbi Spero's article appeared, Planned Parenthood ran a full-page advertisement in major newspapers across the country. As it appeared in Cleveland's *Plain Dealer*, the advertisement was headlined: "Five U.S. Supreme Court Justices Just Had Their Say on Abortion. Now it's Your Turn." There followed a summons for American women to defend their right to abortion: "Planned Parenthood is committed to fighting in every state to keep abortion safe, legal and available for all women." Then Planned Parenthood threw down the gauntlet to elected officials:

> Elected representatives can no longer be allowed to remain equivocal on abortion. They can't permit themselves to be bullied or intimidated by a few vocal and violent anti-abortion extremists. We must send all elected representatives a strong, clear message: *We'll support them only if they keep government from interfering with our private and personal decisions.* From now on, there will be no middle ground.

The ad then turned on those who think differently: "When an intolerant, fanatical few seek to impose their will on the rest of us, we can and must fight back."[93]

In view of the long, almost universal tradition condemning abortion, as recounted by Rabbi Spero, it is disingenuous of Planned Parenthood to speak of the pro-life group as a "fanatical few." If the label "fanatic" is apropos, it would wear truer on the coat of those out to upset the long, universal tradition.

But what of the debate and the awful cleavage that it is causing across the nation? Can any good come of it? Probably not, if the opposing parties merely go at each other in anger. It is obvious that we are in the throes of a culture war, and nothing epitomizes that war more than the abortion issue. We lived through one Civil War — a war fought over the inalienable right to be free. But the unborn no less than slaves cry out, pleading the inalienable right to be born and to live. No one wants another Civil War. We must, then, have recourse to intelligence, reason and respect for our sisters and brothers, whoever they are.

The Planned Parenthood position seems to boil down to: Because we want it, we're going to have it. That, it seems to me, is a weak and unprincipled position that cannot long stand. As a nation we need to think about abortion far more seriously than we are now doing. "I have a right to choose, therefore, I have a right to murder." Is that really our ethical position as a nation? Can we live with that?

I said that no one wants a war of guns. Of course, I am not unmindful that some hot-headed pro-lifers have taken to guns, and threats with bombs. Already people have been killed. That is not the American way. It is unlawful, unchristian, and stupid. We don't want another Civil War.

The only way people can live reasonably and civilly together is if they agree to abide by legitimately established laws, as long as those laws do not require of citizens acts that are immoral. This is especially true of a democratic society such as ours that prides itself on being a society of laws, not persons. In a society of laws, individuals may not take the law into their own hands. To do that is to make of the civil community a jungle. If we don't like the laws, there are civil ways to attempt to change them. That is our right, and it may even be our responsibility. As long as we benefit from the society in which we live, we have an obligation to live under its legitimately established laws.

Moreover, even though abortion is murder, that does not give one the right to bomb abortion clinics much less to kill doctors and nurses who perform abortions. It is a thoroughly unchristian sentiment that one wrong justifies another. Evil is not overcome by yet another evil. As He was lead off to a barbarians death, Christ's words were: "If you live by the sword, you will die by the sword."[94] The only thing that will ever overcome evil is good. Hatred has never won a convert to any cause. But love has. So the bombing of abortion clinics is unchristian; and the murdering of abortionists is unchristian. It was love that overcame the hatred of the Romans who persecuted the early Christians. In time they became the Holy Roman Empire — all Christian. Our world will never be perfect, but each person has within his power to make his social space on earth a bit more agreeable and peaceful. Remember that song: "Let there be peace on earth and let it begin with me." Love, like peace, is spread one person at a time.

Bombing clinics and murdering abortionists is also stupid. It does not accomplish the objectives that anti-abortionists would like to accomplish. It backfires, because burning and killing simply says to the public that those who do these things are fanatical and murderous people. So, the National Right to Life Committee has strongly condemned this type of anti-abortion protesting.

Let us hope that someday we will solve the abortion issue that threatens to split our society. But that issue won't be solved by hatred. It might be solved by intelligence, good will and love.

Some good might come from seriously and sincerely discussing such questions as: What is human life? How does it differ from other forms of life? What rights do pregnant women have relative to their fetus? What obligations with regard to them? What rights and what obligations does the State have with reference to the unborn? These are philosophical questions. One would hope that we are not so removed from philosophy, or so committed to what Robert Novak called "vulgar relativism"[95] that these questions are beyond us.

ON LAWS AND LOGIC

Philosophers search for consistency of thought, — logic, they sometimes call it. They are notorious for that, we all know. The ordinary run of human being gets exasperated with philosophers because they seem to live in a world that is too logical. They reason from principles and seek compatibility among those principles and among the conclusions that are derived from principles. So they talk about such things as "the unity of being," and "the unity of knowledge," and "order in reality," and logical thinking is supposed to assist one in discovering those unities and that order. They abhor contradictions, and say such seemingly idiotic things as "[i]t is impossible for the same thing at the same time both to be-in and not to be-in the same thing in the same respect."[96]

So much for the pure philosophers. In addition to this pure breed, there are also social philosophers and legal philosophers, who also cherish logic and consistency in laws and public policies. They realize the difference between moral propositions and personal preferences; and at least the philosophers among our lawyers hold that law should be based on the former, not the latter. It is not consistent with moral logic to say that "X is morally wrong," and at the same time to encourage people by law or policy, to pursue "X."

This was the point Lincoln made in his debate with Stephan Douglas: There is a difference between a moral principle and personal preference, and when you're dealing with laws you have an obligation to be logical in the laws and consistent in the moral principle that the laws uphold. As Lincoln said, attacking Douglas:

> When Judge Douglas says "[I] don't care whether slavery is voted up or down." ...he cannot thus argue logically if he sees anything wrong with it: ...He cannot say that he would as soon see a wrong voted up as voted down. When Judge Douglas says that whoever, or whatever community, wants slaves, they have a right to have them, he is perfectly logical if there is nothing wrong in the institution; but if you admit that it is wrong, he cannot logically say that anybody has a right to do a wrong.[97]

But although legal philosophers and legislators know that there should be a logic in our laws, they also recognize that, because politics and other preferences get in the way, it doesn't always work out so logically.

The legalization of abortion by the United States Supreme Court has created an absurdity of those state laws that condemn and sentence mothers who may harm their babies by drug and alcohol abuse, but keep them and deliver them alive. The state laws say: "Don't you dare harm them!" while Federal law says: "But you can kill them!" So state prosecutors charge the mother with transferring drugs to her infant while pregnant by ingesting those drugs. As a result, Baby Michael is born addicted to cocaine and hospital tests show signs of cocaine in the infant's urine. The hospital reports the case to the State Department of Health and Rehabilitative Services as required by law when pregnant women appear to be drug users. The State subpoenas the hospital's records, which indeed show cocaine in the mother's body. Pediatric experts testify that the only way a newborn infant could be addicted to cocaine would be if the mother used the drug. So, the mother is sentenced to jail for child abuse.

Meanwhile down the block in the Abortion clinic a pregnant woman is being worked on by abortionists who lawfully suck, scrape, burn, and cut up millions of fetuses in the wombs of mothers.

So this is where we find ourselves: A mother may not abuse her fetus by consuming drugs while pregnant — it's child abuse, and against the law. But a mother may abuse her fetus lethally by dismembering it in her body or burning it with saline solutions until dead, and then aborting it — it's legal, doctors do it every day.

In the former case, the fetus is so assaulted as to be born alive, but afflicted, and that's unlawful. In the latter case, the fetus is so assaulted as to be killed, but that's lawful. The obvious lesson that laws like these teach an addicted pregnant mother is to make sure she gets the fetal infant well chopped up before the delivery.

What the philosopher immediately asks is: How can both of these things be right? If the mother is allowed to kill her fetus, she should also be allowed to abuse it to any degree she chooses. Or if the law forbids her to abuse her fetus by drugging it, it should also forbid her to abuse the fetus by killing it.

True, our nation is not celebrated for its philosophers. But if our laws are this messed up, even with the philosophers we have, think what they would be without them. Or is it the philosophers we have who have led us to the state that we're in?

"YES, ABORTION KILLS BABIES, BUT..."

The major moral issue in the abortion debate is similar to the moral issue in the Lincoln-Douglas debates over slavery, and to the moral issue embedded in the Nazis' so called "solution" to "the problem" in Germany. In all three events, there is the evident domination of the powerful over the powerless. In all three cases the powerful defined the powerless as legally "nonpersons," and thus justified what they wanted: in 19th Century America, slavery; in Nazi Germany, the elimination of Jews; and in modern democracies, the elimination of fetal life.

Naomi Wolf wrote a piece for *The New Republic* and later for *The New York Times* that attracted some attention because the author acknowledged that the moral issue cannot be avoided, and she therefore exhorted pro-abortionists to develop their own moral argument to justify abortion. Since the moral issue will not go away, says Wolf, to pretend to ignore it is bad politics. So Wolf offers a "moral frame,"[98] as she puts it.

Since pro-choicers stand on no decent moral ground, Wolf says that the pro-abortion movement has a poor image that has resulted in three bummers that must be overcome. The first bummer is that pro-choicers come across as heartless and uncaring. When they refer to fetuses as "material" or "a mass of dependent protoplasm," they appear to the public as "uncaring." When Dr. Jocelyn Elders said so casually, "'We really need to get over this love affair with the fetus,' we are seen," says Wolf, "as both uncaring and brutal." Rather than speak so heartlessly, we should "treat abortion with grief and reverence."[99] When we speak heartlessly about children whom we willfully abort, what does that say about the children whom we choose to bring to term and to nourish? When we dehumanize the creatures that are within us during pregnancy, are we not seen as dehumanizing all fetuses?

The second bummer, says Wolf, is that pro-choicers are downright un-truthful. Call it what you want, everybody knows it's a baby. When pro-lifers say: "Abortion stops a beating heart," that is certainly true. Of course, we don't like to see those gruesome pictures of violent death in the womb, such as are presented before congressional committees; and we call this a cheap shot and label it "political polemic." "But," she says, "the pictures are not polemical in themselves: they are biological fact. We know this." So, pro-choicers can't have it both ways: How can we expect the public to believe us when we say: wanted fetuses are charming; but unwanted fetuses are "uterine material." "How can we charge that it is vile and repulsive for pro-lifers to brandish vile and repulsive images if the images are real? To insist that the truth is in poor taste is the very height of hypocrisy."[100]

Wolf cited a recent statement by abortion-clinic doctor Elizabeth Karlin who said: "There is only one reason I've ever heard for having an abortion: the desire to be a good mother." That, says Wolf, is hogwash. Having once herself chosen to take a morning-after pill, Wolf admits that she was thinking only about herself: "There were two columns in my mind — 'Me' and 'Baby' — and the first won out." "I acted — and was free to act — as if I were in control of my destiny, the way men more often than women have let themselves act. I chose myself on my own terms over a possible someone else, for self-absorbed reasons. But 'to be a better mother'? ... Nonsense."[101]

It's clear that Wolf approaches abortion as a champion of the feminist movement: In her view abortion is a right that women must have if they are to achieve equality with men, even if it means taking their child's life. So, she admits that abortion is a battle in the war for dominance; it is not for the faint hearted. If women want equality, they must be strong enough to kill: Women who are "too inherently weak to face a truth about which they have to make a decision," are "unworthy of feminism. Free women must be strong women, too; and strong women, presumably, do not seek to cloak their most important decisions in euphemism."[102] Therefore, to achieve equality "wom-en must be free to choose self, or to choose selfishly," even if it means choosing to kill her child. There's no mistaking Wolf's meaning: "A wom-an's equality in society must give her some irreducible rights unique to her biology, including the right to take the life within her life."[103] I can interpret this only as saying: A woman has a right to kill the innocent child so that, presumably, she will achieve equality.

One is reminded of Lady Macbeth, responding to Macbeth's resolute: "We will proceed no further in this business." She calls him a coward, and he defends his conscience: "I dare do all that may become a man; who dares do more is none." Her response: When you had the resolve to kill for power, "then you were a man." To shame her husband, she boasts a manliness that will unravel, but for the present achieves its purpose: "I have given suck, and know/ how tender 'tis to love the babe that milks me —/ I would, while it was smiling in my face,/ Have pluck'd my nipple from its boneless gums,/ And dash'd the brains out, had I so sworn/ As you have done to this."[104]

The final bummer in Wolf's trilogy is that the abortion movement is failing politically. In the political center, she says, "there is a hunger for a moral framework that we pro-choicers must reckon with."[105] So, she says, feminists must stake out some moral ground on which they justify abortion. She recognizes that encouraging morality in the debate is risky, because morality moves the debate onto God's turf. "Now," she says, "the G-word is certainly a problematic element to introduce into the debate."[106] Nevertheless, God has got to be brought in; if not God, then at least "conscience" or "soul."

In addition to the "G-word" there is another word that the "center" likes, and must be recognized. "We on the left tend to twitch with discomfort at that word…" but it is so deeply rooted in all the major religious faiths, that it can't be avoided. That word, says Wolf, is "sin."[107] While the word "sin," like the "G-word," is also risky, it can be balanced off by recognizing atonement and forgiveness.

So, there you have one person's winning political formula: Pro-abortionists should show themselves to be more tenderhearted, they should be more truthful, and their strategy should include the "G-word" and "sin," along with "atonement," and "forgiveness." With that "moral frame," says Wolf, abortion advocates stand a much better chance of winning back "the center."

And what a "moral frame" it is! writes J. Bottum in *First Things*. Faced with overwhelming medical evidence, abortion proponents now acknowledge that "the fetus is a living human being." This admission, however, does not mean that the abortion debate is over. Pro-abortionists, says Bottum, "are now willing to acknowledge that abortion kills babies. But they are willing to claim the necessity for allowing abortion anyway."[108]

The moral significance of this is monumental. Again Bottum: "Unlimited abortion is now the reality, and honesty about abortion's murderousness no longer necessarily means its rejection." We are arriving at a major cultural divide. "Any medical procedure performed a million and a half times a year — at a rate far outstripping any other developed nation — argues a cultural investment of enormous proportions."[109] Pro-abortionists seem not likely to turn back. Rather they seem intent on discovering or resuscitating a moral system that justifies killing babies. In which case, the nation faces "so fundamental a clash between ethical systems that any sort of argument becomes impossible."[110]

The defense of abortion contains in itself the defense of infanticide. As Bottum observes, Naomi Wolf joins Peter Singer in advocating infanticide "in fact if not yet in rhetoric." What they both advocate is the overthrow of over 3,000 years of the Judeo-Christian tradition of morality. Bottum challenges Singer: "Why — in the absence of religious beliefs about being made in the image of God, or having an immortal soul — should mere membership of the species *Homo sapiens* be crucial to whether the life of a being may or may not be taken?"[111]

Where does that leave us? It may be true that many people live their lives "in the absence of religious beliefs." However, I think that "the center" as well as great numbers both on the left and the right believe in an "immortal soul" that is "made in the image of God," and accept that law laid down so long ago: "Thou shalt not kill."[112]

John Paul II's Encyclical titled *The Gospel of Life*[113] deals with killing the innocent, with abortion and euthanasia. The Encyclical could have been titled "the culture of death" — a phrase the Pope used frequently — because recent generations, even in Christian nations, are dealing so casually with death. *The Gospel of Life* addresses especially the Western democracies, which for many generations have been bold defenders of "the right to life." These democracies, protectors of the defenseless and defenders of their rights and freedoms, now suddenly seem to have turned on the defenseless, allowing the weakest of all to be cut down at the whim of the strong.

Human persons are destined for life, the highest of all life — union with God. Whether they be geniuses or imbeciles, strong or weak, in the prime of life, in their dotage, or in their mother's womb, they are all created "in the image of God."[114] The Author of life owns His creations. "Thou shalt not kill" means that no one shall interfere with the life destiny that God plans for those whom He creates in His own image. No one has the right to proclaim himself a "pro-choicer" when that choice means killing what God reserves for Himself. Naomi Wolf knows this. She is familiar with the Genesis account of that first murder. Yahweh asked Cain: "What have you done?" Confronted by his Creator, Cain was dumb struck. Yahweh said to him: "Listen to the sound of your brother's blood, crying out to me from the ground."[115] Wolf's bizarre ethics — resolve to kill the child, kill it, repent if that seems necessary, then everything's O.K. — doesn't wash, even to a high school student, it won't wash.

"THE SOUND OF YOUR BROTHER'S BLOOD"

What Naomi Wolf apparently is saying in her *New Republic* article is that the pro-abortion cause needs some moral ground to stand on; and she attempts to show the way. She recognizes that the public square cannot stand naked forever; and abortion needs some moral justification. She says that we must admit that it is murder and sinful, but abortion is with us and is going to stay; so we must find some moral ground that justifies it. However, I question that America will accept the garment that Wolf has draped over the naked square.

Years ago in the 1940's Supreme Court Justice Harlan Fisk Stone had observed that the only check upon the High Court's power "is our own sense of self-restraint."[116] Faced with *Roe*, the Court would not or could not restrain itself, and chose rather to exercise, as Justice Byron White said, "raw judicial power." And that spells, as American philosophers are saying "the end of democracy."

Commenting on the Court's ruling, the editors of *First Things* wrote: "Among the most elementary principles of Western Civilization is the truth that laws that violate the moral law are null and void and must in conscience be disobeyed."[117]

Pope John Paul II in his encyclical *Evangelium Vitae* underscores the editor's statement: "Laws which authorize and promote abortion and euthanasia are radically opposed not only to the good of the individual but also to the common good; as such they are completely lacking in judicial validity. A civil law authorizing abortion or euthanasia ceases by that very fact to be true moral binding law.... Abortion and euthanasia are crimes which no human law can claim to legitimize. There is no obligation in conscience to obey such laws; instead there is a great and clear obligation to oppose them by conscientious objection."[118] We are now in a great conflict between "the culture of life" and "the culture of death."

Alistair MacIntyre knows where Naomi Wolf is coming from: a society cannot get along without a morally binding ethic; it requires "some kind of religion, however barbaric and totalitarian it may be." And the "Barbarians are already at the gate." The barbarians whom MacIntyre sees "are some of the most sophisticated and educated elites of our society." They are no less barbarian, for they "in principle refuse to recognize a normative ethic or the reality of public virtue." [...] "The barbarians are the party of emancipation from the truths civilized people consider self-evident."[119]

Robert P. George of Princeton University thinks that the crumbling of our American democracy may have been going on for quite some time. Recently he wrote: "One of the saddest lessons of American history, however, is that Courts exercising the power to invalidate legislation as unconstitutional can themselves trample upon fundamental rights and, indeed, can do so precisely in the name of protecting such rights." This happened as is well known in the *Dred Scott* case and then in our own time in *Roe v. Wade.* Our Supreme Court struck down the abortion laws of all 50 states; and following the *Roe* decision by our Supreme Court, Federal Courts of appeals for the Second and Ninth Circuits "invalidated laws prohibiting physician-assisted suicide in New York and California."[120]

"The hour is late," wrote Robert George; the refusal of the Courts over all these years to reverse *Roe* v. *Wade* "must then be accounted a failure of American democracy."[121]

The basis upon which our democracy was established in 1776 has markedly changed. Comments George again: Our democratic institutions have been "manipulated so that 'right' ceases to be such, because it is no longer firmly founded on the inviolable dignity of the person."[122]

Even Pope John Paul II joins in the criticism: "Democracy itself fundamentally is a system of government, and as such is a means, not an end." "Its moral value," he explains, "is not automatic, but depends on conformity to the moral law to which it, like every other form of human behavior, must be subject."[123] This doctrine of the conformity of civil to moral law is not new, but dates back to Plato and Aristotle and to St. Thomas Aquinas, and has long been in papal social teaching.

Mary Ann Glendon's summary is equally appalling: The abortion license in *Roe* and *Planned Parenthood* v. *Casey* "is more sweeping and destructive than that of any other democratic nation on the face of the earth. What a disgraceful censure of our society; No other democracy is so careless of the value of human life."[124]

Thus Robert George labels *Roe* v. *Wade* along with the *Casey* decision "one of the saddest lessons of American history; the inability of the Court to reverse itself moves America slowly along a road to totalitarianism."[125]

This refusal of the Court, over all these years to reverse itself is surely "a failure of American democracy." Quoting John Paul II, George concludes:

> As the Pope says, 'given such a grave situation, we need now more than ever to have the courage to look the truth in the eye and to call things by their proper names, without yielding to convenient compromises or to the temptation of self-deception.' Let us, therefore, speak plainly: The courts...have imposed upon the nation immoral policies that pro-life Americans cannot, in conscience, accept.... People of good will — of whatever religious faith — cannot now avoid asking themselves, soberly and unblinkingly, whether our regime is becoming the democratic "tyrant state" about which he warns.[126]

NOTES

1. *The Declaration of Independence*, 1.

2. Aristotle and W. Rhys Roberts, *Rhetoric*, Dover thrift eds ed. (Mineola, N.Y: Dover Publications, 2004), 48, http://catdir.loc.gov/catdir/enhancements/fy0618/2004052176-d.html.

3. Edward Samuel Corwin, *The "Higher Law" Background of American Constitutional Law*. (Ithaca, N.Y: Great Seal Books, Div. of Cornell University Press, 1929), 7.

4. Aristotle and Ostwald, *Nicomachean Ethics*, 1-2.

5. Aristotle and J. E. C. Welldon, *The Politics of Aristotle* (London: Macmillan and Co, 1883), 154.

6. Marcus Tullius Cicero and others, *Tusculan Disputations: On the Nature of Gods, and the Commonwealth* (New York: Cosimo Classics, 2005), 437-8.

7. Corwin, *The "Higher Law" Background of American Constitutional Law.*, 5.

8. Ibid., 6.

9. Martin Luther King Jr. and Jesse Jackson, *Why we can't Wait* (New York: Signet Classic, 2000), 70.

10. ROBERT P. GEORGE, "God and Gettysburg," *First Things: A Monthly Journal of Religion & Public Life*, no. 205 (Aug, 2010), 17, http://search.ebscohost.com/login.aspx?direct=true&db=a9h&AN=52092771&site=ehost-live (accessed 12/27/2010).

11. William Eaton, *Who Killed the Constitution?: The Judges v. the Law* (Washington, D.C; New York, NY: Regnery Gateway; Distributed by Kampmann, 1988), 203.

12. John Courtney Murray, *We Hold these Truths; Catholic Reflections on the American Proposition* (New York: Sheed and Ward, 1960), 307-8.

13. Dostoyevsky, Pevear and Volokhonsky, *The Brothers Karamazov: A Novel in Four Parts with Epilogue*, 263.

14. Murray, *We Hold these Truths; Catholic Reflections on the American Proposition*, 308.

15. United States. Congress. House. Committee on the Judiciary. Subcommittee on the Constitution, *Origins and Scope of Roe v. Wade: Hearing before the Subcommittee on the Constitution of the Committee on the Judiciary, House of Representatives, One Hundred Fourth Congress, Second Session, April 22, 1996*, 125.

16. *Planned Parenthood v. Casey*.

17. Gregory C. Sisk, "The Moral Incompetence of the Judiciary," *First Things*, no. 57 (11/01, 1995), 37, http://search.ebscohost.com.proxy.foley.gonzaga.edu:2048/login.aspx?direct=true&db=rfh&AN=ATLA0000902481&site=ehost-live (accessed 8/21/2010).

18. Bottum, *Facing Up to Infanticide*, 42.

19. Ibid., 42.

20. Peter Singer, *Rethinking Life and Death: The Collapse of our Traditional Ethics* (New York: St. Martin's Griffin, Projected Date: 1111, 1996), 210, http://catdir.loc.gov/catdir/bios/hol056/96003653.html.

21. Ibid., 1.

22. Peter Singer, *Practical Ethics*, 2nd ed. (Cambridge ; New York: Cambridge University Press, 1993), 169-71, http://catdir.loc.gov/catdir/description/cam025/92023819.html.

23. "The Oregon Death with Dignity Act," *Issues in Law & Medicine* 11, no. 3 (Winter95, 1995), 333, http://search.ebscohost.com/login.aspx?direct=true&db=a9h&AN=9602261647&site=ehost-live (accessed 4/3/2011).

24. In my correspondence with Dr. Montgomery he wrote that "This quotation is indeed mine, but I believe that it comes from a letter I sent to the A.B.A. when I resigned my membership." Dr Montgomery's publications in this area include: *Slaughter of the Innocents* (Westchester, IL: Crossway Books, 1981), *Christians in the Public Square* (Calgary, Alberta: Canadian Institute for Law, Theology and Public Policy, 1996), *Christ Our Advocate* (Bonn, Germany: Verlag fuer Kultur und Wissenschaft, 2002), and the forthcoming, *Christ As Centre and Circumference* (Verlag fuer Kultur und Wissenschaft, 2011). These titles are available from: www.ciltpp.com.

25. Jones, *The Jerusalem Bible*, 1 Cor. 3:19.

26. Dean C. Curry, "Written on the Heart: The Case for Natural Law," *First Things*, no. 77 (11/01, 1997), 58, http://search.ebscohost.com.proxy.foley.gonzaga.edu:2048/login.aspx?direct=true&db=rfh&AN=ATLA0000335890&site=ehost-live (accessed 8/21/2010).

27. *Planned Parenthood v. Casey*.

28. Vinton R. Anderson Bp, "We Hold these Truths: A Statement of Christian Conscience and Citizenship," *First Things*, no. 76 (10/01, 1997), 52, http:// search.ebscohost.com.proxy.foley.gonzaga.edu:2048/login.aspx?direct=true&db=rfh& AN=ATLA0001004834&site=ehost-live (accessed 8/21/2010).

29. Pope John Paul II and Joseph Durepos, *Go in Peace: A Gift of Enduring Love* (Chicago, Ill: Loyola Press, 2003), 196.

30. Ibid., 197.

31. Ioannes Paulus PP. II, *Address of His Holiness Pope John Paul II to H.E. Mrs. Corinne (Lindy) Claiborne Boggs, New Ambassador of the United States of America to the Holy See* (The Vatican, Rome, Italy: Libreria Editrice Vaticana, 1997).

32. Oliver Wendell Holmes, "The Path of the Law," *Harvard Law Review* 10, no. 8 (Mar. 25, 1897), 459, http://www.jstor.org.proxy.foley.gonzaga.edu/stable/1322028.

33. *Bill of Rights*, (1789): http://www.archives.gov/exhibits/charters/bill_of_rights.html (accessed 28 Dec 2010).

34. *Torcaso v. Watkins*, No. 373 *Torcaso v. Watkins*, (SUPREME COURT OF THE UNITED STATES.

35. Donald A. Giannella, *Religion and the Public Order: Number Five: An Annual Review of Church and State, and of Religion, Law and Society* (Ithica, NY: Cornell Univ, 1969), 99.

36. *McGowan v. Maryland*, No. 8 *McGowan v. Maryland*, (SUPREME COURT OF THE UNITED STATES.

37. *Cochran v. Louisiana State Bd. of Education*, No. 468 *Cochran v. Louisiana State Bd. of Education*, 281, 370 (SUPREME COURT OF THE UNITED STATES).

38. *Everson v. Bd. of Educ.* No. 52 *Everson v. Bd. of Educ.* (SUPREME COURT OF THE UNITED STATES).

39. *Illinois Ex Rel. McCollum v. Bd. of Educ.* No. 90 *Illinois Ex Rel. McCollum v. Bd. of Educ.* (SUPREME COURT OF THE UNITED STATES).

40. Ibid., 247.

41. Ibid., 248.

42. *Zorach v. Clauson*, No. 431 *Zorach v. Clauson*, 343, 306 (SUPREME COURT OF THE UNITED STATES).

43. Ibid.

44. Donald A. Giannella, *Religion and the Public Order. Number Four* (Ithaca, N.Y: Cornell University Press, 1968), 112.

45. *Sch. Dist. of Abington Twp. v. Schempp*, No. 142 *Sch. Dist. of Abington Twp. v. Schempp*, 374, 203 (SUPREME COURT OF THE UNITED STATES).

46. Schempp Kauper and Sherbert, "Studies in Neutrality and Accommodation," *Religion and the Public Order* 3, no. 14 (1963), 14.

47. *Board of Education v. Allen*, No. 660 *Board of Education v. Allen*, 392, 236 (SUPREME COURT OF THE UNITED STATES).

48. *Tilton v. Richardson*, No. 153 *Tilton v. Richardson*, (SUPREME COURT OF THE UNITED STATES).

49. *Lemon v. Kurtzman*, No. 71-1470 *Lemon v. Kurtzman*, 411, 192 (SUPREME COURT OF THE UNITED STATES).

50. Terry Eastland, *Religious Liberty in the Supreme Court: The Cases that Define the Debate Over Church and State* (Washington, DC: Ethics and Public Policy Center, 1993), 232.

51. *Roemer v. Bd. of Public Works*, No. 74-730 *Roemer v. Bd. of Public Works*, 426, 736 (SUPREME COURT OF THE UNITED STATES).

52. Ibid.

53. Mark De Wolfe Howe and Frank L. Weil Institute for Studies in Religion and the Humanities, *The Garden and the Wilderness; Religion and Government in American Constitutional History* (Chicago: University of Chicago Press, 1965), 180.

54. Giannella, *Religion and the Public Order: Number Five: An Annual Review of Church and State, and of Religion, Law and Society*, 108.

55. Giannella, *Religion and the Public Order. Number Four*, 109.

56. Ibid., 112.

57. Ibid., 113.

58. Murray, *We Hold these Truths; Catholic Reflections on the American Proposition.*

59. United States Congress, "Congressional Record Containing the Proceedings and Debates of the 108th Congress, First Session," 149, pt. 20 (5 November 2003 to 11 November 2003, 2003), http://www.bibliothek.uni-regensburg.de/ezeit/?2139924.

60. Thomas Jefferson and Eric S. Petersen, *Light and Liberty: Reflections on the Pursuit of Happiness*, Modern Library ed. (New York: Modern Library, 2004), 75, http://catdir.loc.gov/catdir/toc/fy0606/2003044283.html.

61. Thomas Jefferson and Merrill D. Peterson, *The Political Writings of Thomas Jefferson* (Charlottesville, Va.: Thomas Jefferson Memorial Foundation, 1993), 60-1, http://catdir.loc.gov/catdir/description/unc041/94112063.html.

62. Murray, *We Hold these Truths; Catholic Reflections on the American Proposition*, 40.

63. Richard John Neuhaus, *The Naked Public Square: Religion and Democracy in America* (Grand Rapids, Mich: W.B. Eerdmans Pub. Co, 1984), 95.

64. Ibid., 86.

65. Ibid., 87.

66. John M. Patton, Conway Robinson and Virginia, *The Code of Virginia: With the Declaration of Independence and Constitution of the United States; and the Declaration of Rights and Constitution of Virginia* (Richmond: Printed by W.F. Ritchie, 1849), 34.

67. King and Jackson, *Why we can't Wait*, 70.

68. Ibid., 72.

69. Vatican Council II, *Declaration on Religious Freedom* [Dignitatis Humanae] (The Vatican, Rome, Italy: Libreria Editrice Vaticana, 1965).

70. Murray, *We Hold these Truths; Catholic Reflections on the American Proposition*, xii.

71. John C. Calhoun and R. M. T. Hunter, "Life of John C. Calhoun Presenting a Condensed History of Political Events from 1811 to 1843," Harper & Brothers, http://www.gale.com/ModernLaw/; http://www.gale.com/ModernLaw/.

72. Junius P. Rodriguez, *Slavery in the United States: A Social, Political, and Historical Encyclopedia* (Santa Barbara, Calif: ABC-CLIO, 2007), 41, http://catdir.loc.gov/catdir/toc/ecip077/2006101351.html.

73. Abraham Lincoln and Joseph R. Fornieri, *The Language of Liberty: The Political Speeches and Writings of Abraham Lincoln*, Rev. bicentennial ed. (Washington, DC: Regnery Pub, 2009), 150.

74. Madeline Buckley, "Protesters Line Entrance to Campus," *The Observer: The Independent Newspaper Serving Notre Dame and Saint Mary's*, sec. News, 17 May 2009, 2009, http://www.ndsmcobserver.com/2.2754/protesters-line-entrance-to-campus-1.254833 (accessed 28 Dec 2010).

75. Barack Obama, "Text of President Obama's Address to Graduates," *The Observer: The Independent Newspaper Serving Notre Dame and Saint Mary's*, sec. News, 17 May 2009, 2009, http://www.ndsmcobserver.com/2.2754/text-of-president-obama-s-address-to-graduates-1.254844 (accessed 28 Dec 2010).

76. Ibid.

77. Ibid.

78. Archibald Alexander Hodge, Presbyterian Church in the U.S.A and Board of Publication, *Popular Lectures on Theological Themes* (Philadelphia: Presbyterian board of publication, 1887), 283-4.

79. Ibid., 281.

80. Robert N. Bellah, "The Church in Tension with a Lockean Culture," *New Oxford Review* 57, no. 10 (December 1990, 1990), 11.

81. Ibid., 11.

82. Jones, *The Jerusalem Bible;*, 1 Cor. 13:2.

83. Arayeh Spero, "Therefore Choose Life: How the Great Religions View abortion," *Policy Review* 48 (Spring 1989, 1989), 38-44.

84. Ibid., 38.

85. Michael Levi Rodkinson, Isaac Mayer Wise and Godfrey Taubenhaus, *New Edition of the Babylonian Talmud* (New York: New Talmud Pub. Co, 1896-1903), 170.

86. Jean Calvin, *Commentaries on the Four Last Books of Moses: Arranged in the Form of a Harmony* (Edinburgh: Printed for the Calvin Translation Society, 1852-1855), 41-2.

87. *State v. Cooper*, [NO NUMBER IN ORIGINAL] *State v. Cooper*, 22, 52 (NEW JERSEY SUPREME COURT.

88. Karl Barth, Geoffrey William Bromiley and Thomas F. Torrance, *Church Dogmatics*, 1st pbk. ed. (London ; New York: T. & T. Clark International, 2004), 415-6.

89. Helmut Thielicke and John W. Doberstein, *Theological Ethics. Volume 3, Sex* (Grand Rapids, Mich: Eerdmans, 1979), 228.

90. Timothy W. Crusius and Carolyn E. Channell, *The Aims of Argument: A Rhetoric and Reader*, 2nd ed. (Mountain View, Calif: Mayfield Pub. Co, 1998), 458.

91. Bashiruddin Mahmud Ahmad, *The Holy Quran: With English Translation and Commentary. Uniform Title: Tafsir-i Kabir. English* (Tilford, Surrey, U.K: Islam International Publications, 1988), 15:29.

92. Crusius and Channell, *The Aims of Argument: A Rhetoric and Reader*, 420.

93. "Five U.S. Supreme Court Justices just had their Say on Abortion. Now it's Your Turn. (Advertisement)," *Plain Dealer* July 12, 1989, 1989.

94. Jones, *The Jerusalem Bible;*, Matt. 26:52.

95. Novak, *Awakening from Nihilism: The Templeton Prize Address*, 18.

96. Aristotle and Hugh Lawson-Tancred, *Metaphysics* (London ; New York: Penguin Books, 1998), 88.

97. Hadley Arkes, "Abortion and Moral Reasoning," *Human Life Review* (Winter 1987, 1987), 42.

98. Naomi Wolf, "Our Bodies, our Souls," *The New Republic* 213, no. 16 (Oct 16, 1995), 26, http://proxy.foley.gonzaga.edu:2048/login?url=http://proquest.umi.com/pqdweb?did=7722286&Fmt=7&clientId=10553&RQT=309&VName=PQD.

99. Ibid., 28-9.

100. Ibid., 32.

101. Ibid., 33-4.

102. Ibid., 32.

103. Ibid., 33.

104. William Shakespeare and Nick De Somogyi, *Macbeth: The Tragedie of Macbeth* (London: Nick Hern Books, 2003), 34-5.

105. Wolf, *Our Bodies, our Souls*, 34.

106. Ibid., 34.

107. Ibid., 34.

108. Bottum, "Facing Up to Infanticide," *First Things*, no. 60 (02/01, 1996) 42-3.

109. Ibid., 42.

110. Ibid., 43.

111. Ibid., 43.

112. Jones, *The Jerusalem Bible;*, Deut. 5:17.

113. Ioannes Paulus PP. II, *Evangelium Vitae* (The Vatican, Rome, Italy: Libreria Editrice Vaticana, 1995).

114. Jones, *The Jerusalem Bible;*, Gen. 1:27.

115. Ibid., Gen. 4:10.

116. *United States v. Butler*, No. 401 *United States v. Butler*, (SUPREME COURT OF THE UNITED STATES).

117. Muncy, Neuhaus and Anatomy of a controversy, *The End of Democracy?: The Celebrated First Things Debate, with Arguments Pro and Con: And, the Anatomy of a Controversy, by Richard John Neuhaus*, 6.

118. Ioannes Paulus PP. II, *Evangelium Vitae*.

119. Neuhaus, *The Naked Public Square: Religion and Democracy in America*, 87.

120. Robert P. George, *The Clash of Orthodoxies: Law, Religion, and Morality in Crisis* (Wilmington, Del: ISI Books, 2001), 129.

121. Ibid., 134-5.

122. Ibid., 128.

123. Ioannes Paulus PP. II, *Evangelium Vitae*.

124. George, *The Clash of Orthodoxies: Law, Religion, and Morality in Crisis*, 130-1.
125. Ibid., 129.
126. Ibid., 135.

Chapter Four

Education

THE MELTING POT

The schools copy the culture. What society values intellectually, socially and morally is reproduced in its schools. Criticism of the schools, then, might well be directed at the culture.

If, as a people we place a distorted value on conformity, egalitarianism, and secularism, as some say we do, how this influences our formal education is instructive.

Consider, first of all, conformity, and the role it plays in our schools. Social cohesion depends on conformity, and we rightly value it. We expect our schools to require a measure of conforming behavior. The issue, boldly stated, is this: Are schools primarily to socialize children to someone's ideal citizen or to instruct them? We selected a "melting pot" philosophy in the 19th century out of concern that the immigrant families and religious and ethnic groups that flooded into the United States would be factious elements in an otherwise homogeneous people. The "melting pot" was the solution. It was the beginning on a national scale of conformism in American education and of the politicization of the American school system.

That conformism is still with us. A group of experts recently met under the sponsorship of the Carnegie Foundation for the Advancement of Teaching to discuss the aims of general education. The group's published report did a creditable job but when it zoomed in on education's central purpose, it all but forgot the child in its concern to maintain the melting pot.

No one questions, of course, that schools should educate students in social and citizen responsibility. But this report, like so many others, says more: that the school is primarily a social agent to achieve a social purpose;

that education is the "tool we reach for in our search for renewal of the frayed social compact;" and that it is "an institutional affirmation of society's claim on its members."[1]

Such an educational philosophy invites a lot of questions: A "tool" in whose hands? Who decides that the social compact is frayed? And who decides how children and their education should be molded to mend it? And what are the political, social and philosophical beliefs of this claimant who wields that tool in renewing society through the classroom?

The language used by melting-pot theorists suggests manipulation of the student's mind. This is not what one would expect the purpose of education to be. Supreme Court Justice Jackson, writing in *Thomas v. Collins* said: "The very purpose of the First Amendment is to foreclose public authority from assuming guardianship of the public mind."[2] No public agency should be guardian of thought. An educational system which sees itself as an agent exercising a "claim" on children, and as a "tool" for correcting society's ills, sounds awfully like a guardian of the public mind. This is neither nitpicking nor needless philosophizing. Clarity about primary purpose is all important because purpose determines everything else that follows.

To hold that the primary aim of education is anything other than the intellectual, emotional, social and spiritual development of the student, is bound to lead to an educational program and curricula where the student is shortchanged. The person to be educated must come first and then, only afterwards, social conformity.

The second distortion that permeates public education is egalitarianism. For two decades it has been high on the social agenda, especially by those who consider it a political absolute and are committed to realizing equality of result in America. One of their battle grounds is the classroom.

Hard-line egalitarians seem surprisingly blind to the fact that, apart from being human beings, people are unequal in every respect. One excels in math, another in art, another in languages; one is physically weak, another strong; one seems brilliant in everything, but lacks sensitivity to others; one is an outgoing, vibrant personality, another lethargic, still another nervous and high strung. In the eyes of man and God, we are not all equal, and no one benefits by pretending that we are.

By assuming that we are all the same, egalitarians in the schools have devastated academic standards. Egalitarians argue that comparing children damages the psyche of the lesser achievers. So requirements, academic standards and grading have been downplayed. The result is that children who are poorly qualified are nevertheless passed on from grade school to high school. Each level adjusts by lowering its standards.

Egalitarianism is unreal. In the long run, it damages both the individual and society. The average student knows he is average; he recognizes the difference between himself and a more intellectually gifted student. He can accept that reality, if others — his parents and teachers — can accept it, as long as he is loved and valued as a person as much as the superior student. The fact that a child is less intelligent than some others does not mean that he or she is inferior in all other characteristics. The response to the fact of inequality is not to deny it, but to take the effort to discover each child's endowments and personality, to accentuate them and lead the child to value them and to value himself or herself.

The problem is not with the child, but it may be with our need to deal with people in impersonal masses. We don't take the time to discover the personality of each individual; so we mass-treat individuals as though they were all the same. The children down the block knew, when they heard him play his own compositions at age seven, that Mozart was special, and we have all benefited from the talent that God lodged in Mozart. There are signs on the horizon that egalitarianism in the schools has worn itself out. People are talking about requirements and standards again.

Thirdly, we place a high value on secularism. America was not from the beginning a secular society. All the early documents reflect a people who were God centered and state governments that officially supported religion. But today, we assign high priority to pragmatism and moral relativism, which is poor soil for religious faith. This is reflected in our laws and court decisions, in textbooks and curricula.

Harvard psychologist B.F. Skinner is one of the most influential figures in modern American education. At least three elements in his brand of behaviorism continue to have a powerful deleterious influence in the schools. Knowledge for Skinner is a mechanized, conditioned response; there is no place in his system for intention and poetic insight. Secondly, his world is purely materialistic: what cannot be observed does not exist. God does not exist. Thirdly, he rejects personal freedom, and allows no place in his system for individual responsibility; people are always motivated out of self-interest. As Jeffery Kane observes, this thoroughly colors his educational aims. "Instead of nurturing independent and self-directing human beings, education is meant to control human mechanisms and to shape them into units of a cohesive society."[3] Skinner unabashedly holds that schools should manipulate students' minds toward his social goals.

Perhaps no one influenced the course of modern American education as did John Dewey. His colleague, John Childs, in *Education and Morals*, acknowledged to no one's surprise that "education is a value-conditioned activity. The school seeks to cultivate selected values in the young."[4] Philip Phenix of Columbia Teachers College agrees when he writes: "the really significant outcome of education is the set of governing commitments, the aims for living, that the learner develops. The various subjects of study are simple means for the communication and appropriation of these values."[5] In the case of the American common schools today, the "selected values" are behaviorism, materialism and moral relativism; in a word, secularism, and it has a dulling effect on our schools.

Many professionals hurry to deny that this is the prevailing ethos of the schools. They point to courses and training such as Value Clarification and Cognitive Moral Development. But these are processes of reflection devoid of any content of values. They simply offer students a framework for selecting values. This approach is supposed to lead to the free development of personal values, since no values are recommended, only a process is taught and adhered to. "Values clarification," it is called; all moral positions are acceptable; there are no moral absolutes.

If I am critical of the educational philosophy that pervades many of our schools, it is not to thrash either their teachers or their school boards. They don't create but inherit the values that characterize their schools, and indeed we charge them with the task of perpetuating those values. Conformity, egalitarianism and secularism place many teachers in a bind, and create an atmosphere in which many children are downright poorly educated.

There are few things more important to the health of our nation than education — all of it, from kindergarten through the university. And the fact that parents are increasingly concerned about what's going on in their children's classrooms is a healthy sign.

ARCHITECTURE OF SOULS

Bill Bennett recently made the following poignant statement: "We desperately need to recover a sense of the fundamental purpose of education, which is to engage in the architecture of souls."[6] Because the public schools have lost the sense of the soul in the student, some parents, Catholic and non-Catholic, have decided to create their own schools which profess the existence of souls and place interest in their architecture.

That's what's happening now down in the Tri-Cities in southeastern Washington If education, these parents are saying, were simply a process for teaching kids reading and writing, geography, mathematics, science and the arts, they might entrust their children's education without fear to state-run schools. But they believe that education should be concerned with far more than simply the disciplines that are taught. It is first of all about young people, eager, idealistic and open to the world, and what takes place in their minds, hearts, and souls during those important years of youth. And knowing that I share their beliefs about education they came to me to discuss their ideas and aspirations.

Like Bennett, the Tri-Cities folks are convinced that education deals with the soul, and that youth is a time that comes only once and then is gone, its opportunities never to return. They think that the state schools miss this opportunity which the souls of young people will never have again. They don't blame the teachers, administrators or public school boards. But they do not accept the increasingly secularized culture that pervades the public schools. The courts and the laws have shoved aside the things of the soul, declaring religion, faith, and God off limits in the state-run schools. And the Tri-Cities folks believe that when you remove religion, faith and God from education, you've robbed youth of its deepest aspirations and gutted the schools of the most important things of all. Indeed, you've not only gutted the most important things, you've insidiously made a powerful negative statement about those things: That they are trivial and unimportant, that they are not necessary in an educated person's life.

In his book *Crossing the Threshold of Hope*, Pope John Paul II tells of a Roman journalist's question of him: "Is there really hope in the young?"[7] John Paul's response, which every parent and teacher should read, begins with the question: What is youth?

Youth, replies John Paul, is a time of idealism. Young people today may reflect that idealism in ways different from their parents and grandparents. But everyone who works with youth realizes that they are as idealistic as ever, that they, no less than their forebears, dream of what they would like to be and of the accomplishments they hope to achieve in the course of their lives. It is a time when no challenges seem too formidable, no risks too frightening.

Youth is a time of searching for the meaning of life, and for youth's concrete place in life. It is not just a period of years to be lived through, but a time of fundamental importance, a time given by God for fashioning a personality. So youth is both an opportunity and a responsibility. It is a time when the human being first begins to ask philosophical questions, without realizing they are philosophical. It's the story of the young man in the Gospel, searching how he might respond to what God places before him, and calls him to be: "What must I do to have eternal life?" It is a time of looking beyond the playground and the sports field to the world of ideas and intellectual accomplishments. I like to ask students, especially freshmen and sophomores: "Are you experiencing the joy of learning?" That sometimes draws only a blank and empty stare — which says to me, "Is studying supposed to be a joy?" But there are many times when my question is rewarded with flashing eyes and bright smiles that say: "Yes, I know what you mean!"

Youth is a time to learn to be one's own person. That doesn't mean "to do what I want." It means to learn to be responsible for one's self, to set goals, the right goals, and to direct one's self in their accomplishment. Youth needs help. It also needs boundaries, and youth knows that it needs boundaries, even though it may often not admit it and even fight against their imposition. But it does not want to be smothered with help, so the boundaries should be ever expanding with the years.

And youth, as it is a time for acquiring knowledge and advancing intelligence, is a time also to learn love — to love and to be loved. Youth, of course, has been loved since even before its birth. But only later on, as it looks back, does it realize that it has so long been the recipient of parental love. As young men and women learn that life has meaning, they want to share in its meaning. They, too, want to grow into adulthood, and to take on the joys and responsibilities of love. You may say that love cannot be learned or taught. But it is learned, and it is taught. And it is what youth seeks most of all — the dignity, purity, truth and beauty of love. In its idealism, youth wants to grow to the unselfish maturity of love. I'll say more. Youth senses in ways it cannot explain that ultimately only God can fulfill the love that youth seeks. When they first come upon "You have made us for yourself, O God, and our hearts are restless till they rest in Thee,"[8] every young man and woman hears those words as an echo in the heart. Not so profoundly at first — profundity will come later — but youth realizes the truth of St. Augustine's words, nevertheless.

So, youth is a time when adults, parents and teachers especially, have this great opportunity: to introduce the young to the ultimate questions and mysteries of life, questions about their own life's cause and purpose, and ultimate loves and friendships.

But the problems that many school teachers and administrators face are on an entirely different level — like "illiteracy": many of America's adult population can't read and write well enough to hold a moderately paying job. When asked why so many parents and families are illiterate, Lynn Martin, Secretary of Labor during the Bush Administration, said: Because so many of them are families of "children who have children."[9] The great increase of teenage single-parent families has virtually guaranteed the educational failure of increasing numbers of children. Children who have children cannot take care of themselves, much less of their children.

Children perform poorly because parents perform poorly, and they both belong to families that perform poorly. The student-teacher ratio is important, but more important is the student-parent ratio. In recent decades the proportion of children living in single-parent families rose rapidly and school performance measured by standardized tests, declined. The message is obvious: If families are illiterate, you can expect their children to be illiterate.

Lynn Martin blamed the culture for encouraging single-parent families. "It's no great surprise," he said, "that the number of unmarried women having children has increased. From a time not too long ago when a pregnancy without marriage was almost unthinkable and kept hush-hush, we have moved unwed motherhood to prime time and celebrated on the covers of glossy magazines." Martin doesn't advocate a return to the days when illegitimate children were branded and their mothers ostracized. "But it strikes me," he says, "as equally damaging to ignore the economic and social realities faced today by single teenage mothers, and to avoid the policy changes that are needed to discourage unwed pregnancies and help girls who have children get their lives in order." These parents are themselves children who "stop their education, have few economic opportunities and often lack support systems for parenthood. That means problems for them and their babies."[10]

Delayed school openings — increased costs, decreased benefits — school violence — a rise in single-parent families — illiterate families — children who have children. Can the school system sustain these burdens?

Syndicated columnist Cal Thomas says: No! Parents are fed up. They see no return on their investment. They no longer trust the National Education Association.[11] The NEA says: "If school performance is poor, you've got to pump more money into the school." Parents are saying: Stop measuring productivity in terms of dollars spent. We want something more. Measure the outcome. What are kids learning?

This was a favorite subject of former Secretary of Education, Bill Bennett. More than once he riled the educational establishment in general and the NEA in particular for spending its time and the public's money tinkering with frills while avoiding the essentials of education. He recently blasted that establishment and moved the debate to another level: "We desperately need to recover a sense of the fundamental purpose of education, which is to engage in the architecture of souls."[12] That must have raised some eyebrows! Is there a single public school in the country that teaches kids about souls?

Don't rush to lay all the blame at the doors of the public schools. There's plenty of blame to go around. The schools are handcuffed. "The schools can do nothing about too-soon sex, illegitimate births, teen suicide and a plate full of social diseases," said Cal Thomas, "unless they instill and affirm a purpose for living beyond consumption and glandular satisfaction. Public education should be about preserving those cultural, social — and not excluding religious — values that have induced the type of well-rounded individual once considered essential."[13] But the culture and the courts don't seem to understand "architecture of souls!" Raise that in the Supreme Court and you'll have a howl up and down Constitution Avenue.

So parents are rebelling. Tired of paying more and getting less, they are turning in larger numbers to private schools, and are drumming louder for charter schools, home schooling and vouchers. They want schools that know something about souls.

It is a lamentable scene — that of the public schools slowly digging their own graves. One after another Supreme Court decision has saddled soullessness onto the back of a profession whose job deals precisely with souls. Bill

Bennett summarized the recent years of our nation's cultural decline: "Perhaps no one will be surprised to learn that America's cultural condition is far from healthy. What is shocking is just how precipitously American life has declined in the past 30 years, despite the enormous governmental effort to improve it."[14]

These are the things that are motivating the folks in the Tri-Cities to do something about their schools. I know that there are some who hold that those things are the job of the family and the church, temple and synagogue, not the schools. I disagree. If there is any truth in the adage, "it takes a village to raise a child," the education of youth is the job of all of us. This is especially true in a society such as ours where the education of youth is so difficult, where the values of the family are challenged outside the family, where so many are so muddled about the soul, where so much diseducation takes place on the streets and in the schools, in the movies and on television, and even in the courts.

So, more power to the Tri-Cities folks in Washington State and others who have the vision, courage and trust to launch so worthy an enterprise as a school where the architecture of souls is the highest priority.

DO PUBLIC SCHOOLS STILL SERVE THE PUBLIC GOOD?

Back in the nineteenth century, the proposed ideal American education was in the "common schools," as they were called. Horace Mann sold the nation on the common schools in the 1830's and 40's.[15] Being a "melting pot" of European nations, the United States needs common schools, he said, where immigrants would learn to be Americans. In time that idea became so popular that private and especially church-related schools were suspect, so suspect in fact that Oregon legislated out of existence the Catholic schools, until an historic Supreme Court decision in 1925 reversed the Oregon Court, saving private education in the United States.[16]

In the course of time the ground on which the common schools were built has shifted, and scads of reformers are now hurrying to prop up those schools. Were he here today, Horace Mann would applaud their efforts, but the work of Anthony Bryk, Valerie Lee, and Peter Holland would leave him flabbergasted. Bryk is a Professor of Education at the University of Chicago, Lee an Associate Professor of Education at the University of Michigan, and Holland is Superintendent of the school system in Belmont, Massachusetts. These three began collaborating on a research project in 1981, worked for ten years, and spent two years writing the manuscript which was published in 1993 by Harvard University Press titled *"Catholic Schools and the Common Good."*[17]

The purpose of their research was to learn how Catholic high schools achieve relatively high levels of student learning, distribute their learning more equitably with regard to race and class than do the public schools, and sustain high levels of teacher commitment and student engagement. [18]

The basic argument of the book is that academic structure, communal organization and an inspirational ideology are the major forces that make Catholic schools so effective. "The Catholic school contrasts sharply with the contemporary rhetoric of public schooling...." The "common good," which Horace Mann saw as the purpose of the common schools, is today achieved in the Catholic school. "While the Catholic school, like the Catholic Church itself, has become increasingly public, the public schools have become increasingly private, turning away from the basic social and political purposes that once lent them the title of 'common school.'" [19]

The broad conclusions of the study derive from many specific findings. One concerns curriculum and requirements. Students in public high schools have fewer required courses than those in Catholic schools. Public school students are typically presented with a smorgasbord of "outwardly appealing courses that may entice some students away from more traditional academic offerings." [20] Students in Catholic schools, by contrast, face more of a core curriculum that is required of all students, the course of study being set by school graduation requirements.

Another difference concerns students' sustained intellectual interests. Catholic schools give direction and encouragement toward more vigorous intellectual work than do public schools. In the authors' words: "Catholic schools take a proactive stance encouraging academic course work among their students." [21] As a result there is more enthusiasm among Catholic students, regardless of race or class, to pursue a college education than among public school students. Again, the authors:

> This analysis provides further evidence suggesting an institutional pull by Catholic schools toward academic pursuits. This again contrasts with public schools, where some incongruity exits between students' academic efforts and their educational aspirations. In public high schools, a continuous process of discouragement appears to be at work, as increasing numbers of students abandon post-secondary educational plans. [22]

Another differentiating factor is the responsibility that schools take for the formation of personal character. Historically the common schools included in their mission the religious and moral formation of students. But since World War II that responsibility has largely been abandoned. To be sure, public schools "have extensive codes of conduct and elaborate systems for adjudicating misconduct," as this is necessary to maintain order in the buildings and on the campus. "Beyond safeguarding this basic social order in schools, however, the contemporary public high school appears relatively silent about any larger socialization aims." By contrast, say the authors, "In the Catholic schools we visited, the approach to student conduct was much richer than maintenance of a minimal social order."[23] Teachers in the schools seek "to shape the kind of people students should become — engage in what might be called 'character building.'" While among teachers and administrators there frequently exist substantial divisions on matters of morality and theology, "such internal differences co-exist with a solid core of principles on which the faculty do agree: that education is fundamentally a moral enterprise; that the person is composed of both intellectual [*sic*] and will; and that both these components are properly the focus of teachers' efforts."[24]

The final chapter summarizes four "foundational characteristics" that the authors suggest the public schools might borrow from Catholic high schools. First, there is "a long standing Catholic tradition about what constitutes a proper humanistic education."[25] Elements of that tradition might well serve the public schools, replacing the enticing smorgasbord of trendy courses, the educational value of which is questionable.

Second, "the academic structure of Catholic high schools is embedded within a larger communal organization that is formed around three core features," which enhance the students educational experiences but receive scant emphasis in public schools. These features are: numerous formal and informal school events that provide interaction of students and adults; a definition of the teacher's role that includes extra-classroom interaction with students; and shared beliefs about curriculum, norms of instruction and student behavior.[26]

Third, "the governance of Catholic high schools is decentralized." In marked contrast to the public sector, Catholic schools are "a very loose federation. Virtually all important decisions are made at individual school sites." This promotes creativity, camaraderie, and a sense of ownership by faculty and administrators in the local school.[27]

Fourth, "An inspirational ideology" characterizes Catholic schools. In the 1960's serious questions were raised by many Catholics, including Bishops, about continuing a separate Catholic school system. Thirty years later those questions are rarely heard. Catholic educators may differ about details, but there is renewed commitment to education and broad agreement on certain spiritual principles that may not lend themselves to statistical measurement, but are not thereby unimportant. Say the authors:

> There is much evidence that the ideology of Catholic schools shapes the action of its members. This influence of ideology is seen in an academic organization that uses conventional instruments...in the explicit content of the shared values that ground the Catholic communal organization... To ignore the importance of ideology because it cannot be easily captured in statistical analysis or summarized with numbers would be a serious mistake.[28]

Two important ideas shape life in those schools that set them apart from public schools: Christian personalism, which "calls for humaneness in the myriad of mundane social interactions that make up daily life;" and subsidiarity, which requires that "instrumental considerations about work efficiency and specialization must be mediated by a concern for human dignity."[29]

It is impossible in a piece such as this to summarize and transmit all the findings and arguments of such a piece of research, much less to capture the richness of the ideas and ideals that the book contains. But about the time that the Bryk, Lee and Holland study challenged the effectiveness of the public schools, another book, by Rockne McCarthy, studied another aspect of the public schools, raising the surprising question: Are the public schools still public?[30]

One once heard the parochial schools lambasted as "un-American" because they were "divisive." You don't hear that anymore because it is recognized that the so-called private schools do a pretty remarkable job of educating the public. But McCarthy's book titled *Democracy and the Renewal of Public Education*, turns the tables on that worn out cliché about divisiveness, arguing that today the public schools, which propose to serve all of America's families, in fact serve an increasingly small minority, and so their public school monopoly on education deserves the serious questioning it now receives.

The public educational system is based on one major assumption: public education should be value-free or nonsectarian. This assumption goes back to Thomas Jefferson's notion that sectarian opinions and religious views were somehow irrational and so had no place in public education. This was foursquare Enlightenment teaching, which Horace Mann, father of the American common schools, proposed as the ground for universal public education for all Americans.

The question this philosophy of education specifically addressed early on is: Can nonsectarian education be carried out without offending those who hold sectarian beliefs? Mann and his successors said "yes." Many Americans, especially Catholics, said "no."

Early in the nineteenth century the argument was joined in New York City. As early as the 1820's, New York citizens publicly supported one school system which had the responsibility of educating children in the "common faith" of the people. It soon became clear that the "common faith" of the people was really the "common faith" of the Protestant majority in New York. The dispute erupted in 1840 when Bishop John Hughes pressed the claim "to a proportional share of the common school fund" for support of the Catholic schools. Appearing before the Common Council of New York City, Bishop Hughes argued that public funds for education were monopolized by a private corporation (The Public School Society), which had as one of its goals the "early religious instruction" of children. In supporting the common fund, said Hughes, Catholic parents are paying for schools that violate the religious conscience of their children. Bishop Hughes did not object to all groups sharing in the common school fund; he objected to the educational monopoly of the Public School Society. In his words:

> Let those who can receive the advantages of these schools; but as Catholics cannot, do not tie them to a system which is intended for the advantage of a class of society of which they form one-third, but from which system they can receive no benefit.[31]

Attorney Hiram Ketchum, representing the Public School Society, objected to Bishop Hughes' charge that the Society's schools offended any of the public school children. He argued that sectarian teaching in the common schools was completely inappropriate; but he stressed, nevertheless, those schools have the obligation to inculcate universal teachings of virtue and morality. In Ketchum's words:

> We have the right to declare moral truths....We thus undertake in these public schools to furnish this secular education, embracing as it does, not solely and exclusively the common rudiments of learning, but also a knowledge of good morals, and those common sanctions of religion which are acknowledged by everybody.[32]

The Bishop argued back: it is impossible for one group to teach a common moral education to another group when they differ on what moral education should be. But Ketchum, like Jefferson and Mann, insisted it was possible and repeated that the Public School Society had "the right to declare moral truths."

Ketchum's argument prevailed, the Common Council rejected the Catholic petition and the Society continued to claim that its schools were nonsectarian even though they taught "a knowledge of good morals, and those common sanctions of religion."[33] And, of course, the Common Council continued to receive all the money from the common school fund to support its schools.

But calling something nonsectarian doesn't make it so.

We are today in what some call the "Post Enlightenment" age. Few any longer support the thesis that education can be, or ever was, value-free or nonsectarian. "By the twentieth century," Rockne McCarthy writes, "the commitment to non-sectarian education was transformed into a commitment to *secular* education. With this development, secular education and public education became synonymous."[34] As Dorothy Massie of the National Education Association said, parents are protesting, not simply against a particular textbook or class or teacher, "but against the whole direction of a curriculum."[35] The disagreements are over fundamental world-views that shape a curriculum and the entire life of an educational institution. What is becoming glaringly evident is that in a pluralist society such as ours a "public" monopolist structure of education very poorly serves the entire public.

The system, as Bishop Hughes had argued, only serves the needs of part of the people, and that part which in the 1840's was a large majority is in the Twenty-first Century a minority. Hence, the very legitimacy of public education as it is presently defined is questioned. The current debate over American education "is making it clearer to many people that if secular or value-free education is not possible, then a monopolist system of public education cannot legitimately serve the needs of a pluralist society."[36]

After he lost his debate before the Common Council in New York City in 1840, Bishop Hughes said he would, nevertheless, continue his struggle for the "claims of justice and equal rights." Years later, Rockne McCarthy, now in an article titled "Public Schools and Public Justice," continued the fight that Bishop Hughes initiated. In his 1987 essay McCarthy said that he not only asks the question: "Is the public school system just?"[37] He asks the further question: Is the public school system any longer public?

Late in his years Lord Beveridge, father of the British welfare state, having noted subsequent trends in public policy, cautioned his followers in these words:

> The State is or can be master of money, but in a free society it is master of very little else. The making of a good society depends not on the State but on the Citizens, acting individually or in free association with one another, acting on motives of various kinds, some selfish others unselfish, some narrow and material, others inspired by love of man and love of God. The happiness or unhappiness of the society in which we live depends upon ourselves as citizens, not on the instrument of political power which we call the State.[38]

WHAT'S WRONG WITH THE SCHOOLS?

Aristotle taught the Western World many wise things, among them the wisdom contained in the statement: "[e]ven a small error at the beginning is comparable in effect to all the errors made at the later stages."[39] This principle may apply to our nation's schools which seem to have so many problems.

One educational expert after another has put the public schools under a microscope in hopes of discovering what they are accomplishing and why they are the failures that their critics say they are. Of course, everyone close to the schools has his or her diagnosis of their maladies and what the cure should be. While I don't profess to be able to give a complete diagnosis, I think I recognize some of the problems. So here are one educator's views.

The student must come first. Years ago Supreme Court Justice Jackson in
Thomas v. Collins wrote to this point: "The very purpose of the First Amendment is to foreclose public authority from assuming guardianship of the
public mind."[40] No public agency should be guardian of thought. An educational system which holds itself to be an agent exercising a "claim" on
children, is un-American. The person to be educated must come first, and
only afterwards, social agendas.

We should be clear about that: the primary purpose of education is the
intellectual, physical, emotional, social and spiritual development of the student. If we begin with any other primary aim, the children to be educated will
find themselves in second or third place, behind someone else's social agenda. As Rudolph Steiner, founder of the Waldorf School's home-based program, put it: "One should not ask 'What does a person need to know and be
able to do for the existing social order?' but rather, 'What gifts does a person
possess and how may these be developed?'"[41]

One young lady who has heard enough about "the terrible failure of our
school system," and decided to do something about it is Michelle Rhee. The
District of Columbia Mayor, Adrian Fenty, hired Michelle to be Chancellor
of the District of Columbia public school system. Initially Michelle refused.
"I knew I would be a political problem. If we did the job right for the City's
children it would upset the status quo."

But she took the job and sure enough within two years Fenty, who had
supported her efforts boldly, lost his re-election for the City Major; and
shortly after that Rhee left her job. But she is still fighting. She recently
stated in a Newsweek article, "[t]he state of American education is pitiful and
getting worse. The U.S. is currently 21st, 23rd and 25th among thirty developed nations in science, reading and math respectfully. The children in our
schools today will be the first generation of Americans who will be less
educated than the previous generation."[42]

A lot of money goes into protecting the job security for teachers, she says,
"but there is no big organized interest group that defends and promotes the
interests of children." The focus of the fight is on the teachers, not on the
children. "Go to any public school board meeting in the country," Michelle
Rhee says, "and you'll rarely hear the words 'children,' 'students,' or 'kids'
uttered. Instead the focus remains on what jobs, contracts and departments
are getting which cuts, additions, or changes. The rational for the decisions
mostly rests on which grownups will be affected, instead of what will benefit
or harm children." The focus is on the bureaucracy.

As a result, "[s]o many great teachers in this Country are frustrated with
the schools they are working in, the bureaucratic rules that bind them, and the
hostility to excellence that pervades our education system."

Determined to continue the fight, Michelle Rhee and her colleagues have started an organization called Students First. "We believe every family can choose an excellent school — attending a great school should be a matter of fact, not luck."

If Michelle Rhee has her way children in this Country will get more attention than they have been getting, and good teachers who are interested in her objectives will fight alongside her. She concluded her article in *Newsweek* with: "There is nothing more worthwhile than fighting for children. And I'm not done fighting."[43]

Michelle Rhee's fight with the schools was recently supported through test scores by the Education Trust. U.S. Education Secretary Arne Duncan told the A.P. that he was "deeply troubled" by the data. "Too many of our high school students," he said, "are not graduating ready to begin college or a career — and many are not eligible to serve in our armed forces."[44]

Data from the test shows that one in four students cannot pass our military's aptitude test. The questions are often basic, such as: "If 2 plus x equals 4, what is the value of x?"

"It's surprising and shocking that we are still having students who are walking across the stage who really don't deserve to be and haven't earned that right," said Tim Callahan with the Professional Association of Georgia Educators, a group that represents more than 80,000 educators.[45]

Because she thought that ends and means were all mixed up in our schools, Virginia Seuffert decided to run her own school. It's a one-room classroom at her home. She's the only teacher for the four students who are her children. Why is she doing this? Because she was totally unsatisfied with the absence of purpose, the aimlessness and lack of challenge in the public schools. Seuffert gave this illustration:

> One typical second-grade social studies text talks about how people live in "communities" or "neighborhoods," and the people who live there are called "neighbors." IIt explains that some people live in single family "houses" and others live in "apartments." There's a chapter on neighborhood helpers: fire fighters put out fires, mail carriers deliver the mail, doctors and nurses help people who are sick, and so on. Based on this text, my kids had mastered second-grade social studies before they started kindergarten. I couldn't subject them to this tedious and pointless curriculum.[46]

So she withdrew them from the public and placed them in a parochial school in upstate New York. She was well satisfied with the parochial school, but then the family had to move to Chicago. She placed the children in a parochial school in a Chicago suburb. But not for long. As she said, "We soon discovered that mediocrity, so prevalent in the public schools of our nation, was seeping into the parochial system as well."[47]

Meanwhile, she had done enough reading to know that there were great historical success stories in home education: Wolfgang Mozart, Thomas Edison, Leo Tolstoy and Abraham Lincoln, to name a few. Then, there was John Stuart Mill, British philosopher and economist, who was educated at home by his father, James Mill. Years later John Stuart wrote that in his case it was an experiment that his father used to prove the ease at which young children could be taught advanced work. You might think he was a boy prodigy, but John assures us that wasn't the case. As he wrote: "I'm rather below than above par; what I could do, could assuredly be done by any boy or girl with average capacity and healthy, physical constitution...."[48]

So Virginia Seuffert thought she would give home-schooling a try. Not all states are equally open to home schooling. Many throw up insurmountable obstacles to parents wishing to school their children at home. Illinois is not one of them. So she shopped around among the various home-school programs and chose the Seton Home Study School Program, primarily because it stressed both academic preparation and moral development. Has she been successful? Here's a sample from her report card: "In five months, six-year old Katie had completed a challenging first-grade program and is beginning second-grade work. Third-grader John is studying the history of major civilizations, world geography, and Latin. My fourth-grade student, Carol, who is learning French and studying the five classes of vertebrates, will soon be starting fifth-grade math."[49]

Not a college graduate herself, Seuffert asks the obvious question: "Why is a college dropout able to accomplish, with relative ease on a heated porch, what a well-funded, beautifully equipped modern school, staffed by highly educated professionals, backed by over a century of education research, seems incapable of doing?" Her answer: "It's simply a matter of goals." Seuffert's goals for her children are not unconventional, but the ordinary goals of middle America: "My children must be morally and intellectually prepared to meet with confidence whatever challenges they may face as adults. Learning to color within the lines or understand the meaning of Mother's Day do nothing to forward my aim; solid, academic preparation and character formation do. Our home life and their time spent in school are wasted when this goal is not pursued."[50]

As Seuffert sees it, what's done in most of our schools will never achieve those goals. Modern educators don't seem to understand what children are capable of achieving. For example, the *Elson Reader*, printed in 1926 for the sixth grade, had as its foundation the recognized masterpieces of American British literature.[51] Students were introduced to the likes of Emerson, Wordsworth, James Russell Lowell, Kilmer, Longfellow, Washington Irving, Dickens, Tennyson, Theodore Roosevelt, Abraham Lincoln, Benjamin Franklin and Woodrow Wilson, even Homer. "Today, in sharp contrast to this," says Seuffert, "much of the information our children are taught in the public schools is frivolous, unpatriotic, anti-religious, and anti-traditional, and too often schools are downright unsafe. Public schools are dismally failing to impart to our children the basic knowledge that they will need to be the future leaders of our nation."[52]

A few years ago, Samuel Blumenfeld, Research Fellow at the Institute for Humane Studies in Menlo Park, California, wrote a book entitled *Is Public Education Necessary*, in which he said:

> Public education does not fail in a totalitarian state where its purposes are clearly defined by the rulers. But in a country like our own, the incompatibility of public education with the values of a free society has become more and more apparent each year. [53]

It is estimated that today children are being taught in one million home-school programs. What we're witnessing is a conflict between the family and the state: Whose authority is primary in the education of children? Who is primary in forming children's minds and behavior?

This is not an advocacy for home schooling. It is a call to examine our public school system more closely and critically than we have done thus far.

HUMANITIES UNDER ATTACK

Once upon a time folks in the academy agreed on the importance of the humanities for a well-educated person. The humanities deal with human beings and human culture and aim to impart understanding of such enduring values as justice, freedom, virtue, beauty and truth. For centuries, and well into present times, everyone acknowledged that to know the best that human beings have known, thought and done in the world was the heart of a university education. But that was once upon a time. Today, the humanities are under attack. The attackers are in the classrooms.

Many years ago the humanities began to be gradually and gently nudged aside by the development of the professions and the need to make room in the curriculum for undergraduate professional studies requirements. But those were friendly nudges. More recently the crisis to the humanities comes from its enemies who are out to bury Western culture and wipe away every trace of the humanities. That was Michael Foucault's aim, his attitude toward the humanities being clearly enunciated:

To all those who still wish to talk about man...to all those who still ask
themselves questions about what man is in his essence, to all those who wish
to take him as their starting-point in their attempts to reach the truth...to all
these warped and twisted forms of reflection we can answer only with a
philosophical laugh.[54]

The assault against the humanities, then, is not a happenstance. As Gregory
Wolfe plainly said: "The Marxists, feminists and deconstructionists have
made it clear that their prime enemy is the Judaeo-Christian tradition of
metaphysics. With that destroyed, terms like truth, good, evil and soul can be
discarded."[55]

Western intellectuals have long been infatuated with Marxism, and many
see themselves playing a major role in the revolution. While the final victory
of socialism was considered far off in history it needed to be prepared for by
radical cultural change. Proletarians could not gain political power until they
achieved control of the culture, and that was a task for intellectuals. The
intellectuals, therefore, not the proletarians, are history's Messianic class.
Their mission was expressed by Frederic Jameson: "To create the Marxist
culture in this country...to form a Marxist intelligentsia for the struggle of
the future — this seems to me the supreme mission of a Marxist pedagogy
and a radical, intellectual life today."[56]

In the 1960's, while I was on the faculty at St. Louis University, a well-
known sociologist, Alvin W. Gouldner, was across town at Washington University teaching the same doctrine, namely that revolutionary intellectuals
constitute a "new class" whose "capital" consists of culture not money. The
culture he had in mind was anti-traditional, what he called "culture of critical
discourse."[57] "We must distinguish," wrote Gouldner, "between the functions universities publicly *promise* to perform....and certain of their actual
consequences which, while commonly unintended, are no less real: the pro-
duction of dissent, deviance, and the cultivation of an authority-subverting
culture of critical discourse."[58] The university is transformed from a place of
learning where culture and literary, philosophical and scientific tradition are
preserved and transmitted, to a political battlefield. It is this political war that
Gouldner had in mind: "To participate in the culture of critical discourse,
then, is a political act."[59]

Under its voluntaristic impulse the critical discourse extends well beyond
discourse to become antagonism, negation, and nihilism. Lee Congdon called
this contemporary Marxism's greatest temptation: "The passion for negation
that often shades into nihilism."[60] So the celebrated Russian anarchist Mikhail Bakunin advocated a "cultural revolution," by which he meant the total
destruction of educational institutions and of the human spirit. In his "Catechism of a Revolutionist," he announced the goal of his Messianic violence:
"The revolutionary despises all doctrine and refuses to accept the mundane

sciences. He knows only one science: the science of destruction. For this reason, but only for this reason, he will study mechanics, physics, chemistry and perhaps medicine. But all day and all night he studies the vital science of human beings, their characteristics and circumstances, and all the phenomena of the present social order. The object is perpetually the same: the surest and quickest way of destroying the whole filthy order."[61] Thus, the target of the destruction is not simply the economic system of free enterprise, but all Western culture and values that are associated with that system. The heart of Western civilization must be annihilated, and Western history must be re-written.

This is not theoretical stuff. Echoes of the Gramsci and Gouldner themes were heard from an annual meeting of the Association of General and Liberal Studies. As reported in the November 11, 1987 *Chronicle of Higher Education*, university educators were told that "higher education should be the steering wheel of cultural change and advancement for the future" and so professors should "stop pretending that teaching is not a political act."[62] According to Henry Giroux of Miami, the purpose in teaching the liberal arts is to achieve "social transformation," otherwise a college will be nothing more than a "Sunday school, a Greek museum, or an arm of the corporate world." It sounded awfully like the campus upheavals of the 1960's, as "professors were urged to value the contributions of students as much as the expertise of great thinkers."[63]

No wonder Secretary of Education, Bill Bennett, was shouted down as he proclaimed like a lone prophet in a wilderness the necessary and essential place of the humanities in the university. It is through the humanities principally that the culture, values, and moral principles of the Judeo-Christian tradition are kept alive in Western society. That tradition does not exist on paper but in the mind and in the soul. Tear down the humanities, you tear away the soul and leave the corpse.

RENDERING GOD'S THINGS TO CAESAR

Schools used to be simply places where girls and boys received an education. Today they are battlegrounds where the nation's political and social issues are fought out. For a longtime, over a hundred and fifty years, we seemed to get along rather peacefully, for we appeared to walk on more or less common cultural and religious ground. But that ground in recent years has been crumbling beneath our feet.

Recall, for example, the various ways our Supreme Court has described our religious culture. In 1931, the Court said in *United States v. McIntosh*: "We are a Christian people acknowledging with reverence the duty of obedience to the will of God." Here is the high Court recognizing a culture that accepts both God and Christianity. One judge wrote that religion, as we understand it, is "belief in a relation to God involving duties superior to those arising from any human relation." A brief thirty years later, the same Court's definition of religion swings around 180 degrees; God no longer need be recognized, the Court wrote: "Among religions in this country which do not teach what would generally be considered a belief in the existence of God are Buddhism, Taoism, Ethical Culture, Secular Humanism, and others."[64] In effect, the Court said that atheism now enjoys the same status as religion.

During most of this century the schools have been arenas of legal contests over the "non-establishment" and the "free exercise" clauses of the First Amendment. These two clauses are, and no doubt from now on will be, in constant tension. The first Amendment says that government shall have nothing to do with religion, but that it shall guarantee its right to exist and flourish. When ruling on education today the Supreme Court holds that, with respect to religion, the public schools must be neutral.

Take the issue of prayer in the public schools and at commencement ceremonies — who knows what the Founding Fathers would do today? They hardly imagined the society we live in. Some will readily dismiss public prayer altogether by quoting Our Lord: "When you pray," He said, "go into your private room, and when you shut your door, pray to your Father who is in that secret place, and your Father who sees all that is done in secret will reward you."[65] Others point out that Jesus, on that occasion, was then speaking against hypocrisy; he was not talking about public policy. On another occasion He said: "Whenever two or three are gathered together in my name, I am there in the midst of them."[66]

There are those, however, who hold that religion is, and should be, a private affair, that it has no place in the public forum, and certainly not in state institutions. Some think that the prayer that convenes the Congress might just as well be stopped, since no one attends anyway — the minister prays in a chamber that is virtually empty. Having on several occasions offered the noon day prayer that convenes the House of Representatives, I can testify that in the House that is the case.

Of course, if one's religion is only a public affair, it is the hypocrisy that Our Lord condemned. But the pertinent question is: What happens if religion is only a private affair, as some would have it, and God is not recognized in the public forum? What happens to the public mores, to the religious and moral fiber of society? People publicly celebrate what they value. What they do not value they leave aside or quietly pass over altogether. But those things that go unnoticed are seen as unimportant, and that notion of unimportance gets passed on from generation to generation until a nation forgets them altogether, and then discards them.

So, those who push for prayer in public schools are concerned about more than simply prayer in schools. The concern is over the godlessness that threatens to permeate public life. The secularist tone in the public schools — not simply the absence of prayer — is the reason that families are taking children out of public schools and demanding tax support for private schools, and the right to teach them at home. It is the issue of godlessness that triggered the argument over evolution and creation in the curriculum. Few are opposed to teaching evolution in the schools; what some people oppose is the teaching of evolution in the context of a materialistic, supposedly godless universe. What many people oppose is having their children instructed in an environment of Secular Humanism. Secular Humanism, which the Court said is a religion, explains itself thus: "Faith in God, assumed to love and care for persons...is an unproved and outmoded faith. [...] As nontheists, we begin with humans not God, nature not deity. [...] We can discover no divine purpose or providence for the human species."[67] Many parents object to having their children captive in a school that indoctrinates that kind of religion, if religion it can be called.

So the absence of prayer and the legal rulings against public prayer are symptoms of deeper-rooted problems.

Consider the Constitution? Should nine judges in Washington, D.C., deny parents the right to have their kids pray at a school, if they want to? People will say that some parents' kids will face embarrassment. But there is no Constitutional protection against embarrassment.

The Court protects the freedom of speech of the television industry, thus allowing into the living room scenes of brutality and sexual violence that upset and embarrass kids and their parents. The Court allows this even if some people are embarrassed and offended. Freedom of speech is that important. And freedom of religion? In the case of the schools when kids enter the classroom they lose freedom of religion for they must follow the "religion" of the public schools. If Secular Humanism is a religion and secularism is the culture of our schools, then religion is taught, in a great variety of ways, in the public schools.

So it seems, and the argument has been made, that the desired "neutrality" of the public school has resulted in no neutrality at all, but rather a kind of religion all its own. This has come about perhaps because of the very nature of the problem in a pluralistic society, perhaps also because in effect the courts have subordinated the "free exercise" clause to the "non-establishment" clause.

A number of recent studies seem to make this clear. One of these is a study by Professor Paul Vitz of New York University, in which the author demonstrates that the textbooks used in the schools have deleted religion and religious references altogether, thus falsifying western history and culture.[68] For example, from textbooks widely used in the schools, one would never know that it was deeply held religious convictions that motivated Joan of Arc, or that it was religious freedom that the Pilgrims were pursuing, or that the Reformation and counter-Reformation are major movements in western history. Are not, then, the schools engaged in what Richard Neuhaus called, "massive education malfeasance?"

Why the omissions? There are many reasons but probably the most compelling is in order to avoid controversy. Religion is admittedly controversial. Rather than engender controversy and run the risk of offending those who object to the intrusion of religion in the schools, textbook publishers simply eliminate religious history and references altogether. What results is "censorship by omission." Some will defend that on grounds that religion is a subject for church and home, not for the schools.

The result: not, indeed, public schools that are "neutral," but public schools that teach a religion all their own. As Sir Walter Moberly put it:

> It is a fallacy to suppose that by omitting a subject you teach nothing about it. On the contrary you teach that it is to be omitted, and that it is therefore a matter of secondary importance, or of no importance at all. And you teach this not openly and explicitly, which would invite criticism; you simply take it for granted and thereby insinuate it silently, insidiously, and all but irresistibly. [69]

To make matters worse, the courts allow schools to teach not religion, but about religion. So the Sacred Scriptures and other religious texts may be studied as literary historical documents. That is to say, they may be and are used in the schools as secular documents, which altogether misses the point of those documents. In fact, they are documents of faith, and those who wrote them and comment on them, and interpret them, are believers. What is important then is not what non-believers think of them but what they mean to believers. What secularists believe religion to be is not very important or enlightening to a believer. The important thing is not what secularists believe religion to be, but what believers believe it to be.

So where does that leave us? If students are being mis-educated, I would think that intelligent and conscientious educators would want to correct that. And if students' consciences are being violated, I would think that educators would want to correct that. More fundamental still, I think that by now we should all have learned that religion and its place in our lives cannot be determined by state control. We should have learned that in a democratic society, people, meaning parents and children, have a right to have belief presented as it appears to the eye of the believer.

When they showed Him the coin of the tributes, Our Lord said: "Render to Caesar the things that are Caesar's and to God the things that are God's." [70] It appears that our present regime is rendering to Caesar some things that are God's.

ON BULLHORNS AND BASEBALL BATS

Some years ago the National Commission on Excellence in Education came out with a report on education titled "A Nation at Risk."[71] A few years later, when he was Secretary of Education, Bill Bennett came out with his report card on the nation's schools which concluded: "We are still at risk."[72] National Education Association president, Mary Hatwood Futrell, not one to pass up a scrap, challenged Bennett: "Since you're not supporting more federal funding for education, what do you expect? Lack of funding is strangling education reform in state after state."[73]

Not one to walk away from a fight, Bennett countered: "It seems unlikely that we will ever spend enough money to satisfy the N.E.A."[74] Then he added: "In this country when it comes to education, we reward poor performance. Poorly performing schools complain: 'We need more money!' So we give them more money. They continue to perform poorly and complain again, 'we need more money!' So we give them more money."[75]

About this time some school administrators, angry at being blamed for schools' failures, and at wits end over charges of poor performance and lack of discipline, took matters into their own hands. Joe Clark and his methods were in every paper across the nation. Clark kept students in line at East Side High School in Paterson, New Jersey by wielding a bullhorn and baseball bat. One of Clark's colleagues, high school principal Melvin Smoak, at Orangeburg-Wilkinson, South Carolina, patrols his schools corridors with a walkie-talkie and a computer.[76]

While Clark's and Smoak's colleagues agreed that walkie-talkies and baseball bats will get kids' attention, most thought that there must be more enlightened roads to reform than the old shillelagh.

John Chubb thought so, too. This Senior Fellow at the Brookings Institution came out with a thoughtful article in 1988 which is still very pertinent, titled "Why the Current Wave of School Reform Will Fail."[77] Most schools are poor, says Chubb, because they are poorly organized: their goals are unclear, they lack leadership, collegiality and autonomy. Good schools have definite organizational qualities that influence student learning. Educational practices such as how teachers test or assign homework, or how teachers themselves are evaluated, are far less important than the school's organization as a whole — its goals, leadership, and educational climate. "Their institutional structure and character is shaped by their environments — by their relationships with parents, of course, but more pertinently by the way they are controlled, by their connections to administrative and political superiors."[78]

Schools at the top, Chubb elaborates, "have strikingly superior organizations;" their goals are spelled out in terms of "academic excellence;" they have a sense of mission; leadership is "more pedagogical and less managerial than in low-performance"[79] schools; the leadership style is not authoritarian but collegial — successful schools "seem like a big family;"[80] organizational qualities approximate those associated with teams rather than hierarchies. How important are these qualities? In Chubb's view, they add a year to learning in high school. "All other things being equal, attending an effectively organized high school for four years is worth at least a full year of additional achievement over attendance at an ineffectively organized school."[81]

The essential ingredients of a good school are "such things as academically focused objectives, pedagogically strong principals, relatively autonomous teachers, and collegial staff relations." But — and here comes the hooker — for these elements to exist and flourish, superintendents, school boards, and other outside authorities must be willing "to delegate meaningful control over school policy, personnel, and practice to the school itself." School autonomy in the hands of the right administrators and teachers is critically important. "Efforts to improve the performance of schools without changing the way they are organized or the controls they respond to will have only modest success; they are even more likely to be undone."[82]

Having said all that, Chubb, not surprisingly, joins those who favor more of a free market in education. Better organizational effectiveness, stronger leadership, a sense of mission, collegiality, more professional teaching — these goals will be achieved only "by increasing school autonomy." And the only way to increase school autonomy is "to rely less on relationships of authority and more on the signals of the market."[83] But he has no expectation that that will take place in the current educational environment: those in control will not change the way schools are organized.

That's where school reform hits the wall: "Reforms that would transform the controls over schools from political and administrative arrangements to those of the market would shift much of the power over public education from elected and appointed government officials outside of schools to the professionals within the schools and to their essential clientele — students and their parents."[84] But those in control of the educational system want no reform that involves a shifting of power. Therefore, all the talk about school reform will come to naught. Sounds like the old story of the foxes guarding the chicken coop.

However, in the outside chance that the educational establishment will give up its hold on the school system, Chubb has this advice: "[i]f real alternatives are considered, a number of options ought to be taken seriously — among them, magnet schools, open enrollment plans, and full or partial voucher systems. In one way or another, each provides students and their parents more choice among schools and more reason to become cooperatively involved in them."[85] That's a long way from bullhorns and baseball bats. But it's not likely to fly with the N.E.A. whose answer, Bill Bennett would say, is already scripted: "We need more money."

THE CULTIVATION OF MORAL MORONS

It should come as a surprise to no one that the secularism, the atheism and moral chaos that pervades our culture likewise pervades our public schools. Some of our state and city boards of education are embarrassed by the box they're in. Efforts to remain religiously and morally neutral as the schools are expected to be, has had the to-be-anticipated effect of undermining moral behavior in students; the religiously neutral in theory is anti-religious in fact. Religion is supposed to be excluded not only from the classroom but from the entire school, on constitutional grounds. Anti-religion is not. If a student or teacher mocks religion, particularly if it is at a state university, he is merely exercising 'academic freedom.'

And the schools get blamed for everything. But schools reflect the culture. If we don't like what's going on in the schools, maybe we should look at ourselves. Take secularism, for example. Ours is a society of materialists, behaviorists and moral relativists — poor soil, all three, for religious faith — and these are reflected in our laws, court decisions, textbooks and curricula.

One of the most influential figures in modern American education was B.F. Skinner, Harvard psychologist, recently deceased. Skinner was a behaviorist with a large following that rigidly adhered to the fundamentals of behaviorism, and his theories have widely influenced American schools. Skinner's world is purely materialist: what cannot be observed does not exist. Hence, God does not exist either in or beyond nature, and the human soul and all human behavior, including intellection and will, are functions of material particles in deterministic interaction. Understanding and knowledge are simply mechanized responses to external stimuli; there is no place in Skinner's system for intention, poetic insight and the integration of experience into a cohesive view of life and reality. Personal freedom is not what it seems, for there is no free will as people commonly understand and experience it. What appears to be freedom, and virtues such as love and loyalty, are in reality programmed responses to as yet undiscovered stimuli. People are always motivated out of self-interest. Personal responsibility are words without meaning.

Given all that, B. F. Skinner's followers consistently hold that "[i]nstead of nurturing independent and self-directing human beings, education is meant to control human mechanisms and to shape them into units of a cohesive society."[86] Skinner unabashedly believed that educators are and should be manipulators of those material particles and stimuli that are bouncing around in students' bodies.

The influence of behaviorism is easily seen in a report a few years ago by a group of "experts" assembled by the Carnegie Foundation for the Advancement of Teaching. Skinner would come down four-square in agreement with the report's position that the schools are primarily social agents to achieve a social purpose and that education is a "tool we reach for in our search for renewal of the frayed social compact."[87]

It would be one thing if these were simply idle fantasies that psychologists played around with after hours. But these things are for real, and are translated into policies in the schools. The Federal government and the states have greatly expanded their funding and control over public education.

Educators openly recognize and parents also recognize that their children are in the schools precisely to be influenced and molded toward certain patterns of behavior. Here is John Childs, a colleague of John Dewey, considered by many the father of American education: "The school seeks to inculcate selected values in the young by means of both the subject matter and the methods that it emphasizes in its program."[88] And here is Philip Phenix, professor at Columbia Teachers College, with the same message: "the really significant outcome of education is the set of governing commitments, the aims for living, that the learner develops. The various subjects of study are simply means for the communication and appropriation of these values."[89] And what are the "values" that are inculcated in the young? Behaviorism, materialism and moral relativism — in a word, secularism.

Education professionals hurry to deny that this is the prevailing ethos of the schools, and point to the flurry of recent courses that aim at moral development. They still teach courses that carry such titles as "Values Clarification" and "Cognitive Moral Development" to which they point with pride as filling that moral vacuum created by behaviorism and secularism. But one has only to scratch beneath the titles of these courses to discover that they simply introduce the student to processes of reflection that are utterly devoid of any content. What they do is all that moral relativism can do — give students a framework, as they say, for selecting values, any values they wish, since both teacher and textbook are committed to accepting all values whatsoever. No values are recommended as superior and preferential over others, and students are taught to freely develop their own personal value system. This is the "values clarification" process that teachers and textbook authors point to with pride.

I said that this educational approach assumes that no values are superior to or preferential over others. That needs one qualification. Implicit in this approach are the assumptions of behaviorism, materialism and secularism — they are the values of choice. The game assumes that one ground rule. As

Kane observed, "the unflinching acceptance of all moral positions denies the existence of any moral absolutes as doggedly as fundamentalism, for example, insists on them."[90]

Those who have thoroughly studied values clarification as it is used in the schools summarize it thus: The students may embrace racism, fascism or any cultural position as long as they go through the process of values clarification taught by the nation's educational theorists. This is the moral chaos that this kind of education leads to. And it should be no surprise. Moral philosophers and historians of philosophy have long known that if you are consistent in espousing moral relativism, this is where you end up.

But what can a local school board do? What can the superintendent, principal and teacher do? If we the public believe these things, promote these values and shape the culture in which the schools operate, and then tell the public school educators to run the schools according to that game plan, what are they to do but pass on that stuff. We the people charge them to teach the kids what we believe. We give them an awful job, not because we don't give them large enough budgets, but because we demand that they educate human beings by principles and assumptions that don't fit human beings. If you want teachers to teach school kids in materialism and moral relativism, then recognize, as Joseph Sobran does, that you have established a secular religion, and expect that the schools will send back to you what the New York State Superintendent of Public Instruction admitted his schools were sending back to his community, "moral morons."

"...IT STINKS..."

Does character building belong in the schools? As a lot of people ask that question, the Gallup poll organization back in 1988 did a survey. To the question: Should courses on values and ethical behavior be taught in the public schools or left to parents and churches, forty-three percent said it's the job of the schools; thirty-six percent said that it's for parents and churches. To the question: Who should have most say about the content of values and ethical behavior courses, forty-two percent said the parents; twenty-four percent said the local school board; fourteen percent, the teachers; ten percent, school administrators; the rest said either the state or the federal governments. And to the question: Should students be excused from character education classes if their parents object to what is being taught, fifty-two percent of the adults said they should be excused, thirty-seven percent said they should not, and eleven percent did not know.

Intrigued by the data, *The Wall Street Journal* ran a story back in September 26, 1988. "Kids today are rudderless," said the *Journal*. "The task of building character has fallen to teachers largely because nobody else is doing the job. The American family is fragmented. The influence of religion continues to decline. And the lessons taught on television are often the wrong ones. Add it all up, and today's children have been left 'rudderless in a turbulent world.'"[91]

A Baltimore school official recalled that in his many years as principal, he often brought up to his students the Golden Rule. But some time during the 1970's he stopped that because the only response that the "Golden Rule" drew from students was blank stares. "They didn't know what I was talking about."[92]

According to the Gallup poll, most people have no objection to schools teaching responsible citizenship, but many think that the re-introduction of character education is liable to be abused. "The American Civil Liberty's Union, for example, is concerned that 'values education is sometimes a ruse for teaching religious values,' says Colleen O'Connor, an ACLU spokeswoman."[93] The way the present system works, schools and teachers must be value-free, leaving students to choose their own values.

Eleven-year-old Sean Hooks' assessment of the system didn't mince words: "We have freedom in this country, but it stinks — drugs, alcohol, crime. There's no good news anymore. I'm hoping we get a president who cleans out America."[94]

Education wasn't always this way. In its long history, character building was considered the central responsibility of educators. Plato said that the purpose of education is to make good men — today I'm sure he would say, "Good men and women." Moral understanding and the ethical foundations of behavior were all important in the early centuries of education in this country; philosophy, theology and the study of moral principles were recognized as the summit of an education. It included not just theoretical understanding of moral principles, but practical programs in the schools to inculcate those principles in the students so that they became integral to their characters. School boards and administrators placed high importance on example and the influence of teachers as models. There were clearly defined behavioral expectations of teachers as well as students, and personal character and example were considered in the hiring and retention of faculty. In a word, there were ethical, moral and character expectations as well as intellectual and academic expectations.

But early in this century, courses in moral philosophy disappeared from the catalogs of most universities, and character development as a university responsibility fell by the wayside. Educators, in their love affairs with scientific methodology, prided themselves on being "value-free." Universities no longer considered themselves moral guides for students, and indeed communities no longer expected or wanted moral guidance from them.

In short order, this evaporation of moral teaching and expectations sifted down to influence secondary and primary education. Soon high school and grade school teachers were telling students to find their own beliefs and commitments, and to motivate themselves in the pursuit of virtue, as best they can. So for several generations the public schools have endorsed the notion of "values clarification," and teachers now tell students: "Virtue is not our business; good and bad is not our business; just clarify things for yourselves and choose what seems best for you."

But many parents and educators, seeing what Sean Hooks sees — "drugs, alcohol, and crime; there's no good news anymore" — think it's time to reevaluate value-free education. The educational system has operated too long under the influence of cultural and moral relativism, which says: one culture is as good as another; no one moral standard is better than any other; no one should press his or her moral views on another, and so no one should attempt to influence the character of students through the inculcation of any set of moral principles. There's not likely to be a change soon. But maybe I'm wrong. If an eleven-year-old can see that "it stinks," maybe there's hope for the rest of us.

VOUCHERS, ANYONE!

Nothing in our culture is more American than freedom, and the right to choose with regard to things that affect our lives. We have the right to choose our public officials, the juries who judge us, the gods we worship, the laws we're governed by, the airlines we fly, the economic system we want and the structure of government that serves us; large segments of our population even believe that a woman has the right to kill the fetus in her womb or to let it live. We support freedom and diversity in most every social and cultural institution you can imagine — except the prison system and the public school system.

We want, and we demand, the right to choose just about everything under the sun, until it comes to schools and prisons. Then on behalf of the schools, the educational establishment — National Education Association, the American Association of School Administrators, and the National Association of Secondary School Principals — says "NO!" There the educational establishment draws the line: school choice, they say, is trouble with a capital "T."

Chester Finn, former professor of education and public policy at Vander-
bilt, outlined that establishment's four arguments against choice: (1) Choice
is the monster seeking to get its foot in the door: public-school choice is the
wedge that leads to the inclusion of private schools. Nothing strikes horror in
the establishment like the "V" word — vouchers! And the greatest bugaboos
are the church-related schools; (2) Choice will work to the detriment of poor
and minority families because they are "too disorganized to make and execute complex decisions of this kind."[95] In a word, the educational establishment (the NEA and the States) needs to protect the poor from themselves and
their inadequacy; (3) Choice makes running schools a chaotic exercise, for it
leaves too many uncertainties. Better to organize bureaucratically from the
top, and make families and children fit the mold; (4) Choice will be seen as a
panacea for our educational ailments, and nothing else will receive public
attention. This last is the only criticism that Finn thinks "half-reasonable."[96]

Finn, who would like more freedom than the establishment will allow,
points across the border to Canada where educational vouchers have long
been in vogue. Finn believes he is supporting a revolutionary idea, and maybe he is. But eight hundred years after the Magna Carta and over two hundred
years after the Bill of Rights, one doesn't expect freedom in education to be
considered such a revolutionary idea. However, surprising as it may be, for
most families in North America it is revolutionary.

Public education whether in Canada or in the United States, is designed
on the idea of convenience. Convenience dictates that each neighborhood
should have a school offering the same curriculum and embodying essentially the same values. In this model the school, like the convenience store, is
part of a "delivery" system in which education as a packaged commodity is
brought to the consumer. The neighborhood public school is part of a state-
wide delivery system. There is considerable pressure to conform to the delivery system, and the possibility of meaningful parental choice in education is
virtually non-existent. Only high-income families can select the schools of
their choice because only they can afford to pay for education in the independent sector.

The virtual lack of alternatives in public education is made problematic
by the system's hierarchical administrative structure. It is not designed to
accommodate diversity. Public school boards and administrators resist diversity, and they vehemently object to the exercise of freedom by parents.
Searching for improvement and diversity is considered disloyalty to friends
and neighbors.

Many teachers within the system, of course, recognize the "convenience
model," and the pressure to conform, because they live with it every day.
However, if education is to develop the potential that exists in every child, it
must allow the best in the teacher to develop the best in the child. Children
are different, their intellectual capacities vary, the families they come from

vary, and the value systems that those families have instilled in them from their earliest years vary. Simply to "deliver" them all one prescribed curriculum misses the mark of what education is all about.

Opponents to vouchers say that since the community has a large stake in education, the state should run the show. Of course, they have a point. But this gets a bit tricky when you think of who has an interest in education: nonparents with no direct interest in the schools, professional educators who earn their living through the system, and parents with no budgetary power. History shows that professionals and educational hierarchy allow political and social agendas to greatly influence educational decisions. While parents are not disinterested in political and social agendas, they are much more inclined to put in first place the comprehensive education and development of their children, with all the individualization that accompanies a good education. So parents have a point when they object to the "convenience" model and assert their right to a say in that education.

That's why parents recently have been talking a lot about educational vouchers. A voucher represents the family's taxes, and with an educational voucher in hand parents are financially empowered and free to purchase education at a school of their choice.

This educational voucher system would have a number of desirable effects: (1) it would add freedom and choice in public education, (2) it would promote educational diversity, and (3) it would improve standards because it would add the element of competitiveness — teachers and schools would no longer have a captive audience. The public schools would then have the opportunity to earn the loyalty of their clientele, because the clientele would have the power to "vote with their feet." It's a free enterpriser's dream. How, then, can one not support it? Like many other public issues, it comes down to money and power. Who's going to be in the driver's seat? As *The Christian Science Monitor* recently observed: "'empowering the parents with the money' will 'drastically increase' what is already 'a slow movement of influence and power to the parents.'"[97]

Nevertheless, the idea of school choice has been gaining much momentum especially among parents and business leaders. Several states have adopted state-wide public school choice plans, and other states are considering them. A number of cities have already experimented with school choice.

Take Milwaukee's inner city, for example, which began pioneering school choice. Governor Tommy Thompson pushed choice and the state legislature approved the program. Thompson proudly called it a "laboratory of democracy." Messmer High School is an independent school, originally Catholic, but no longer affiliated with the Archdiocese. It is in a predominantly poor, black section of Milwaukee. The Principal is Brother Bob, a young Capuchin.

Not unlike other big city schools, Milwaukee's public schools had long performed so horribly that Governor Thompson put his foot down: business-as-usual had to go. Not unlike other big city schools, Milwaukee had responded by throwing money at problems; and as problems got worse, the city simply threw more money at them. Black students were suffering the most.

When Brother Bob looked into this, he thought he would offer Milwaukee an opportunity it couldn't refuse. Messmer's students were predominantly black, and the public schools were spending over $6,000 per pupil, compared to Messmer's $4,400.[98]

So Messmer's application to the Wisconsin School Choice Program, was initially approved, and Messmer began receiving $2,500 in tuition aid for low-income students. Almost immediately Messmer was flooded with applications from black students. The inclusion of Messmer in the choice program was considered a godsend by poor parents. And it was a bargain for the taxpayers of the state.

That's the good news. Then came the bad. When the educational establishment learned that black students were applying to Messmer to take advantage of the choice, it flew into a tizzy. The establishment was outraged: empowering parents can be a dangerous idea and so the result: Messmer was dropped from Wisconsin's School Choice program. The powers that be were not afraid that choice would fail, but that it would succeed.

Amazing! Nothing is so American as freedom of choice. Yet the educational establishment appears to say: "Poor black families are too ignorant to make wise choices. We will make them for you."

It's a hot political button. The National Education Association is aware that it is a hot button. But they are a mighty political force which neither political party wants to offend. On the other hand, parents are fed up with paying for poor education; and they are furious at being forced to send their kids to schools where they are indoctrinated with values that undermine what parents are teaching them at home.

There are a lot of Messmers doing a better job of education than many public schools, and at half the cost. The last I heard from my Milwaukee friends is that, unfortunately Governor Thompson's "laboratory in democracy" seems still to be mired in politics.

Chester Finn thinks that the Voucher is an idea whose time has come; at the very least, it deserves to be tested. Why is it resisted so? In Finn's view the educational establishment has so dug in its heels because "Choice augurs a rearrangement of power and authority relationships in American education, and the farther-reaching and more comprehensive the choice policy, the more total the reallocation of power." Choice is "the reassertion of 'civilian control' over the system." If implemented it will mean "as large a shift as one can imagine in the hoary ground-rules of the public-education system."[99]

So, "Whose is the right to educate?" is a critical question. I think it is a shared right. And I believe parents are willing to share it. That's not the problem. As many parents see it, the problem is that they have so long been frozen out that now many policymakers no longer concede them any effective right in their children's education. Nevertheless, many parents want to regain what was once theirs, and are calling for vouchers; and many others who have been sitting on the fence, are now, with the increase of violence in the public schools, hopping onto the voucher bandwagon.

ON HOMEWORK AND RESTLESS FEET

I remember how, as a kid, at the beginning of every school year, my feet were restless. It was difficult for me to leave off the long days of play, sports and running out of doors, and all that, and settle down to hours at a schoolroom desk, and the homework in the early evening before going to bed.

There was a time when education was done entirely at home. Later the task was split between home and school; there was schoolwork and homework. Today, unfortunately and for whatever reasons, homework for many children is non-existent. Where it still exists parents often are scarcely involved. As a result, formal education now is almost entirely the work of the schools. For a time, schools didn't mind shouldering the entire burden. But now, most teachers and school boards look back to the good old days when mom and dad were more involved in the education of their children. And all things considered, that system probably turned out a better product.

There are some things the school can't do. Schools can teach. And if they are good schools, they teach well and have a great influence on helping students learn. But educating the student to become an adult is a bigger and more difficult job. Education includes not only reading, writing, and 'rithmetic, but the much more challenging task of character formation and self-discipline. Without that, students fall short of being responsible adults, however old they may grow. Educating, as distinguished from teaching, is the job of the family, peer groups, the church and society at large, as well as the schools. Education embraces total human development of mind, will, personality and character.

Highly acclaimed sociologist Amitai Etzioni did a study on this subject and published his views in a lengthy article entitled, "Self - discipline, Schools and the Business Community." According to Etzioni, the fundamental failure of our K-12 educational systems is "not that millions of high school graduates have great difficulty in reading, writing, and 'rithmetic." These deficiencies are but consequences of a much more fundamental problem. They result from "insufficient self-discipline," and reflect the child's lack of "ability to mobilize self and to commit." If this is true, then the graduates of our educational systems "enter the adult world *twice* handicapped. They suffer both from continued psychic underdevelopment and from the inadequate cognitive preparation this underdevelopment helped to cause."[100] In raw language: if the child can't sit down and study, the child won't learn reading, writing, and 'rithmetic.

Successful school systems, he says, impart more to students than simply knowledge. Successful schools are planned, structured and administered with the view also to developing character and self-discipline, a central and essential ingredient of character, without which, knowledge will make a painful entrance, if at all.

And this brings me back to homework. Etzioni's study built upon a study done earlier in the 1980's by Harvard's Professor James Coleman. Coleman's was one of the first recent studies that compared the public to the private schools in which the public school made a poor showing. On any number of test performances, children in the private schools consistently outperformed children in the public schools. Coleman accounted for this difference by a number of variables such as attendance at class, vandalism of school property, fighting and disobedience, drug and alcohol use, verbal abuse of teachers, etc. In every case, there was a much higher incidence of these disciplinary problems in the public than in the private schools.[101]

Another variable that Coleman studied was homework. According to his data, the private schools assigned much greater importance to homework than did their public counterparts. For his investigation, he divided grade schools into the average and the high-performing schools. His data is from the spring term of 1980. That semester, of all the public schools in the country, only 5.5 percent were requiring 10 hours or more of homework a week, as compared with 11.5 percent of the Catholic schools, and 19.5 percent of other private schools. Among the high-performing schools, only 16 percent of the public schools were requiring 10 hours or more of homework a week, as compared with 51 percent of all private schools.[102]

Building on Coleman's data, Etzioni searched for a deeper underlying cause of good and poor performances by students. According to Etzioni, high-performing students succeed, not simply because doing homework increases their knowledge beyond that of the low-performing student, but because it develops their self-discipline. In his words:

> The role of homework is pivotal. First, not because it provides more hours to pump information into pupils, but because it both encourages and measures the development of self-discipline and associated good working habits. Homework is typically done not under close supervision of teachers or parents, but by pupils, "on their own" to be evaluated later. Hence, when systematically and fairly evaluated, it fosters the crucial internalization of discipline, the foundation of self-discipline.[103]

To accomplish intellectual tasks, energetic bodies and restless youthful personalities have to be controlled and disciplined so the mind can concentrate on the learning task at hand. This is difficult even for adults who supposedly have been at the self-discipline business for years. Again Etzioni:

> Think what it would take you to memorize, say, a telephone number of 26 digits — a considerable amount of effort, but not cognitive effort; instead, concentration, control of impulse, self-motivation, and ability to face and overcome stress (in order to resist distractions and accept the "routine" work involved in memorizing), are required. This element of psychic organization, or capacity to mobilize and commit psychic energy to a task, is what those who are not learning well seem to me to be most lacking.[104]

If there is validity in Etzioni's conclusions, what practical recommendations might parents take from them? Well, a parent might ask the child: "Did your teacher give you any homework today?" If the answer is "no," perhaps the parent might point out to the teacher at the next PTA meeting the value to children of homework, not merely for the child's acquisition of knowledge, but also and more importantly, for the child's self-discipline and character formation.

Moreover, as the school year goes on, and your child comes home and shows you the homework assignment, now graded by the teacher, you might make a big fuss over it, regardless of the grade, because your child mustered up enough self-discipline to sit down and do the homework. Not a small achievement for a youngster.

If teachers, students and parents — all three — did that week after week over the course of a school year, imagine what great changes are taking place in that little will and mind, and what mighty footprints will someday be left by those restless feet.

ON EGALITARIANISM

Egalitarianism, whatever its merits in other areas of life, is a value misplaced in the schools. Egalitarianism, of course, may be dissected many ways. My comments here concern academic standards.

Hard-line egalitarians seem blind to the fact that, apart from being human, people are unequal in virtually every respect. One excels in math, another in art, another in languages; one is physically weak, another strong; one seems brilliant in everything, but lacks sensitivity to others; one is an outgoing, vibrant personality, another lethargic, still another nervous and high strung. After the Declaration of Independence says that "all men are created equal," it goes on to explain. "Equal in what?" In that they are all endowed by their

Creator with certain inalienable rights, which are rooted in the human nature that all share. Beyond that, in the eyes of man and God, we are not all equal. By pretending equality in all things, we mess things up. By assuming that all children are the same, egalitarians in the schools have not only devastated academic standards they have also deceived the students.

Standards in the schools imply requirements, performance, measurements and grades, which involve recognizing inequalities among students. That upsets the egalitarian assumption. It is argued that comparing children damages the psyche of the lesser achievers. So requirements, academic standards and grading have been downplayed. The result is that children who are poorly qualified are nevertheless passed on from grade school to high school, and then, poorly prepared, graduate from high school and enroll in college. Thus, some children find themselves in high school, frustrated and unable to cope. Enter, "remedial education" — which simply means that the high schools do what the primary schools fail to do, and the colleges do what the high schools failed to do. Each level adjusts by lowering standards.

School boards across the country have voted to do away with honor rolls and letter grades in the schools. Everyone needs to be honored, they say, so all students will get the same grades as long as they eventually meet the school district's curriculum objectives. In some places grades are simply eliminated. The paramount consideration is to encourage the students' self-esteem and avoid damaging youthful egos. This is understandable and well-meaning. It's understandable that educators and school boards in a democratic society would choose such a policy. It stems from our exaggerated fascination with egalitarianism.

We recently had an exhibit in the University's art museum. When I left, I said to one of our art professors: "This is beautiful! How I wish I could do that!" I remember when I was studying philosophy — I, an average student, marveling at the philosophical quickness and insight of Bob Johann — he inhaled the stuff like air, while I and others plodded along. But to pretend that we are all intellectually equally gifted, is simply to ignore the obvious. We are all unequal, in every respect, except one: we are all human beings, created "in the image of God,"[105] children of our Creator and Eternal Father.

Egalitarianism is unreal: it's socialist and untruthful, and so in the long-run damages both the individual and society. Average students know that they are average; they recognize the difference between themselves and other both more and less gifted students. They can accept that reality, if others — their parents and teachers first of all — can accept it, as long as they are loved and valued as persons, in the image of God, as much as the other students. The fact that a child is less intelligent than others does not mean that he or she is inferior in all other characteristics. The response to the fact of inequality is not to deny it, but to take the effort to discover each child's endowments and personality, to accentuate them and lead the child to value them and to value himself or herself.

The problem is not with the child, but with the society, which is not accustomed to looking beyond surface values, and is in too great a rush to deal with children in impersonal masses. So we miss-treat individuals as though they were all the same. And with that, everyone loses. We need to take the time and effort to discover the personality, talents and interests of each individual. They all have their own families, interests and talents, friends and aspirations which in time fill out the circles of their lives. It is ironic: egalitarianism, which on the surface appears concerned for the individual, in reality debases him or her, because it doesn't take the time to know the young student.

Some years ago, a University graduate student of mine turned in a term paper for a required course a week before she was to graduate. It was a very shoddy, carelessly done piece of work, which I graded F, and she failed the course, which was required for graduation. Her parents were already driving from the East Coast to St. Louis for the graduation ceremonies, in which she now would not participate. After venting her anger against me, she phoned her parents and headed them off. She was a person of considerable intelligence and charm, and maybe the charm interfered with her intelligence and personality. However, that summer she repeated the course, passed, and graduated. In time, her anger subsided, and one day before leaving the University, she came to my office to thank me for being the first teacher in all her years who made her measure up. False love rests on a falsehood. No good can come of it. One who is never asked to measure up may never know what he or she can really do. It is often the beginning of self-discovery, and sometimes greatness.

I said that egalitarianism is humanly debasing. Being unreal, it ultimately betrays itself. What starts out as a zealous mission by a teacher or parent to elevate ends up debasing the student. Soviet communism purported to be an experiment in egalitarianism on a grand scale. From all accounts we have, it was a colossal and tragic failure. There was no equality, and a high privileged power class ruled the masses by force, terror and lies. In the 70 year experiment in egalitarianism in the Soviet Union the masses were not elevated, but debased.

None has written more poignantly about the suffering of the masses under communism's egalitarian experiment as have the Russian writers. Dostoevsky vividly captures the debasement in *The Possessed*:

> We shall extinguish every genius in his infancy. Everything must be reduced
> to the common denominator, total equality. Each belongs to all, and all to
> each. All are slaves and equal in slavery....we will cut out Cicero's tongue,
> gouge out Copernicus's eyes, stone Shakespeare to death — slaves must be
> equal...[106]

But to return to the schools, and their egalitarian experiments, advocates of giving all kids the same grade are apparently afraid of damaging youthful egos. But I don't think that the truth damages egos or lowers self-esteem. To act as though a student with an I.Q. of 160 is the same as a student with an I.Q. of 115 serves no good purpose for either student.

Students can take the truth about themselves if adults can take it, especially their parents, loved ones, relatives and teachers. Self-esteem and love come from being loved and esteemed. And all egos grow in the sunlight of truth and love.

An educational psychology that says you'll damage students' egos by telling them the truth, is simply bad psychology. It assumes that the student is too dumb and self-centered to accept that the student sitting next to him, who always has the right answers is probably brighter than most in the class. It assumes that students can't understand that though they may not be the brightest, they are still able and loved, prized and cherished simply because they are who they are.

It's bad psychology because it fails to understand where self-esteem and ego strength really come from. Self-esteem doesn't come from brains. Some very bright people have low self-esteem. Not telling students the truth about their scholastic abilities is bad psychology because it tells students that they are not valued for who and what they are. People you can depend on, who care and love you, and whom you can love and trust — that's what makes self-esteem and strong egos.

Students are damaged by falsehood and by a lack of love, a lack of trust and support, attention, caring and encouragement by the right people. Students can accept the truth about themselves if their parents, friends, loved ones and teachers can accept who they are, regardless of their standing in the class. But if they are deceived about this central human concern, sooner or later they will learn that they were deceived, and then they will struggle with trust. "Why did they deceive me? Were they ashamed of me?" Sooner or later as adults they will stand alongside their peers and learn that in the real world not everyone gets the same grade. And then they will know that their teachers did not tell them the truth, and will be prone to distrust both themselves and other people.

If helping the young to develop self-esteem were just a matter of grades, it would be easy. Being more a matter or truth, trust and love, it's not easy at all. But the rewards are great — the rewards are priceless.

IT'S A SOCIALIST SYSTEM

Syndicated columnist Warren Brookes recently had some bold words to say about the need for openness and choice in public education: It's a matter of national survival; for all our talking about it to date, we've "only tinkered at the margins"[107] of educational reform. Yet, in Brookes' view, our very economic survival depends on radical reform of public education that allows for choice.

Economic success or survival is linked to education because we live in an information and knowledge age. Some say that the reason we are falling behind in productivity and in the economic competition is because we are falling behind in education. To the question, "Is the test score decline responsible for the productivity growth decline?" Cornell University economist John H. Bishop responds: "Yes, the primary reason for declining productivity in the United States is the rapid decline in the trend of the 'knowledge factor.'" As a result of declining test scores, "the labor quality shortfall was 1.3 percent in 1980, and 2.9 percent in 1987...is projected to be 6.7 percent in 2010."[108]

In a knowledge society, if you lose in education, you lose the game. "In the 1970's less than 25 percent of the new jobs created were in what are classified as managerial or professional occupations...by the mid-1980's, contrary to the spurious misinformation of organized labor, over half the new jobs are in these higher paying and more demanding skills."[109]

What buried the Socialist world's economy threatens to bury our education. That's Brookes' concern; American public education is "a kind of collectivist millstone around the neck of our nation which is now in the battle of its life for survival." Cast off the millstone, says Brookes; unless we free up our educational system, unshackling it from bureaucracy and political infighting, we're going to fall far behind. "Spirituality and freedom," says Brookes, "will always triumph over materialism and totalitarian tyranny."[110]

Serious educational reform will put education into the marketplace. "Socialist systems fail not only because they fail to energize the most productive asset of all, the individual human mind, but because as entrenched monopolies they are so totally unaccountable to the individual consumer — because they provide no market in which competing ideas and products can be tested, priced, approved or rejected, modified or abandoned."[111] Socialist systems fail primarily because they have no marketplace in which failure or success can be judged or priced. Similarly, public schools have no marketplace where failure or success is judged and priced.

So with all the voice he can muster, Brookes trumpets for parental choice in education, for privatization of the public schools, and for vouchers. And he points to a cadre of heavyweights who play in the same band: Milton Friedman, who said when asked why American students graduated from high school with a surprisingly socialist perspective: "Because they're products of a socialist system — mainly public education. How can you expect such a system to inculcate the values of free enterprise and individual entrepreneurship and competition when it is based on monopoly, state-ownership, abhors competition, and strives only through compulsion and taxation?" Bill Bennett, when after advocating a system of vouchers, was asked: "What if this kind of voucherized, private market approach kills off some schools?" replied: "So, give them a funeral. No one gives a funeral to the kids who are now dropping out of those bad schools, and maybe out of life itself." David Kearns, Chairman of Xerox concurred: "The new agenda for school reform must be driven by competition and market discipline...the objective should be clear from the outset: complete restructuring. The public schools must change if we are to survive."[112]

Brookes concludes: "Serious education reform...is essential to our economic future survival. We cannot expect to compete in a world which is decentralizing power and freeing up economic wealth, with an education system that is still choking on its past centralization, and chained to a stagnating bureaucracy."[113]

David Boaz of the CATO Institute agrees that trying to reform the present system is all in vain. The present system is a socialist system. It doesn't work, because it ignores the consumer. "Private schools," wrote Boaz, "do a much better job at educating students, but most parents find it difficult to pay once for the public school system and then pay again for private school. If they didn't have to pay school taxes, they could afford to purchase education in the marketplace."[114]

Most incongruous of all, say some critics, is leaving the reform in the hands of the educators. "Not only are test scores declining, but businesspeople complain that graduates of American high schools are not prepared for work. American students tell survey researchers that their reading, writing, and math skills are good, but employers have a different view."[115]

These critics are not opposed to certification of teachers or teacher testing. But they don't think that teacher testing and more stringent standards of certification will solve the problems of the public schools. There is a more fundamental problem: the students are a captive audience; and their parents have no choice. To summarize the critics: a system that is unaccountable to the consumer is fundamentally flawed. It's a socialist system. Real reform, say critics, will come only when all parents are able to choose where they will send their children to school.

That would require a major about-face in American public education. And the feet of the educational establishment, pointed in the opposite direction, are frozen in concrete.

This reminded me of Robert Novak's search a few years ago for a good restaurant in Moscow. Along with other members of the press corps, he was interested in seeing the extent to which the free market had affected the service and quality of food in Moscow's restaurants. His first test came at lunch at the hotel where he was staying. The menu was copious with English translations provided. When he asked the unsmiling, run-down-at-the-heels waitress for smoked fish, she responded, "Not have." When Novak asked: "What do you have?" He learned that they actually served about one-fifth of what was listed on the menu. What is "chicken tabaka?" Novak asked. "Fried chicken, very good."[116]

Well, he ordered broiled fish, but a half-hour later, the waitress, nevertheless, brought out "chicken tabaka." It was preceded with a huge bowl of what passed for chicken soup. In the bowl was a dark, bony thing that one day might have been a piece of chicken. It provided no flavor to the watery soup, as but one spoonful demonstrated. By the time the "chicken tabaka" was served, Novak had conjured up images of Colonel Sanders. What he actually received, the Colonel could never have imagined. It might have been fried; but it was scrawny, no crust, greasy and with a foul odor. Novak felt he had met his match. The taste matched the order; and Novak settled with sliced onion on the side, bread and mineral water.

Nevertheless, he survived the afternoon. That evening Steve Hurst, an old Moscow hand with CNN, invited Novak to accompany him to one of the new *perestroika*-spawned "Georgian" restaurants.

By contrast with what he had at lunch, the dinner restaurant and service was immaculate, the maitre d' and waiters alert and attentive. But the real contrast was the food. It was varied, plentiful, and delicious — seafood, pickled meats, fresh vegetables, veal, foul, good wine, etc. It was a feast made all the more pleasant by a violinist and pianist. It was dining that could compete with 3-star restaurants in London, Paris and New York.

Novak's reflections on his dining that day: the contrast between these two restaurants is not just the difference between a good and bad restaurant. They are different in kind. The luncheon restaurant grew out of and still operated on the socialist system — we'll pretend to work and you pretend to pay us. The dinner restaurant had moved away from that system and, as a fledgling enterprise in the private sector, had dipped its toes into the market economy.

Novak concluded that unquestionably *perestroika* had improved Moscow's restaurants. Maybe a little *perestroika* would improve our education.

HURRAH FOR ADELE JONES!

In some schools, egalitarianism has run wild, an example of which was reported in the press some time ago. The incident occurred in Sussex Central High School in Georgetown, Delaware. There the Board of Education sent a bad message to the students and teachers in Delaware and to the Schools of Education that teach the teachers. The Board fired Adele Jones, 33, because she was too demanding and flunked too many high school kids.

The school principal explained to the School Board, which upheld the firing, that D's and F's are "negative grades," and added: "My goal is to use positive reinforcement to improve the self-esteem of kids."[117] This was no surprise to Rita Kramer, longtime critic of United States schools. Having recently studied teachers' colleges where the philosophy of American education is set and future teachers indoctrinated, Kramer commented: "Over the last 20 years professors of education have preached to their students, who go out to become our children's teachers, that teaching kids the basic skills of language and numbers should take a back seat. Teachers now are indoctrinated with the idea that the schools exist to promote self-esteem and make kids feel good about themselves."[118]

But Adele Jones had a different idea, one that was bound to collide with the principal and the Board: "The message I kept getting from my supervisors was: 'Keep the kids happy, even if you have to lower your standards.' But it doesn't do any good if we keep passing students on, then they get a rude awakening when they get to college and find they can't do the work." Summing up her attitude she said quite simply: "I believe in hard work and don't accept excuses."[119]

And she does one other important thing: she holds herself to the same standard, giving her kids all the tutoring and assistance they ask for. And the kids know it, and are her strongest supporters. Said Kevin Brittingham, 18: "After I failed algebra, Miss Jones got in touch with me. She said I'd no reason to fail because I was the brightest kid in class. So I took the course over, did the work this time, and got a B-plus. If she hadn't spoken to me like that, who knows if I'd gone on to college?"[120]

There's no question that the teachers in the schools have a tough job. It's tough enough to teach kids Algebra 2, as Jones was doing. It's doubly tough to teach Algebra 2 to kids who have a low self-esteem. And it's all but impossible to teach kids where the peer pressure is against the very idea of an education. As the news reported recently, bright black kids in inner-city schools have to fight off their own black peers who aren't as bright. How dare an uppity black talk about Shakespeare, much less use four syllable words. "That's white talk, man! Stop that white talk! You black!"

A tough job, yes. But the answer is not to give up teaching black kids Shakespeare and four syllable words. Knowledge and learning are spiritual realities that cross all barriers — national, ethnic, religious, sexual, and color. Aside from God's grace, the human mind is each person's greatest asset. Not to try to cultivate it is an awful waste.

And self-esteem? I never saw a case of low self-esteem cured by concealing the truth. Hard work doesn't hurt self-esteem; and expectations are necessary for building self-esteem. As one of Adele Jones' students said, self-esteem is built by challenging, not coddling, young people. This was from a 17 year old: "I'm proud of my 92 average! Why? Because I actually earned it. Probably this is the first time I had to earn a grade."[121]

Kids see through the sham of a teacher who gives passing grades for failed work, and they don't admire that teacher. The first to protest the firing of Adele Jones were the students she had failed. Virtually the entire student body protested, carrying signs protesting the firing. One read: "I failed Ms. Jones' class and it was my fault," and another: "Just because a student is failing doesn't mean the teacher is."[122]

If the expectations are reasonable, come from love and a sincere wish to help, and if extra assistance is offered when needed, students measure up to those expectations. The classroom is not the place for "I'm okay, you're okay" pop psychology. It is the place of expectations, without which both teacher and student wander around without direction, in a fog of normlessness. "Anything you do is okay," is absolute relativism applied to the profession of education. It is a formula that fails our kids, fails ourselves, and fails society.

Education has always thrived on Adele Jones' old-fashioned formula: "I believe in hard work, and don't accept excuses." It's the old fashion way, and it works.

"ON CARING AND THE PROFESSOR'S JOB"

In a world where bureaucracy and bureaucratic mechanisms are rapidly replacing personal encounters, universities must remind themselves that students are persons straining toward adulthood, and that successful growth takes place only in personalized and stimulating environments. Therefore, universities should be places that genuinely care about the students who people their campuses.

Unfortunately, a number of social changes since World War II and the Vietnam era are obstructions to a personalized and caring campus. In addition to the sheer size of campuses and numbers of students, two social processes adversely influence relations between students, on the one hand, and university administrators and faculty, on the other.

The first is the dying notion of "in loco parentis." It once was that universities were assumed to function with quasi parental authority and responsibility. No more. With the breakdown of the family and familial authority, the state has entered into many areas of private life, asserting itself between parents and children, and between children and other intermediate institutions. While civil rights legislation and court decisions have protected many children who suffer because of inadequate parenting and harmful family relations, they have in many cases messed up relations between children and institutions such as colleges and universities.

Legislation dealing with the right of privacy, for example, sometimes prohibits universities from sending students' records and reports to parents without the prior consent of the student, even though parents are paying the bills. Parents complain, but sometimes the university's hands are tied by the law. Students sometimes claim the right of privacy against university administrators who enter their rooms to search for alcohol and drugs, against the consent of the student. Cohabiting students challenge the right of universities to interfere with their right of privacy. In these ways, legislation erodes the authority of both the university and the family.

With their hands thus tied, some universities gladly wash their hands of "in loco parentis" responsibility. "Okay," they say to students and parents, "you're on your own. What you do is not our responsibility. The quasi parental responsibility that we once accepted, we no longer accept. It is yours, to sink or swim." Legalism breeds depersonalism, which in turn can breed an uncaring campus.

The second process that has rained disaster on not a few schools and colleges is egalitarianism, which when coupled with cultural relativism has potential to level everything. I have written about the problems that arise from egalitarianism. In a recent discussion on standards and measures of success at Gonzaga, one of our deans spoke about caring for our students: "Any university that accepts only top students," he said, "can easily graduate top students. Our challenge and the measure of our success should be how much we help them to grow, intellectually and personally; not what others have done with them, before we get them, but what we do with them while they are here."

This took our discussion into the cheapness and damages caused in education by cultural relativism. If all are equal, then one view is as important as another, one area of knowledge as significant as another, one piece of literature as valuable as another. If there is no hierarchy of knowledge or values, there is no point in being concerned about academic planning and curricular development. If every viewpoint is true, there is no falsehood. If every action is good, there is no evil. This is intellectual and moral nihilism.

This is the dart that Alan Bloom fired at American higher education. We have become so accepting, permissive and open as to have our minds totally closed to reason: "Openness used to be the virtue that permitted us to seek the good by using reason. It now means accepting everything and denying reason's power [...] Cultural relativism destroys both one's own and the good [...] To deny the possibility of knowing good and bad is to suppress true openness."[123]

You can't run a good university on the basis of cultural relativism, University people must care intensely about the truth, and about right and wrong. If there is no difference between truth and falsehood, good and bad, then university presidents, trustees, administrators and faculty will idly slide along, just holding a job without purpose, marking time. To care about truth is to care about priorities and curricula and course content. To care about quality is to care about faculty, who they are, what they know and do, and what they teach. To care about students is to have standards that are high but attainable. To care about students is to see that they get things straight and they really understand what they're learning, and not just parrot back what the professor says. To care about students is to experience a joyful excitement when students piece things together, find meaning and put purpose in their lives.

At commencement some years ago I summed up three things that I hoped the graduates would take away from Gonzaga as permanent baggage:

First, human intelligence is a precious gift, and its development a matter of high importance. Short of divine grace, it is the only thing we have to work with. So the cultivation of the mind is a very high priority. Our students' personal futures and the future of society and the world depend on the use of right reason and sound judgment. Not just any kind of sloppy thinking will do. If the Jesuits over their 450-year history have had an enduring commitment to education, at great cost and expenditure of vast resources, it is because civilization and culture depend on intelligence, good judgment, wisdom, clear sightedness.

Second, a comprehensive knowledge of life and its parts includes knowledge of the human spirit and its longing for God. Faith, too, is a source of knowledge and understanding. Therefore, a complete education integrates the world of human endeavors, science and arts with faith and the things of eternity. Mind and spirit were never meant to be separated because human life in its fullest is one. Divine grace and God are not opposed to human wisdom, but rather are its aspiration and fulfillment.

Third, the unselfish life is the happy life. A selfish life is small and circumscribed, and the more selfish it is, the more it shrivels and withers away. The unselfish life is a life that loses itself in others and in a grander vision. We need the courage to entrust ourselves to something bigger than ourselves; when we do, we become our very best. God has not given us such marvelous talents and opportunities just for ourselves alone, but for others, especially for the less gifted and less advantaged. It is only in giving that we receive; only when we lose our lives that we find them.

Universities that value truth and assign a high priority to intelligence will take great care that students learn to distinguish truth from falsehood, the real coin from the fake. Universities that value faith and humanity's spiritual nature will take great care that students weave together concern about the things of this world with concern for eternity. Universities that value the unselfish life will take great care that students look beyond themselves and the narrow confines of their own lives, to search for something far higher to which they may dedicate themselves, and in which they find themselves.

I say without exaggeration or misrepresentation, that these things we must aim to achieve straining all our powers to accomplish. It is a trust, the magnitude of which we must accept gladly, even cherish, for the prize is of incomprehensible worth.

NOTES

1. Ernest L. Boyer and Arthur Levine, *Common Learning: A Carnegie Colloquium on General Education* (Washington, DC: Carnegie Foundation for the Advancement of Teaching, 1981), 18-9.

2. *Thomas v. Collins*, No. 14 *Thomas v. Collins*, 323, 516 (SUPREME COURT OF THE UNITED STATES).

3. Jeffrey Kane, *In Fear of Freedom: Public Education and Democracy in America* (New York, NY: Myrin Institute, 1984), 47.

4. John L. b. 1889 Childs, *Education and Morals; an Experimentalist Philosophy of Education* (New York: Arno Press, 1971), 16.

5. Philip Henry Phenix, *Education and the Common Good; a Moral Philosophy of the Curriculum*, 1st ed. ed. (New York: Harper, 1961), 18.

6. William J. Bennett, "Quantifying America's Decline," *Wall Street Journal* Mar 15, 1993,   http://proxy.foley.gonzaga.edu:2048/login?url=http://proquest.umi.com/pqdweb?did=4321929&Fmt=7&clientId=10553&RQT=309&VName=PQD.

7. Pope John Paul II and Vittorio Messori, *Crossing the Threshold of Hope* (New York: Knopf, 1995), 118.

8. Saint Augustine Bishop of Hippo and others, *The Confessions* (Chicago: Encyclopaedia Britannica, 1955), 698.

9. Lynn Martin, Deloitte,Lynn Martin , who was Secretary of Labor in the Bush Administration, advises the accounting firm and Touche on women's issues., "For Children Who have Children," *The New York Times* September 8, 1993.

10. Ibid.

11. Cal Thomas, *Things that Matter most* (New York: Harperperennial, 1995), 179.

12. Bennett, *Quantifying America's Decline*, A12.

13. Thomas, *Things that Matter most.*

14. Bennett, *Quantifying America's Decline*, A12.

15. Horace Mann and Edward A. Newton, *The Common School Controversy: Consisting of Three Letters of the Secretary of the Board of Education of the State of Massachusetts, in Reply to Charges Preferred Against the Board by the Editor of the Christian Witness and by Edward A. Newton, Esq., of Pittsfield, Once a Member of the Board ; to which are Added Extracts from the Daily Press, in Regard to the Controversy* (Boston: J.N. Bradley, 1844).

16. *Pierce v. Soc'y of Sisters*, Nos. 583, 584 *Pierce v. Soc'y of Sisters*, 268, 510 (SUPREME COURT OF THE UNITED STATES).

17. Anthony S. Bryk, *Catholic Schools and the Common Good* (Cambridge: Harvard University Press, 1995).

18. Ibid., 297.

19. Ibid., 11.

20. Ibid., 119.

21. Ibid., 119.

22. Ibid., 22.

23. Ibid., 133.

24. Ibid., 135.

25. Ibid., 297.

26. Ibid., 298-9.

27. Ibid., 299.

28. Ibid., 303-4.

29. Ibid., 301.

30. Richard A. Baer and Richard John Neuhaus, *Democracy and the Renewal of Public Education: Essays* (Grand Rapids, Mich: W.B. Eerdmans Pub. Co, 1987), 169.

31. Ibid., 63.

32. Vincent P. Lannie, *Public Money and Parochial Education; Bishop Hughes, Governor Seward, and the New York School Controversy* (Cleveland: Press of Case Western Reserve University, 1968), 83.

33. Ibid., 83.

34. Baer and Neuhaus, *Democracy and the Renewal of Public Education: Essays*, 70.

35. Ibid., 72.

36. Ibid., 71.

37. Ibid., 81.

38. William Henry Beveridge Baron, *Voluntary Action; a Report on Methods of Social Advance* (New York: Macmillan Co. 1948, 320.

39. Aristotle and C. D. C. Reeve, *Politics* (Indianapolis, Ind: Hackett Pub, 1998), 141.

40. *Thomas v. Collins*, 516.

41. Mary Caroline Richards, *Toward Wholeness: Rudolf Steiner Education in America*, 1st ed. (Middletown, Conn; Irvington, NY: Wesleyan University Press; distributed by Columbia University Press, 1980), 31.

42. Michelle Rhee, "What I've Learned. (Cover Story)," *Newsweek* 156, no. 24 (12/13, 2010), 36-41, http://search.ebscohost.com/login.aspx?direct=true&db=a9h&AN=55695685& site=ehost-live (accessed 1/13/2011).

43. Ibid.

44. Christine Armario and Dorie Turner, "Nearly 1 in 4 Fails Army Entrance Test," *Journal - Gazette* Dec 22, 2010, http://proxy.foley.gonzaga.edu:2048/login?url=http://pro-quest.umi.com/pqdweb?did=2219989841&Fmt=7&clientId=10553&RQT=309& VName=PQD.

45. Ibid.

46. Virginia Seuffert, "Home Remedy," *Policy Review*, no. 52 (Spring90, 1990), 72, http://search.ebscohost.com/login.aspx?direct=true&db=a9h&AN=9608140357&site=ehost-live (accessed 9/30/2010).

47. Ibid., 73.

48. Ibid., 73.

49. Ibid., 74.

50. Ibid., 74.

51. Ibid., 75.

52. Ibid., 75.

53. Samuel L. Blumenfeld, *Is Public Education Necessary?* (Old Greenwich, Conn: Devin-Adair Co, 1981), 9.

54. Michel Foucault, *The Order of Things: An Archaeology of the Human Sciences* (London; New York: Routledge, 2002), 373.

55. James V. Schall S.J., "Intelligence and Academia," *International Journal of Social Economics* 15, no. 10 (1988), 71.

56. Frederic Jameson, "Marxism and Teaching," *New Political Science* 1, no. 2/3 (1979/1980), 33.

57. Alvin Ward Gouldner, *The Future of Intellectuals and the Rise of the New Class: A Frame of Reference, Theses, Conjectures, Arguments, and an Historical Perspective on the Role of Intellectuals and Intelligentsia in the International Class Contest of the Modern Era* (New York: Oxford University Press, 1982), 28.

58. Ibid., 45.

59. Ibid., 59.

60. Lee Congdon, "Culture War," *Virginia Viewpoint* 2005-5 (September 2005, 2005), http://www.virginiainstitute.org/viewpoint/2005_09_5.html (accessed 14 January 2011).

61. Sergei Gennadievich Nechaev, Mikhail Aleksandrovich Bakunin and Black Panther Party, *The Revolutionary Catechism* (United States: Black Panther Party, 1970-1979).

62. Scott Heller, "'Radical Critique' Says Reform of Higher Education is Timid and Narrow," *The Chronicle of Higher Educationi* 34, no. 11 (11 Nov 1987, 1987), A13.

63. Ibid., A21.

64. *United States v. Macintosh*, No. 504 *United States v. Macintosh*, 283, 605 (SUPREME COURT OF THE UNITED STATES).

65. Jones, *The Jerusalem Bible*, Matt. 6:6.

66. Ibid., Matt. 18:20.

67. *Humanist Manifesto II.*

68. Paul C. Vitz and New York Univ, NY Dept. of Psychology, *Religion and Traditional Values in Public School Textbooks: An Empirical Study*,[1985]), http://search.ebscohost.com/login.aspx?direct=true&db=eric&AN=ED260019&site=ehost-live (accessed 1/14/2011).

69. W. H. Sir Moberly b.1881, *The Crisis in the University* (London: SCM Press, 1949), 56.

70. Jones, *The Jerusalem Bible*, Matt. 22:21.

71. David P. Gardner, National Commission on Excellence,in Education and And Others, *A Nation at Risk: The Imperative for Educational Reform. an Open Letter to the American People. A Report to the Nation and the Secretary of Education*,[1983]), http://search.ebscohost.com/login.aspx?direct=true&db=eric&AN=ED226006&site=ehost-live (accessed 1/14/2011).

72. William J. Bennett and of Education Department, *American Education: Making it Work. A Report to the President and the American People*, 1988), 65, http://search.ebscohost.com/login.aspx?direct=true&db=eric&AN=ED289959&site=ehost-live (accessed 1/14/2011).

73. Francisco, MELINDA BECK with TESSA NAMUTH in New York, MARK MILLER in Washington, LYNDA WRIGHT in San and Bureau Reports, "'A Nation Still at Risk'," *Newsweek*, May 2, 1988, 55.

74. Ibid., 55.

75. Bennett and Department, *American Education: Making it Work. A Report to the President and the American People.*

76. Ibid., 55.

77. John Chubb, "Why the Current Wave of School Reform Will Fail," *Public Interest*, no. 90 (Winter, 1988), 28, http://proxy.foley.gonzaga.edu:2048/login?url=http://proquest.umi.com/pqdweb?did=1439702&Fmt=7&clientId=10553&RQT=309&VName=PQD.

78. Ibid., 29.

79. Ibid., 33.

80. Ibid., 34.

81. Ibid., 36.

82. Ibid., 29.

83. Ibid., 48.

84. Ibid., 48.

85. Ibid., 49.

86. Kane, *In Fear of Freedom: Public Education and Democracy in America*, 38.

87. Boyer and Levine, *Common Learning: A Carnegie Colloquium on General Education*, 18.

88. Kane, *In Fear of Freedom: Public Education and Democracy in America*, 38.

89. Phenix, *Education and the Common Good; a Moral Philosophy of the Curriculum*, 18.

90. Kane, *In Fear of Freedom: Public Education and Democracy in America*, 39.

91. By Ellen Graham, "Children — Coping with Change: 'Values' Lessons Return to the Classroom — Educators Say Kids Today are 'Rudderless'," *Wall Street Journal* Sep 26, 1988, http://proxy.foley.gonzaga.edu:2048/login?url=http://proquest.umi.com/pqdweb?did=27392891&Fmt=7&clientId=10553&RQT=309&VName=PQD.

92. Ibid.

93. Ibid.

94. Ibid.

95. Chester E. Finn Jr., "The Choice Backlash," *National Review* 41, no. 21 (11/10, 1989), 31, http://search.ebscohost.com/login.aspx?direct=true&db=a9h&AN=8911130305&site=ehost-live (accessed 1/14/2011).

96. Ibid., 31.

97. Rushworth M. Kidder, "Tuition Vouchers: Should Parents Set School Policy?" *Christian Science Monitor (Boston, MA)* April 8, 1985.

98. Source Unknown.

99. Finn Jr., *The Choice Backlash*, 32.

100. Amitai Etzioni and Chamber of Commerce of the United States, Washington, DC National Chamber Foundation, *Self-Discipline, Schools, and the Business Community*,[1984]), http://search.ebscohost.com/login.aspx?direct=true&db=eric&AN=ED249335&site=ehost-live (accessed 1/15/2011).

101. James Samuel Coleman and Public and private schools, *Coleman Report on Public and Private Schools: The Draft Summary and Eight Critiques* (Arlington, VA: Educational Research Service, 1981).

102. Ibid., 30.

103. Etzioni and Chamber of Commerce of the United States, Washington, DC National,Chamber Foundation, *Self-Discipline, Schools, and the Business Community*, 7.

104. Ibid.

105. Jones, *The Jerusalem Bible,* Gen. 1:27.

106. Edward Wasiolek, *Dostoevsky: The Major Fiction* (Cambridge: Mass, M.I.T. Press, 1964), 41.

107. Warren T. Brookes, "Public Education and the Global Failure of Socialism," *Imprimis* 19, no. 4 (April 1990, 1990), http://www.hillsdale.edu/news/imprimis/archive/issue.asp?year=1990&month=04 (accessed 15 Jan 2011).

108. John Bishop and State Univ of New York, Ithaca School of Industrial and Labor Relations at Cornell Univ, *Is the Test Score Decline Responsible for the Productivity Growth Decline? Working Paper no. 87-05*,[1987]), http://search.ebscohost.com/login.aspx?direct=true&db=eric&AN=ED299282&site=ehost-live (accessed 1/15/2011).

109. Ibid.

110. Brookes, *Public Education and the Global Failure of Socialism*.

111. Ibid.

112. Ibid.

113. Ibid.

114. David Boaz, "Libertarianism," *The Free Press* (1997), 244-5.

115. Ibid., 244.

116. Source Unknown.

117. Ron Grossman, "Firing of Teacher for Flunking Students Offers a Lesson to American Teachers," *Chicago Tribune* 2 Aug 1993, 1993.

118. Ibid.
119. Ibid.
120. Ibid.
121. Ibid.
122. Ibid.
123. Bloom, *The Closing of the American Mind*, 38, 40.

Chapter Five

Faith

THE TWO STANDARDS

Everything Jesuit, sooner or later, takes one back to St. Ignatius Loyola, the founder of the Order, and to his little book, *The Spiritual Exercises.*[1] The book has been called a manual, suggesting a military handbook, in turn suggesting the spiritual struggle which living the Christian life demands, and which St. Paul said is a struggle "not against human enemies but against the Sovereignties and Powers who originate the darkness in this world, the spiritual army of evil in the heavens."[2]

That manual is still in use. Commentaries by the thousands have been written on it, and still are being written. Yet, popular as it has been, most people today would probably judge it downright Neanderthal. That's because the two leading characters in *The Spiritual Exercises* have today, unlike the era when Ignatius wrote, been rather written off as mythical. Nevertheless, those characters and their influence live on, and the major theme of Ignatius' book recurs in today's media and popular publications, and in scholarly journals as well.

One of the key meditations in *The Spiritual Exercises* is on Two Standards: one of Christ, "our supreme Leader and Lord"; the other of Lucifer, "the deadly enemy of our human nature."[3] The purpose of the meditation is to realize more fully what it means to follow Christ, and to understand Satan's strategies that lure us away from that following. The success of the meditation depends on our grasping the reality of Satan's existence, his intentions and power, and Christ's call to follow Him.

The term "standard" is reminiscent of Ignatius' military days when companies marched, as they do today, under descriptive banners. The "standards" of the meditation are two sets of spiritual values. Ignatius, presuming that we realize the spiritual conflict we are engaged in, asks us to meditate on its opposing leaders and their "standards."

Being the "mortal enemy of our human nature," as Ignatius describes him, Satan's ultimate goal is that we deny God, or at least reject him and his authority over us. Wise and crafty, says Ignatius, Satan does not go about his work crassly; he proceeds by stages, luring us at first, not to deny or reject God, but to exaggerate our own importance. Generally Satan tempts us: first, to covet riches, possessions and the alluring things of the world; secondly, to seek honors and recognition, position, power and prestige, and to indulge in excessive self-esteem; and thirdly, vain from an exaggerated notion and love of ourselves, "to overweening pride." From pride, says Ignatius, humans are easily led "to all other vices."[4]

Pride, like its antithesis humility, is not easily understood. It seems to be the most intellectual of sins. Webster defines it as: "an overhigh opinion of oneself; exaggerated self-esteem; conceit."[5] Satan, whom Christ said he saw "fall like lightning into hell,"[6] must know something about pride. Theologians and spiritual writers have long agreed that, being angelic spirits, the fallen angels succumbed to a sin of pure mind and will, no allurements of flesh or material honors being involved, an act in which, from whatever reasoning, they placed themselves above other spiritual beings who were actually superior to them, perhaps even above God himself. In its basest form, pride replaces God by one's self, saying in effect, "I am so important, eminent, and deserving that I will have whatever I want; no one must stand in my way." Pride is a stupid inflation of human nature, and a foolish trivialization of God.

Someone recently asked me: "Do you believe in angels?" The question comes even from Christians, who for thousands of years believed in a spiritual world but whose Christianity in recent ages has been layered over by rationalism and materialism. Few people today take angels, including Satan, seriously, in spite of the horrifying evils and hatred that afflict all of us. And, though it's impossible to know what people really think, I would wager that where Satan is not taken seriously, neither is God; and if that is so, it must please "the mortal enemy of our human nature," assuming that Satan, enigma that he is, can be pleased by anything. Not taken seriously, he has at least achieved a partial victory, on the way to the ultimate victory, the denial of God, or His trivialization. Nietzsche must have thought that Satan had achieved at least a temporary victory. "God is dead," epitomizes the rationalism of the late 19th century: God, if there is a God, is uninfluential, uninterested in, and unnecessary for human nature, for we humans are sufficient unto ourselves. Nietzsche put the exclamation mark on the rationalist movement, and that mark has not been erased. This is pride's apogee.

Stephen L. Carter is an Episcopalian professor of law at Yale University. His book, *The Culture of Disbelief*, gives no indication that its author is familiar with St. Ignatius or his meditation on Two Standards. But if ultimate pride is the substitution of human beings for God, Carter sees a lot of pride in our culture today. "American law and politics" he says, "trivialize religious devotion." So an American who wishes to get ahead and be taken seriously, if he believes in God, had better play down his faith or, better, "keep it a secret." Otherwise he will surely "risk assignment to the lunatic fringe."[7] The predominant culture led by its intellectuals, regards belief in God and religious devotion as simply superstition. The message from the culture is: Believe in humans, not angelic spirits, good or bad; trust in yourselves, not God; and if you want to be important and looked up to, and at the same time must have religion, "kept it in its proper place; and still more, in proper perspective. There are, we are taught by our opinion leaders, religious matters and important matters, and disaster arises when we confuse the two."[8]

In a Colorado public school recently a teacher was called on the carpet for keeping a personal Bible in his desk, which he would occasionally read while students were engaged in other activities. He was told that the Bible had to go. "He was also told to take away books on Christianity he had added to the classroom library, although books on Native American religious traditions, as well as on the occult, were allowed to remain." The teacher appealed the case that eventually went to a federal court. The court upheld the school system: "the teacher could not be allowed to create a religious atmosphere in the classroom, which, it seems, might happen if the students knew he was a Christian."[9]

Educators recognize the importance of role models in the education of young people. In this case the court seems to say that the teachings and the role models from occult and some religious traditions are OK, but not Christianity. Why? I don't know. Perhaps it's that Christianity insists on being taken seriously. It's not a pastime.

Speaking of pastimes, Carter titles one chapter, "God as a Hobby." Some people collect stamps, others coins, others like to garden — then, some take to religion. Carter is ironic: "…it is perfectly all right to believe that stuff — we have freedom of conscience, folks can believe what they like — but you really ought to keep it to yourself…"[10] No question about it, Ignatius is sure to say, that's Satan's standard.

Ah, you will say, but look how presidents and politicians recognize God in their speeches, calling on Him to bless us and bless America. And who are more public than presidents and politicians? Columnist William Safire had an answer for that. Don't be fooled, he said, by the public utterances of office seekers, who use God for their own purpose:

> Analysts of American culture have long recognized the civil religion concept. The platitudes of America's civil religion are expected and accepted — but they are only platitudes. It may be that we are comfortable with them precisely because they demand nothing of us.... they make virtually no demands on our consciences.... God is thanked for the success of an enterprise recently completed or asked to sanctify one not yet fully begun. God is asked to bless the nation, its people, and its leaders. But nobody, in the civil religion, is asked to do anything for God. [11]

Do something for God? One must first take God seriously. That brings us to the other standard, which basically is Christ's life and the primary virtues that inspired Him. In Ignatius' meditation the spiritual values of Christ's standard are directly contrary to those of Satan. First, poverty of spirit: detachment from riches and possessions, and all things created; this leads to indifference to honors, prestige and esteem among people so that one's heart may be free to follow Christ and serve God; and these virtues lead to humility.

Humility is as difficult to understand as pride. It is pride's opposite. Fundamentally, it seems to be truthfulness about one's self and one's relationship to others and to God. We are free beings, yet utterly dependent on God because created; we are the peak and wonder of the material world, made in God's image, a little below the angels, but fallen from grace; we are sinful, but redeemed and forgiven; finite, but destined for all eternity to live with God. These are thoughts that inspire us to hold our heads high, but allow no place for pride; thoughts that lead us to believe how blessed we are because we are so loved by God, but likewise lead us to ask, as St. Paul did: "What is it, O man, that you have that you have not received? Why then, if you have received, do you behave as though you had not received?" [12] Thoughts that also make reasonably generous persons ask of themselves: "What can I do for God?"

Every spring our nation sets aside a day for a national prayer breakfast. Large numbers in cities and towns all across the land turn out to hear public speakers who entertain with funny one-liners, then exhort the crowds to thank God for our nation and His blessings, and to ask His continued beneficence. We feel good about ourselves, and then go to work.

A few years ago Mother Teresa spoke at the prayer breakfast in the nation's Capitol. She had no one-liners. Something was heavy on her mind. Just a short time before she had addressed the U.S. Supreme Court, presenting an *amicus curiae* brief on behalf of several abortion cases in New Jersey. In that brief she reminded the Court of our history: that our nation was founded on the belief that all people are created equal; that through the years we have held certain sacred principles about human dignity which made America an inspiration to all mankind; that our country "has ever been an inclusive, not an exclusive society"; but that, in the Court's decision in *Roe v. Wade* we decided to exclude the unborn child from the human family; and that in defending that position the Court said that it did not need to "resolve the difficult question of when life begins." However, said Mother Teresa, "That question is inescapable. If the right to life is an inherent and inalienable right, it must surely obtain wherever human life exists…It was a sad infidelity to American's highest ideals when this Court said that it did not matter, or could not be determined, when the inalienable right to life began for a child in its mother's womb." She concluded her brief: "I have no new teaching for America. I seek only to recall you to faithfulness to what you once taught the world." [13]

Following this statement to the Supreme Court, the little nun spoke at the prayer breakfast before the President, Vice President, and a roomful of political leaders. She spoke on love and peace. She spoke on the family as the center of love in society. She spoke on love of the child, "which," in her words, "is where love and peace must begin." Then she said: "I feel that the greatest destroyer of peace today is abortion, because it is a war against the child, a direct killing of the innocent child, murder by the mother herself. And if we accept that a mother can kill even her own child, how can we tell other people not to kill one another?" [14]

With each word she spoke, the hall grew more hushed, the silence stunning. There was a thunderous applause as many in the audience rose to their feet, for not everyone was clapping. Supporters of abortion shifted in their seats and fumbled with their water glasses. She hurled no blames. She spoke with love. She simply and peacefully called our leaders and all of us, as she had the Supreme Court, to that faithfulness to what our nation once taught the world.

That address and the *amicus* brief were skimpily reported in the media. But, that apparently surprised no one. That we no longer teach what we once taught the world, is not news. By its silence in reporting the news the media seemed to say; "Mother Teresa, you should have known better. It is perfectly all right to *believe* that stuff, but you really ought to keep it to yourself."

But Mother Teresa cannot keep it to herself. "From the abundance of the heart the mouth speaks." [15] This woman was so committed to the Standard of Christ that keeping it to herself is impossible. Riches and possessions? There she is in that simple white robe and sandals, working with the poor. Honors and esteem among people? She had told that breakfast audience about one day of her work in Calcutta: "There was the man we picked up from the drain, half eaten by worms and after we had brought him to the home, he only said, 'I have lived like an animal in the streets, but I am going to die like an angel loved and cared for.' Then, after we had removed all the worms from his body, all he said, with a big smile, was: 'Sister, I am going home to God' — and he died."[16] Humility? She said to the breakfast audience: "We have been created to love as He loves us. Jesus makes Himself the hungry one, the naked one, the homeless one, the unwanted one."[17] "What can I do for God?" We really don't have to look very far.

Ignatius' insight into the spirit of Christ and the spirit of Satan, into the nature of good and evil, and his understanding of both the depravity and the sublimity that human nature is capable of, is profound. The central roles he assigns to pride and humility as determinants in human character and events is not misplaced. Neither are Satan and Christ mythical characters, nor is the war they are engaged in a fictitious war.

As Christ's life and message is history's central event, Ignatius' meditation belongs in the worldview of every educated person, and in the curriculum of every university. These spiritual dimensions of an education are the most difficult to take hold of and become familiar with, but they endure longer and more profoundly transform the human person than all others. To achieve their promise in a university they obviously must take hold in the thoughts and lives of faculty, staff and administrators, before they may be expected to become realities for our students.

OH, I'M NOBODY

I met him as I was walking across the campus. It was a Saturday morning when the campus is quiet as a ghost, and I caught sight of him through the falling leaves of autumn. He was still at a distance, and I knew that he would soon be crossing my path. He appeared not to be a student but a young laborer, I would say, in his mid twenties, who was probably taking a shortcut across the lawns. Hands in his pockets, head downcast, his mood mirrored the fall morning. As he looked up, I said, "Hello."

"Oh, hello," he said, "who are you?" I responded, "I'm Father Coughlin."

"Oh, pardon me," he said. "I'm sorry, I didn't recognize you."

To which I responded, "Well, I didn't recognize you either. Who are you?"

"Oh, I'm nobody ..."

"Of course, you're somebody," and I engaged him in a brief conversation: What is your name? Where do you live? Where are you heading this Saturday morning? And in a short time we went our separate ways. That's all there was to it.

Except that it stayed with me a long time, and is still with me: "Oh, I'm nobody." I recalled some recent reading I had done. In his little book *Existence and the Existent*,[18] Jacques Maritain wrote about the subject and the object in knowledge. As an object of knowledge, the human person is differently perceived when the knowing subject is another person, when the knowing subject is the self-knowing person and when the knowing subject is God. The first instance is knowledge that other persons have of me, the second is knowledge I have of myself, and the third is knowledge that God has of me.

The knowledge in each case is very different. When another person knows me, an image of me is internalized in the mind of that knowing subject, while I remain an object apart. However well another knows me, I am never fully grasped and understood; never known are the real depths of my desires, ambitions, sins and virtues, accomplishments, hopes, beliefs, loves and hates. However much another person may know me and love me, his knowledge is through fractured images, incomplete, and so both his understanding and love are halting and reserved.

The knowledge that I have of myself is quite different. There the knowing subject and the object known are identical. I know myself immediately and intuitively, not merely through images. Hence, I understand, realize and experience far more completely and intensely the depths of my own loves and hopes, jealousies, desires, pains, anguish, fears, vice and virtues. I know myself not only as object through fractured images, but as subject. I know myself knowing, loving, and experiencing the ups and downs of my life. My knowledge of me goes to the profound heart of me. In seeking to explain, Maritain appeals to Somerset Maughan who wrote:

> To myself I am the most important person in the world; though I do not forget that, not even taking into consideration so grand a conception as the Absolute, but from the standpoint of common sense, I am of no consequence whatever. It would have made small difference to the universe if I had never existed.[19]

To paraphrase Maughan: When I compare myself to all of creation, to all the great, gifted and holy men and women in the universe, I realize how insignificant I am; and certainly, I know how insignificant I am when compared to the Absolute, the Infinite Being of God. I know perfectly well that "I am of no consequence whatever." I know, as Maritain added, "that I am one of the herd... I shall have been a tiny crest of foam, here one moment, gone in the twinkling of an eye, on the ocean of nature and humanity."[20] It was what the youth said that Saturday morning: "Oh, I'm nobody."

Yet, "to myself, I am the most important person in the world." Others know me merely as an object of knowledge, one among many. But I know the deepest recesses of my being that others can never know. I know me so much more profoundly because I myself am both object and subject of knowledge. Again, Maritain: "I am at the centre of the world... With regard to my subjectivity and act, I *am* the centre of the world... My destiny is the most important of all destinies. Worthless as I know myself to be, I am more interesting than all the saints. There is me, and there are all the others. Whatever happens to the others is a mere incident in the picture; but what happens to me, what I myself have to do, is of absolute importance."[21]

So, there is the way that others know me, and there is the way I know myself. And, then, there is God who knows me. Like everything about God, so His knowledge also surpasses our understanding. Yet we can know something of God's knowledge of us, and He has revealed some things about Himself as subject and ourselves as objects of His knowledge. We know that He knows each of us as distinct beings. Yes, there are billions of us — but God doesn't turn to His memory, as to some kind of giant computer, and punch the keyboard to draw me up on the screen to say: "Ah, yes, that's Coughlin; of course I know him." Rather, He knows me as the individual recipient of His creative love, as one to whom He continually gives being, and whom He holds and guides in His loving Providence.

In the Sistine Chapel Michelangelo portrays a vibrant God The Father, reaching out to touch a lifeless Adam, quickening him with life. It is beautiful art that attempts to portray the Infinite Being, as if saying: "of all the possible humans to whom I, from my Infinite ocean of Being, could give being, I give it to you." He knows me in Himself, immediately, as the source and cause of my being, without any need of mental reflection. His love causes me, and everything about me, to be. His knowledge of me is a loving knowledge. He knows me as a person who is receiver of that love. He knows me as a person whom He draws both by nature and grace to Himself. He knows me, then, as being from Him and as guided by Himself toward Himself. He knows me as a person for whom He humbled Himself, "taking the form of a slave."[22] He knows me as a person for whom He lays down His life, so great is His love. He knows His own Infinite love for me, which no one, not even I, can know. He knows all that of me, and more, without records, memories or images, but simply in the loving act whereby He causes me to be and to continue to be through His creative love and power. No one knows me as God knows me, and I don't even know myself as God knows me. Again Maritain: "To Him alone am I uncovered. I am not uncovered to myself."[23]

Remember the tale of the three umpires? Having called the third strike that sent the batter to the dugout, the first umpire, as the player stamped and raged in protest against the call, said to the unfortunate man: "Listen, I calls 'em as I sees 'em." The second umpire, having made the same call, said to the batter as he slammed his bat to the ground: "Listen, I calls 'em as they are." The third umpire, also having made the same call simply said: "Listen pal, they ain't nothin' till I calls 'em."

I ain't nothin' till He calls me to be. And everything about me —
thoughts, words, disposition, temperament, hopes, fears, loves and hates, sins
and virtues — they ain't nothin' till He gives them being. Nothing about me
escapes His knowledge and His love. The young man was right: "I'm nobody" — except that God causes me to be somebody. And that makes all the
difference. All this He says Himself in Psalm 139. Notice how the Psalm
speaks of God's knowledge as a loving knowledge:

> Yahweh, you examine me and know me,
> you know if I am standing or sitting,
> you read my thoughts from far away,
>
> The word is not even on my tongue,
> Yahweh, before you know all about it; [24]

But, billions upon billions of us? How can He keep us all straight? We can't
understand it because we think in finite terms. He is Infinite Being and the
cause of *my* being. He doesn't create and love humanity, which is an abstrac-
tion. He creates and loves individual persons made, as He said in Genesis, "in
His own image." [25] Every finite being of us is from Him, in Him and for Him.
Psalm 139 continues:

> Such knowledge is beyond my understanding,
> a height to which my mind cannot attain.
>
> It was you who created my inmost self,
> and put me together in my mother's womb;
>
> You know me through and through,
> from having watched my bones take shape
> when I was being formed in secret,
> knitted together in the limbo of the womb.
>
> You had scrutinized my every action,
> all were recorded in your book,
> my days listed and determined,
> even before the first of them occurred.
>
> God, how hard it is to grasp your thoughts!
> How impossible to count them!
> I could no more count them than I could the sand,
> and suppose I could, you would still be with me. [26]

From the window of my office I spotted the young man who had said, "Oh,
I'm nobody." He was crossing the University Mall, heading toward town.
Soon there disappeared among the tawny falls of autumn "the most important
person in the world."

I'M SOMEBODY

This time, I was at beautiful, hidden Priest Lake, tucked away in the hills and mountains of northern Idaho. It was full winter now, and the scenery was a picture postcard. Atop a snow-covered bluff I looked through tall evergreens, down upon the water. It was morning and the winter sun, filtering through the mist, fell soft on the snowcapped mountains and shone an orange glow on the lake below. It was a scene for contemplation; and I recalled that young man who said, "Oh, I'm nobody."

This time I had been reading another favorite, one of Maritain's associates, Etienne Gilson. In his chapter "A Metaphysics of the Name of God,"[27] Gilson writes about God's presence to us. And I found that God's knowledge of us and His presence to us was like turning a crystal and seeing the same wonder reflecting different brilliances.

We are present to things and to people in many different ways. Things are present to other things simply by being juxtaposed. Trees are present to other trees, because they grow up together and drink from the same earth. Calves are present to their mothers, on whom they feed, and both slurp from the same drinking hole. Wolves are present to one another as they run in packs. Humans are present to one another, in intellectual and loving ways: they live together in the same homes, share meals and work, become two in one flesh, bear children, exchange ideas, pray and grow old together sharing memories, sorrows and joys.

You recall that passage in the third chapter of Exodus where on Mt. Horeb God told Moses to lead the Israelites out of Egypt? Insecure at the prospect of undertaking such a responsibility, Moses said: "Look, if I go to the Israelites and tell them the God of Abraham sent me to do this, they will say to me 'what is his name.' What am I to tell them?" God said to Moses, "I am *he who is*...." Tell the Israelites, "*I am* has sent me to you."[28]

Years later when the Christian philosophers asked the question: What is God? They found their answer from God himself: I am *he who is*. Using this knowledge, Christian metaphysicians for centuries worked it into their philosophizing, somewhat like this: I am a human being, that other being is a tree, that other a bird, that down below is water, that a mountain, that a sun, clouds, snow and mist. Finite verbs define every single created being. A tree possesses the limited being to be only a particular tree; the sun possesses the limited being to be only this sun; I am only this particular human being. I am not the millions of other people and things that have their own being. So every created thing is, yet is not. My hold onto being is so tenuous. Never are the words of St. Paul — "what have you that you have not received?"[29] — so utterly apt, for not only what I am and what I have, but that I am at all, is a received act of being.

But God? God is "He who is;" He simply *is*. There is no predicate, no definition, because He is without limits. He is infinite, so it takes the infinitive to try to explain what He is. So, to the question: What is God? Thomas Aquinas answered: *ipsum esse* — being itself — or however that infinitive can be expressed in language that is finite — subsistent being, the very act of existence, infinite being. And the rest of us? Everything else that is, indeed is, but is limited being, receiving its being from the One who is Being Itself. Limited beings — trees, birds, mountains and mist, humans and angels — are said to participate in Infinite Being.

Now the most perfect and most intimate thing about me is the being, the existence, that I receive from the Subsistent Being, who causes me to be and to be what I am. "In short, the 'to be' of a being is its very core, that which is most intimate in it — the actuality of all its acts and the perfection of all its perfections."[30] At this point Gilson gets excited, you might even say melodramatic, for he tells the reader now to brace himself for "a metaphysical shock." The shock is this saying of St. Thomas: "God is innermost in each and everything, just as its own *esse* is innermost in the thing." A "metaphysical shock," because this is as close as you can get to pantheism without getting sucked in. God, says Thomas, is as intimate to me as my own act of being. Again Gilson: "God is present in all things because He is their cause; so He is in them as the cause is in its effect."[31]

Imagine a violinist performing a sonata. The being of the sounds of the sonata are separate and different from the being of the artist. Though the being of the sound depends on the artist, it nevertheless has its own being. (The sound may be recorded and later played back.) "Still, while it is being performed, the sonata owes its whole existence to the violinist; it is, but only in virtue of the being of the artist. It participates in that being as effects participate in their causes, that is, by deriving their being from that of their causes. Nor is this an idle metaphor. Man or bird, when the singer ceases to sing, the song ceases to be; the being of the cause really is *in* the effect."[32]

St. Thomas, as always, says it in an economy of words: "God is said to be in each and every thing, in as much as he gives to things their own being and nature." And it is a continuous giving, as Gilson explains: "God did not simply give being to creatures at the moment of creation, he is giving it to them all the time; by a simple undivided act, he incessantly causes the world to be, so that if he withdrew his support from his creation, the whole thing would at once cease to be, as the song of the singer who stops singing." Can anything be more present to us? Amazed at the thought of it, Gilson asks: "Do we realize that our whole being — and first of all its actual existence — hangs on the intimate presence of God?"[33]

Poets seek to express the metaphysical reality of God's presence in images and metaphors. Perhaps none as successfully as Hopkins. In "Hurrahing in Harvest," as he walks home on a late summer day, the poet is inspired by "the intimate presence of God" in the sheaves of harvested corn stacked across the fields, in the wind waving the sheaves yet to be cut, and in the "lovely behavior of silk-sack clouds." He wrote:

> I walk, I lift up, I lift up heart, eyes,
> Down all that glory in the heavens to glean our Saviour....[34]

In "The Windhover" he describes a morning when he caught sight of a falcon, flying as in an "ecstasy," hurling and gliding and rebuffing "the big wind." Enchanted, as he was, by mere "brute beauty" Hopkins reflects on his soul filled by God's presence. What must that beauty be! And the poet seems to shout:

> Brute beauty and valour and act, oh, air, pride, plume, here
> Buckle! AND the fire that breaks from thee then, a billion
> Time told lovelier, more dangerous, O my chevalier![35]

The snow crunched beneath my feet. The evergreen branches bowed under the snow, the lake glimmered a dappled-orange, the waters mirrored the distant mountains. There was no sound, but there was a presence, necessary and inescapable, a sense of reverence, of being in a holy place. I heard echoed that young man's "Oh, I'm nobody!" I prayed: May he whose whole being "hangs on the intimate presence of God," someday come to say, if only to himself: "Oh, I really am somebody!"

ON FLAGS AND OTHER SYMBOLS

A few years ago the Supreme Court handed down a decision that had been heatedly debated: a citizen's right to publicly desecrate the American flag.[36] At the time I pondered our American flag and what it represents, and other important symbols in our lives.

The flag is important because it is a symbol of our long history as a nation and of the beliefs and values that have nourished the people over the course of our national life. Symbols are important cultural phenomena, and this hassle over the flag got me to thinking how powerful and influential they can be.

A symbol is "something that stands for or represents another thing."[37] It points to another reality beyond itself. It is a sign, and many sociologists use the two terms interchangeably — sign and symbol. While it has a reality of its own, its primary function is to point to another reality that is often rich with meaning, the significance of which far surpasses the value of the symbol itself.

The sign on the highway — but a piece of tin — symbolizes a curve in the road ahead. Paul Revere warned of the approach of the British with a sign, lanterns in the window of the inn: "one if by land, two if by sea." And the soldier who falls defending the flag knows that he is not sacrificing himself for a piece of cloth.

Poets and philosophers, and scientists too, reflect frequently upon the cosmos as a sign. Chesterton, at once so profound and complex, and yet simple and childlike, wrote of his childhood experiences when the world for him was Elfland, "the realm of fairy tales, enchanted castles, and animals, witches and talking trees."[38] It was his fairyland of baubles and toys.

While he never seemed to outgrow his enchantment with Elfland, as he grew older he searched for ways to explore it more fully and to exhaust its delights and meaning. And one day a new reality, concealed in fairyland, burst upon him, and profoundly shocked him. He later wrote: "The world was a shock, but it was not merely shocking; existence was a surprise; but it was a pleasant surprise." It is always a shock when one first sees what Chesterton saw: "Existence is a surprise," for it is "not a necessity...we do not count on it." What began as fairy tales of childhood, became the basic faith underlying his adult life. And late in life he wrote:

> I felt that life itself is as bright as a diamond, but as brittle as a window pane...
> The wonder has a positive element of praise...and this pointed a profound
> emotion always present and subconscious; that this world of ours has some
> purpose; and if there is a purpose, there is a person.[39]

Chesterton was not the first to be shocked by the existence of things that are "not a necessity." Centuries earlier, St. Ambrose wrote how it burst in on him — the cosmos, that is, into which he was born, and which he took for granted, in which he recognized himself participating and experiencing over and over again since childhood — the cosmos, as sign, shocked him too, and moved him to exclaim, "Why, there is, indeed, *something* rather than nothing!"

In the first chapter of Romans, St. Paul also wrote of the cosmos as a sign: "...what can be known about God is perfectly plain...since God himself has made it plain. Ever since God created the world his everlasting power and deity — however invisible — have been there for the mind to see in the things he has made."[40]

Thus it is that the world and cosmos are sometimes called sacraments. But the seven sacraments of the Christian church, while symbols, are something more. Remember the old Baltimore catechism's definition of sacrament? "An outward sign instituted by Christ, to signify and to give grace."[41] The Christian sacraments are signs or symbols, then, but very peculiar signs. There are no others like them. Unlike every other sign, the sacraments embody and confer the very thing they signify. Like flags and highway signs, the sacraments symbolize another reality, namely, Christ active in our lives, purifying, redeeming, healing, nourishing, and strengthening. But they do more than that, for they actually give the grace that they signify, namely, the life of Christ.

The Eucharist, like the flag, is a sign of a greater reality: It symbolizes the death and resurrection of Christ. But it is also the reality of Christ whom it signifies. The separate consecration of bread and wine symbolizes the immolation and death of Christ who, however, is not symbolically but really present. He is not really but symbolically immolated, but he is really present and acting, giving Himself.

The sacrament of marriage is a sign of another reality, the unity of Christ with his people to whom He gives Himself. St. Paul says that when husband and wife give themselves to each other in marriage, they symbolize Christ's giving of Himself for the redemption of the human family, He so loves us. Christ's giving Himself in love is signified in the marriage commitment, but over and above that sign, Christ is really present in the marriage sacrament, conferring on bride and groom the grace to love, to be faithful, and to bear the burdens of marriage "in good times, and in bad, in sickness and in health, till death..." Thus, husband and wife are bound not simply by a legal bond, but by the bond of God's love which unites them also in His love. Hence the words in the marriage ceremony, "What God has joined, man must not divide."

Indeed, symbols are powerful things, and some are inexpressibly powerful. When I think of symbols, I think of the different ways in which persons are present in symbols, who those persons are, and the claim they have upon our respect.

And whether the Supreme Court handed down a wise decision or not, the Court was surely right when it said that the American flag deserves our respect because it is the symbolic embodiment of all of us, a deservedly proud people, our struggles, history and ideals. The environmentalists are right, too — the earth and the cosmos deserve our respect and protection for they are gifts for the nourishment of our bodies and spirits, and they direct our thoughts and reverence to their Creator and Giver. As we read from St. Paul: "God's everlasting power and deity, however invisible, are there for the mind to see in the things He has made."[42] And the Church is right — the sacraments deserve our respect and reverence for they signify God's presence, but over and above that, sacraments actually convey His grace and presence into our lives and activities, sanctifying us and uniting us with our Supreme Source and final End, Alpha and Omega.

EUCHARIST

The Catholic News Service recently carried an article on a survey that suggests there is widespread confusion among Catholics about the presence of Christ in the Eucharistic celebration of the mass. The Church has long definitively held that Christ is present in the Holy Eucharist under the forms (species, accidents) of bread and wine. As a theology student, I spent the good part of an academic year studying the sacraments. And while those studies never removed the mystery inherent in all the sacraments, I never had any doubt as to what the Church teaches about the eucharistic celebration.

The Incarnation is a redemptive, a salvific act, and the Redeemer is a suffering Savior. St. John the Baptist suggested this when Our Lord first appeared on the public scene and is introduced with these words: "There is the Lamb of God."[43] What must have registered in his listeners' minds? What did "the Lamb" mean to his Jewish audience? They may have recalled God's testing of Abraham's faith, when He ordered him to take his son, Isaac, up to the mountain and sacrifice him to God. When God stayed his hand, Abraham spied a lamb caught in the brambles, which became the lamb of sacrifice.

They may have recalled all the years, since their ancestors' flight from Egypt, during which the Jews celebrated the Passover, when families gathered to kill the Passover lamb and eat the meal in honor of Yahweh, who delivered them from the Egyptians.

A few, but I imagine very few, may have recalled the 40th Psalm: "You wanted no more sacrifices or oblations. So you prepared for me a body. You took no pleasure in holocausts. Then I said, just as it was commanded of me in the scroll of the book: 'God, here I am! I am coming to do your will.'"[44]

Or some may have thought of the 53rd Chapter of Isaiah, very familiar to the Jews. It speaks of that curious Servant of Yahweh, understood by many learned Jews to be the Messiah, but not all because they could not comprehend a suffering Messiah. Here is what Isaiah said:

> My servant grew up like a sapling in front of us....
> Without beauty, without majesty (we saw him),
> A thing despised and rejected by men,
> A man of sorrows and familiar with suffering,
> He was despised and we took no account of him.
>
> And yet ours were the sufferings he bore,
> ours the sorrows he carried....
>
> Yahweh burdened him
> with the sins of all of us.
> Harshly dealt with, he bore it humbly,

> he never opened his mouth,
> like a lamb that is led to the slaughterhouse,
> like a sheep that is dumb before its shearers
> never opening its mouth. [45]

Throughout their history, the Jews, like many other peoples, had sacrificed animals to God as offerings of worship and thanksgiving, and in atonement for sins. The Jews especially offered lambs, because they were a pastoral people.

Against that background, John the Baptist now points to Jesus as he comes along the lakeshore, and says: "Look, there is the lamb of God that takes away the sin of the world."[46] It was not till some three years later that what John meant began to be clear, at least to some. The servant of Yahweh is Himself the lamb of sacrifice. God provides His own lamb, and the Lamb is His Son. At the feast of Passover, He is sacrificed and in the new Christian covenant is known as the Paschal Lamb. At the Holy Thursday institution of that new covenant, He made clear that what they were eating and drinking was, as our Eucharistic liturgy says: "The Lamb of God who takes away the sins of the world." A salvific sacrifice, and a communion with a suffering Redeemer. St. Paul writes of these two realities — the sacrifice of the cross and the sacrifice of the mass — in his letter to the Corinthians (I Cor. 5): "So get rid of the old yeast and make yourselves into a completely new batch of bread, unleavened, as you are meant to be. Christ, our Passover, has been sacrificed; let us celebrate the feast, then, by getting rid of the old yeast of evil and wickedness, having only the unleavened bread of sincerity and truth."[47]

John didn't say that Jesus is like a lamb, as Isaiah had said. He is The Lamb. Likewise Christ did not say that He is like bread, but "I am the bread of life."[48]

That last Passover night when he gathered with his apostles to eat the paschal lamb and bring the Old Covenant to a close, He did so by offering a new victim, Himself, God's Lamb, God's Son. He said: "This is my blood of the new covenant which will be shed for you and for all for the remission of sins."[49] He did not say "this is a symbol of my body" or "a sign of my blood." He said: "This is my body which will be given for you. This is my blood…which will be shed for you."[50] His blood which they then drank was shed the next day. Then looking to the future, beyond Good Friday's shedding of His blood, He said: "Whenever you do this you proclaim the death of the Lord until He comes." Then He said: "Now you do this in remembrance of me."[51]

Then, as He predicted, the body and blood that He gave to his apostles as eucharistic food on Thursday, was really offered and shed on Good Friday.

Then came the Resurrection, then the Ascension. And ever since, and for all time to come, the Lamb, immolated for our sins, stands before God in glory. Even as I write, the Servant of Yahweh stands before His Father in Heaven offering Himself to God as immolated for our sins. To grasp some understanding of the sacrifice of the mass, it is important to realize the permanence and endurance of Christ's sacrifice. Even though His death was a single past historical action which is over and done, Christ's offering of Himself still goes on. It does not cease. Christ always offers Himself. "In His state of glory, as in His earthly state, He adores, gives thanks and offers his humanity. The physical act on Calvary is past, but its value remains."[52] The Lamb is offered and slain, but He lives and continues to offer Himself. He is now and always offering Himself. Christ's glorious state, his state as of one risen from the dead, is the state of a victim always offered and always active. In God's eyes Jesus Christ is forever He who loved even unto death and gave Himself fully and entirely. As the Letter to the Hebrews says: "Christ is always standing before God interceding. He lives always to plead with God on our behalf."[53]

St. John saw him thus in vision, as He relates in the Book of Revelations: "Then I saw...a Lamb that seemed to have been sacrificed....The Lamb came forward to take the scroll from the right hand of the One sitting on the throne, and when He took it....They sang a new hymn:

> You are worthy to take the scroll
> and break the seals of it,
> because you were sacrificed, and with your blood
> you bought men for God
> of every race, language, people and nation
> and made them a line of kings and priests,
> to serve our God...."[54]

Meanwhile on earth, that same victim is present sacramentally, under species of bread and wine as on Holy Thursday, and is offered on earth by Christ's priest and the Christian community. The Lamb, offered and slain in redemption for sins, offers Himself in Heaven, personally, and on earth sacramentally through priest and people whom He has redeemed. It is necessary to grasp this in order to understand that the Sacrifice of Calvary still goes on and that the offering at the mass — "Behold the Lamb of God" — is that same sacrifice. When the priest elevates the host and chalice at mass, he is offering to God on earth what Christ Himself, even now, is offering to God in heaven. What the priest offers in mass is the Lamb who, physically present before God in heaven, is sacramentally present on the altar at mass. Christ, through the priest, offers on earth the same glorified, immolated humanity that He Himself offers to God in Glory. He is offered in Heaven, as immolated and glorified, and He is offered on earth, as immolated and glorified.[55]

Immediately after the consecration in the mass, in all of the Eucharistic prayers, the Church prays, as in the third prayer:

> Father, calling to mind the death your
> Son endured for our salvation,
> His glorious resurrection and ascension
> into heaven,
> And ready to greet Him when He
> comes again,
> We offer you in thanksgiving
> this holy and living sacrifice.

Notice: It is a "living sacrifice." In the Mass, Christ living and offering Himself to the Father in heaven, is present sacramentally and offering Himself on earth.

This is not new doctrine. It has been the belief of the Church from the beginning. And it has been the defined teaching of the Church, defined at many Councils and Synods of the Church. It is indeed mystery. As the Latin Cannon reads in words immediately following the consecration, it is the "Mysterium Fidei," mystery of faith. But it is a teaching so central, so long taught and so often defined, that there need be no confusion about the presence of Christ in the celebration of the Eucharist.

WHO ABIDES IN LOVE?

It was ten minutes before the wedding and in the sacristy I was pacing back and forth going over the gospel reading that had been selected for the Mass: "As the Father has loved me, so I have loved you....This is my commandment: Love one another as I have loved you."[56]

"Love...as I have loved...." I had heard and read these words many times. Now they made me pause. I recalled St. Peter's: "You are partakers of the divine nature."[57] But no one can love as Christ loves. So what did He mean? And I recalled Paul's words to the effect that since the Holy Spirit dwells within us we have "the power to cry Abba, Father..."[58] Does it mean that the Spirit of God living in us empowers us to love as he loves? Hardly.

But it was time to begin Mass, so I found myself in the sanctuary, before the altar, beside the bride and groom, looking out over the two families, relatives and friends who had come to witness the marriage. I'm nervous, but I'm always nervous at weddings. Why? Understandably the bride and groom are wired to a high pitch. But why I, and I presume others? We, after all, are only spectators? All I have to do is say: "Now, John, repeat after me: 'I, John, take you, Mary, to be my wife... 'Now you, Mary: 'I Mary, take you, John, to be my husband....'"

The bride and groom place their lives on the line. But the rest of us? Well, the rest of us are really more than spectators, because what we witness and what they do strikes deep chords in the hearts of every one of us, depriving us of the luxury of being mere spectators. A marriage is, if anything is, about that commandment, "Love, as I have loved you." It is about the most profoundly moving things in our culture: love and honor, trust and faith, truth, integrity, sacrifice, commitment. It strikes the noblest chords in the human being.

We use the word "love" so casually. We "love" everything from God to ice cream cones. Not St. John. I can't tell you how many times St. John uses the word "love" in his Gospel and Epistles. But the word has a prominent place in John's thought. He heard those words when they were first spoken — "As the Father has loved me, so I have loved you;" — and he placed them in his Gospel. And those other words: "Greater love than this no one has than that he lay down his life for his friend."[59] And standing beneath the cross he witnessed that proof of His love. Then, after the resurrection, he saw the Lord turn to Peter and ask: "Do you love me?" and Peter said, "You know, Lord, that I love you;"[60] and the Lord then told Peter what a price he would pay for his love.

The years went by. And throughout a long life, John reflected on these things. Peter had paid the price, and John's own brother, James, had also paid the price, and Paul, too. And His mother Mary, whom Christ had entrusted to John, had joined her Son in heaven. John outlived them all, and toward the end of a long mystical life, he wrote a letter about love in which he said: "God is love. And he who abides in love abides in God, and God in him."[61]

And here we are celebrating a man and woman's love. How many times before this day had they said to each other: "I love you." And now they say to each other: "I will love you and honor you all the days of my life...."

"God is love." "I love you." Now it seems so simple. And, of course, it is a sacrament. It fits a simple syllogism: Marriage is about love; but God is love; therefore, marriage is about God. "I love you," in its deepest and fullest sense, means "I want to give you your highest good, God,"[62] so far as I am able. "I give you God?" Sounds odd, but many things in Christianity sound odd to us.

Christian marriage must be wrapped in mystery. St. Paul said: "Marriage is like Christ." Marriage is like God who "so loved the world that he gave his only Son";[63] like the Son who so loved us that he lay down his life for us. In Christian marriage, Paul said, man and woman give as Christ gave himself for the Church. Christ gave God, He gave Himself.

I look at the man and woman before me and hear them exchange their marriage vows: The man so loves the woman that he gives himself, and if he truly loves, he seeks to give his most precious gift and her greatest good, God, so far as he is able; the woman so loves the man that she gives herself, and if she truly loves, gives her most precious gift and his greatest good, so far as she is able, God. This is what people do who truly love, for "God is love."

People sometimes say that Christians exaggerate the meanings of the mysteries of Christianity. I think that the opposite may be nearer the mark. We don't say enough. We are miserly in our proclamations, because we understand so little the mystery of God in our lives: "God is love, and he who abides in love abides in God, and God in him."

MARY

Mary, the mother of Christ, was the cover personality on *Newsweek* recently. Kenneth Woodward wrote the cover story, titled "Hail, Mary." He introduces his story with: "A growing movement in the Roman Catholic Church wants the pope to proclaim a new, controversial dogma: that Mary is a Co-Redeemer."[64] As it's out of the ordinary for Mary to be the cover personality for a weekly journal, and as many Christians labor under some confusion about Mary's place in the Church, I offer the following reflections.

First of all, people sometimes misunderstand the respect and the special place of honor that the Catholic Church gives to Mary. Informed Catholics know that the Church does not worship or adore Mary. Worship and adoration are of God alone. Mary is honored and revered, as other persons are honored and revered, either because of certain outstanding things they have done or positions of dignity that they hold. But she is honored in a very special way, and holds a special place in Catholic theology, because Mary is unique among all people.

Mary is a human person, like us. Like the rest of us, she is redeemed by Christ, and so is gifted with grace that comes to her through Christ's redemption. But she is gifted in an exceptionally high degree. At the Annunciation when the angel greeted her, the words used were "Hail, full of grace."[65] We have no reason to believe that any of the rest of us are "full of grace," and Holy Scripture has never pinned that honor on any other.

Therefore, Mary is a very special human person. And the reason she is so singular is that she is the mother of God. The Second Person of the Blessed Trinity, the Word of God, became incarnate within her and was born of her. Mary's place in the divine scheme of things, and her exaltation above all other human beings, stems from the great mystery of the Incarnation, which in a word is this: the second person of the Holy Trinity the Son of God the Father, eternally possessing the Divine nature, assumed to Himself a human nature, a human body, soul, mind and will. The Word Eternal became flesh in time and space through Mary's cooperation with God. Thus, whatever

Christ has from His human side, He has because God chose her and Mary assented to be His mother. God could have done it some other way, but this is the way He did it.

The early Church prayed long and argued heatedly over this phenomenon. That Mary bore and gave birth to Jesus, was not questioned. But what that meant, as concerns Mary's relationship to God, was long debated. In the course of the discussions, several formulas from the early Greek vied for the assent of Christians. *Anthropotokos* said some: Mary is the mother of the man. *Christotokos* said others: Mary is the mother of Christ, but understood so as to reject any notion of divine motherhood. *Theotokos* said most of the Bishops and believers of the early Christian world: Mary is the mother of God.[66] And this the Bishops declared at the Council of Ephesus in 431 A.D.[67]

But how can a creature be a mother of God? Well, only if God can be a creature. So the mystery of the Incarnation and the mystery of the divine motherhood of Mary are interrelated mysteries. The Word is God, and the Word became flesh through Mary. "You are the mother of my Lord,"[68] said Elizabeth. Cardinal deBerulle expresses the mystery that has been the firm faith of Christians since the earliest centuries, thus:

> You give life to Jesus, because He is your Son, you receive life from Jesus for He is your God. And thus, at the same time, you are both giver and receiver of life....You are giving life to Christ and receiving life from Him.[69]

The Mother of God: no other honor, title or reverence can be given to Mary comparable to this; every other title and honor that the Church bestows upon her, derives from this.

And this leads us intimately into our subject. The Incarnation is a redemptive, a saving Incarnation. The Son of God became man of Mary to redeem us. What began with the Incarnation culminated in the redemptive death of Christ on the cross. At the Annunciation the angel said: "You must name him Jesus because he is the one who is to save his people from their sins."[70] Even before His birth, therefore, it is prophesied that Jesus will be involved in some kind of redemptive action.

As an infant when Mary and Joseph consecrated Him to God in the temple, the priest Simeon said that his eyes had seen "the salvation prepared for all the nations to see."[71] He went on to imply that that salvation was bound up with suffering. Your child, he said to Mary, is destined to be "a sign that is rejected," and she will share the rejection, because "a sword" would pierce her own soul.[72] As Mary stored up all these things in her heart, it must have become increasingly clear that suffering would be her Son's lot, and hers too.

At the height of this redemptive action, as St. John recorded: "There stood at the Cross of Jesus, His mother Mary."[73] Sacred Scripture gives clear evidence of Mary "as most intimately joined with her divine Son, and as always sharing His lot."[74] She bore Him in her own body, giving Him a body for the sacrifice. Now she stood beside Him, sharing His suffering and death. All Christian writers have thus understood this scene: united with her Son in sorrow, her soul pierced, she offers herself with Him to God.

Turning to His mother Jesus said: "Behold your son;" and to the disciple whom He loved: "Behold your mother."[75] Christian writers from the earliest days have seen in this Mary's spiritual motherhood of all those redeemed by her Son. Mother of Christ, she is mother of all Christians. She is our mother. And Christian writers from the earliest days have admonished us: Stand beside your mother, at the cross of your Brother.

Finally, at His side in glory, as He now offers Himself in heaven to His Father, as once at His side on Calvary where He offered Himself, is His mother. The Church has long believed that Mary, who shared intimately in His conception, nourished Him in her own body, and shared in His suffering and death, also shares her Son's complete victory over sin and death, and so was assumed body and soul into heaven. She lives in glory united with her Son. As she stood by His side at His immolation on the cross, she stands at His side in Glory, offering herself with Him as He continues to offer His humanity to God.

Surely, after her Son, she is the most exalted of all people. She had, probably in some indistinct way, foreseen it: "All generations will be blessed for He who is mighty has done great things for me."[76]

But mediatrix of all graces? and Co-Redemptrix? If that is in the revelation, it will probably someday come to full light. For the present, my knowledge and sense of faith, both admittedly woefully weak, incline me to think that the Church, as always in matters such as these, will proceed slowly on both of these questions, as we continue to reflect on Mary's role in our salvation.

ON DUCKLINGS

It had been a long flight with several changes of planes, and now I found myself at the Madrid airport weary and waiting for another connection in the wee hours of the morning. My only companions long before the sun rose were the cleaning crews mopping the marble floors in preparation for another day and several other near-dead souls who like me were awaiting early morning connections. Only they were much more ingenious than I in improvising beds out of chairs, sofas, coffee tables and luggage, over which they draped as they huffed, snorted, and twisted to find comfort. Some people can curl up anywhere in the midst of turmoil or lack of it, and off they go to sleep. Being too restless to sleep, I simply envied them. Preoccupied with my own fatigue and grime, nothing in my little world at that hour seemed beautiful.

In pursuit of some distraction from the ugly still dark morning, I reached into my bag for a paperback and came up with *Stories and Prose Poems* by Solzhenitsyn. I scarcely recalled grabbing it from my bookshelf at home and throwing it in among the socks and shirts. Paperbacks are light traveling companions. I thumbed around its 200 odd pages, reading bits and pieces, then came across "The Duckling," which I read and reread.

And a question lit up my tired mind — What do humanists do? It came like an echo across the swishing mops and snoring. I had heard it before, educators frequently hear it: What do poets and writers do for us? Engineers give us buildings and bridges, financiers invest our earnings, accountants teach us how to dodge the I.R.S., lawyers keep us out of jail, doctors patch us up, mechanics patch up our cars, and farmers feed us. But poets and writers and humanists....

These thoughts somehow transported me from that unseemly hour with its mops and snoring. I began to see afresh things I had seen before: humanists write beautiful things for us, think thoughts and see things that otherwise we might not see, share with us insights into things that are sometimes awesome and history-determining like the Gulag and sometimes gentle, everyday things like ducklings. Humanists write beautiful things — in the sense that beauty is a transcendental, in the sense that "beauty is truth, and truth beauty"[77] — so neither the Gulag nor the duckling escape the humanists eye. But why try to explain when Solzhenitsyn says it all in but a few lines.

A little yellow duckling, flopping comically on its white belly in the wet grass and scarcely able to stand on its thin, feeble legs, runs in front of me and quacks "Where's my mommy? Where's my family?"

He has no mommy, because he has been fostered by a hen: duck eggs were put in her nest, she sat on them and hatched them with her own. To shelter them from the bad weather, their home — an upturned basket without a bottom — has been moved into a shed and covered with sacking. They are all in there, but this one is lost. Come on then, little thing, let me take you in my hand.

What keeps it alive? It weighs nothing; yet it is warm with life. Its little beak is pale pink and slightly splayed, like a manicured fingernail. Its personality already sets it apart from its foster brothers.

And we men will soon be flying to Venus; if we all pooled our efforts, we could plough up the whole world in twenty minutes.

Yet, with all our atomic might, we shall never — never! — be able to make
this feeble speck of a yellow duckling in a test tube; even if we were given the
feathers and bones, we could never put such a creature together. [78]

A whole new set of thoughts had introduced beauty into my early morning —
thanks to the poet. St. Ignatius would have liked Solzhenitsyn. Over and over
again in his writings he speaks of the presence of God in the universe, "In all
things," he wrote, "we should seek God, for He is in all things, and all things
are in Him." Perhaps no words more capture that spirituality of Ignatius. [79]

The cleaning lady wrung her mop dry. A shaft of early morning, yellow
sunlight seeped through the window of the airport, falling on the face of a
weary traveler. He rearranged his slouched body and pulled a cap over his
eyes, hoping that sleep would return.

"He is in all things, and all things are in Him." St. Paul had said it: "Ever
since God created the world his everlasting power and deity — however
invisible — have been there for the mind to see in the things He has made."[80]
Christian philosophers have explained why it must be so. Why could I not
have seen in mops and buckets and snoring bodies what Solzhenitsyn saw in
a thin, feeble, flopping duckling? He is there, we have only to look for Him.

THOUGHTS FROM ST. EMILION

Have you ever tried St. Emilion? It's a bit more expensive than the wine I'm
used to, but I have had it on special occasions.

St. Emilion, in the wine country of Bordeaux, is a quaint medieval town
that rises on a hill near the Dordogne River. In the 12th Century it sported a
Chateau du Roi, but all that remains today of the Chateau is its tower. I like
to climb to the top of citadels, so up I went along the circular, dark stone
staircase, and emerged into the sunlight, to a tranquil view of rolling hills
ripe with vineyards that stretched as far as I could see.

My trip into the Bordeaux country coincided with Pope John Paul II's
visit to Rheims in September 1996 for the celebration of the 1500th anniversary of the baptism of King Clovis. I still recalled enough of the language to
struggle through the French newspaper and was interested in seeing what the
press might say about the Pope's visit. The press, in anticipation of the visit,
was at best indifferent, often hostile. The issue that preoccupied the journal-
ists seemed to be: Should a high ranking French dignitary go to Rheims to
welcome the Pope? Should France, a professed secular nation, even recognize his presence? Some editorials were strident, protesting that their secular
government should not recognize a church leader, much less the baptism of
their founding monarch.

It was a Sunday morning, and as I felt my way back down the tower staircase and walked the cobbled streets, I thought that, instead of celebrating mass privately on the balcony of my hotel room, I would attend mass that morning with the people of St. Emilion and see for myself Catholics at worship in this once so Catholic, now officially secular, country. So, I sought out the church.

Finding it was not that easy. St. Emilion is crowded with *caves* (wine cellars). One especially caught my eye: "Cave du Couvent." How interesting, I thought: In the Bordeaux country even the nuns have their wine cellars. Then my eye wandered upward to the weathered, worn embossed lettering on the entablature over the entrance to the *cave*. It told the story: "Masion des Ursulines" — once an Ursuline convent, now wine cellar.

Now, on to the church. Earlier in the day, I had spied a Gothic steeple and cross rising above the red tile roofs of this compact little town. I inquired and received directions which led me to a set of grand, arched church doors which I entered only to find myself in the Tourist Bureau. As I learned later, the church in St. Emilion, like so many others, had been confiscated during the French Revolution. What was later restored to the Catholics was the sanctuary and half of the nave, but the entrance and the rest of the nave remained public property. I saw something similar in other French towns, in Rodez, for example, where the former Jesuit high school is now public of-fices, including another Tourist Bureau. Well, the Tourist Bureau people directed me around the block and down a narrow walkway where I joined a small stream of people who knew their way into the secluded sacred half of the old church.

Soon larger numbers of parishioners began strolling in. I was expecting to see mostly little French ladies and a few gray haired and balding men. But there were old and young and middle-aged, mothers and fathers with their children, and teenagers, some in jeans and sandals, others in dress slacks and sport jackets — a scene not unlike many a rural town in the United States. There were hymns, robustly sung, and a homily, and large numbers receiving holy communion. Back in my pew, I recalled that at this very time John Paul II was celebrating mass in the great cathedral of Rheims.

The next morning the news media ate crow: a mammoth and jubilant crowd had the previous day overflowed the Rheims cathedral and public square; and indeed an official delegate from Paris, sent at the last minute, did welcome John Paul II.[81] The proceedings commanded television audiences all over Europe. Of course, I realize that there was, no doubt, an even larger number of Frenchmen still comfortably in bed or in the *caves* that Sunday morning. Nevertheless, I had second thoughts about France's touted secular-ism: the Christian faith, that goes back to King Clovis and beyond, is still deep in the roots of the French soul, and this generation, like its predecessors, continues to be nourished by those roots.

Back home in Spokane, I read an article entitled "Not So Christian America."[82] It summarizes many recent surveys on the religion/secularism issue: how secular or how religious is America as measured by church attendance, religious practice and beliefs. The article concludes that we Americans appear still to be a religious and Christian people even though we have adopted many secular laws and practices; the jury is still out. One is reminded of our Lord's parable of the enemy who sowed weeds in the field. The master said: "Let the weeds grow up with the good grain till the time of harvest."[83]

God is in no hurry; He is supremely patient. See how many years is His creation: 12 to 14 billion, by the best scientific estimates. He is the primary actor in every event in history. He was there for Clovis, and long before. He witnessed the French Revolution and its follies. He was there when St. Emilion's first vines were harvested, saw the work of the sisters at the Maison des Ursulines, John Paul II and all his predecessors, saintly and not so saintly, saw the Romans come to Gaul and the rise and fall of French cities, Flanders Field, Omaha Beach, and all the rest. He rides time, looks neither backwards nor forward, neither hurries nor tarries along the way. In His infinite intelligence, we are all present at once: French and American, Vinedresser and Ursuline, Pope and patriot, past, present and future. As He said: "I am the Alpha and the Omega, who is, who was, and who is to come, the Almighty."[84]

"I WISH YOU TO SERVE US"

Ignatius Loyola was born probably in 1491 at the Castle of Loyola in the Basque region of northern Spain. He entered military service in 1517 under the Viceroy of Navarre, and in 1521 when French troops entered Spain and attacked Pamplona Ignatius defended it, suffering a blow from a cannonball to his right leg that also badly wounded his left. At a nearby hospital he received the crude treatment typical of the day: his leg was set, but improperly, and so was broken again and reset. After suffering several painful operations, the doctors were unable to save him from a lifelong limp.

Recuperating at the Castle of Loyola, out of boredom he asked for books to wear away the tedious hours of his convalescence. Only two books were available, *The Life of Christ* and a worn out copy of *Lives of the Saints*. Moved by the heroism of the Saints' lives, Ignatius found himself asking over and over again: "If they can do it, why can't I?" Dreams of earthly chivalry that previously had infatuated him were, over time, transformed to dreams of chivalry for another Lord. Under the etching of grace, little by little, he knew that he was being led along a new path.[85]

Having convalesced, he made an all-night vigil of prayer in the Benedictine monastery of Montserrat, and early on the next morning on March 24, 1522, he laid his sword and dagger before the altar of Our Lady of Montserrat. He then went to the little town of Manresa where he spent the next 10 months alternately in a monastic cell of the Dominicans and in a hermit's cave outside the town. He fasted, prayed, scourged himself and begged for bread in the streets.

As soldiering was all he had known, he went to school at age 33 with students less than half his age, at Barcelona, then Alcala, then Salamanca, and finally Paris. Along the way he inspired nine fellow students who joined his reformed way of life. On August 15, Feast of the Assumption of Our Lady, 1534, that little band of ten took vows of poverty and chastity, and set off on pilgrimage to the Holy Land. But they never reached the Holy Land, for along the way Christ appeared to him carrying his cross with God the Father at his side. "I wish you to serve us," said Jesus. The Father added, "I will be propitious to you in Rome." So they turned toward Rome and several years later, in 1540, Ignatius founded The Society of Jesus.[86]

Beyond question, the grace of God fueled the new order. Within a short generation or two, Jesuit missionaries carried the Gospel to every continent, theologians broke new ground in the post-Tridentine Church, spiritual directors revitalized the spirit of the Church through Ignatius' little manual of *Spiritual Exercises*, philosophers pioneered modern political theory, writing blueprints for the modern state and for Church-State relations, and educators founded more than 300 colleges, distinguishing themselves as "the schoolmasters of Europe."[87] As Pope Paul VI declared of them: "Wherever in the Church, even in the most difficult and exposed fields, in the crossroads of ideologies, in the social trenches, there has been or is confrontation between the burning exigencies of humanity and the perennial message of the Gospel, there have been and are the Jesuits."[88]

A lot has been written about Ignatius Loyola, and about the Society of Jesus. Most Jesuits are embarrassed at what we read: It's the giants among us who are the heroes, the rest of us hanging on to their coattails. But one thing we all recognize: One person can make a great difference! Ignatius would amend that: One person and God can make a very great difference.

Ignatius made a difference. Leaders and heroes make a difference. But we don't play them up the way we used to. As soon as a hero comes along, we can't wait to cut his legs off, as though no star must shine. We obscure achievers. Even achievers in sin are robbed of their sin. We seem to want no heroes, good or bad. That's our culture, you'll say. That's the way it must be in a culture that has lost the true notion of freedom, and so, of moral goodness and evil. In a mechanical world no one deserves anything, neither sinners nor heroes, for there is no evil and no virtue, no blame or praise, no responsibility, no stars to shine, no villains to be reviled. But, my goodness, how flat and uninteresting is a world without villains and heroes.

Ignatius' life, which began 500 years ago, was anything but flat and uninteresting. Challenged to do great things, saints do them. Like Jacob, they wrestle with God; in the struggle they know that they are more than mere gadgets on a giant mechanical ferris wheel, that the struggle is real, and that honor, courage and virtue are the big stakes in life.

In the last analysis, individuals with vision and through sheer force of will, often standing alone against a storm, make a difference. Ignatius made a difference, as did many of his followers and others from those times: Francis Xavier, Theresa of Avila, John of the Cross, Francis Borgia, Peter Canisius, Robert Bellarmine. They all made a difference. They were to the world of spirit and culture of the 16th and 17th centuries what Winston Churchill was to the free world in the early 20th century. And what Mother Teresa has been to the world of the spirit in our generation. They are the heroes.

They don't have to be on television or heralded on the nightly news. You find them both in private and public places. Once settled in Rome, Ignatius hardly moved from those three rooms at the Gesu where he wrote the Constitutions of the Society of Jesuit. But from there he sent Jesuits all over the world. That vision at Manresa he pursued with stubborn courage his whole life. That's what heroes are made of. Our age needs more of them.

FOLLOW THE CONDUCTOR

Some sixteen entered carrying violins, both men and women dressed in black, the women in formal evening gowns. A second wave came with violas in their hands; then came the cellos; then eight musicians crossed the stage to the back of the orchestra stationing themselves beside eight big bass fiddles that stood like sentinels. What strangely shaped instruments! I wondered who first started making music by sawing a bow across strings that run the length of a sound box.

Now more musicians in black came on the brightly lit stage carrying horns, trumpets and trombones, stranger creations still — shiny, metal pipes that coil around in circles and oblong shapes, sometimes with fancy curls, and then flare open at the end like a conch, or like glistening bells. Others carried seemingly simpler, uncomplicated instruments — flutes, oboes, bassoons and clarinets. Finally, the harpist walked to her harp and the drummer to the snare and kettle drums and hanging brass rings.

There they stood, not quite a hundred in all. Then all eyes shifted to the aisles of the orchestra floor as a seeming endless parade of women in blue gowns and men in black ascended the stage. A larger chorus you'll rarely see; there must have been 300 in all. They took their places filling in row upon row behind the orchestra until the stage was a magnificent scene of near 400 musicians and singers, men and women, young and old, from every conceivable background, race, creed, nation and culture.

Then a single person walked on stage and stepped to the podium. There was silence throughout the hall as the conductor raised his hands, and from the violins came the most beautiful sound, an exquisite melody which lasted no more than a minute. As the violins played on, the violas picked up the melody and repeated it with slight variations. Then the full, sonorous, mournful sound of the cellos played it back again, and all three instruments were now engaged in a musical conversation on the original melody. Then as from under the floor, came the stately ponderous step of the double bass, like eight giants walking in unison through a forest. The strings were joined by the woodwinds, then the brilliant blare of horns and the crashing of drums.

Then 300 men and women in unison rose to their feet as though loosed from a single trap, their full voices almost at a shout, riding in harmony over the music.

Some four hundred human beings under the direction of one baton played and sang that beautiful symphony, composed almost two centuries ago, from an infinite number of notes, each written down in its place, to be sounded at its time and in reference to every other, to form a unity of order and harmony. Out of soundlessness its author created music; as in the beginning, out of the formless void and darkness, God created the universe.

Walking home that evening I thought both about the world of music and order, and about that other world of disorder and discord. Four hundred people come together in harmony and a thing of beauty. Another four hundred never come together, never sing at all; they may live together in the same city, but under intense suspicion of other's intentions. Six million people are snatched from their loved ones and transported into ovens. A woman is raped and knifed. A man is clubbed to death as he enters the peace of his home.

What contradictions human beings are. St. Paul said of us: Our minds are darkened, God has abandoned us to our degrading passions because we exchanged God's truth for a lie. Left to our own thoughts and behavior, we are steeped in all sorts of depravity: rottenness, greed, malice, envy, murder, wrangling, treachery and spite; enemies of God, rude, arrogant and boastful, enterprising in sin, rebellious to parents, without brains, honor, love or piety.[89] A dismal portrait. Yet David said of us: "I look up at Your heavens, made by Your fingers, at the moon and the stars You set in place — Ah, what is man that You should spare a thought for him, the Son of Man that You should care for him? Yet you made him little less than a god, You have crowned him with glory and splendor, made him lord over the work of Your hands, set all things under his feet."[90] Indeed God Himself had at the beginning said of us: "Let us make him in Our own image....and in the image of God He made them, male and female He made them."[91]

We are so good; we are so mean. We make order and harmony out of the worst chaos; we make rubble of the most precious things. We make the most beautiful music; we make the most terrible discord.

We seem divided against ourselves. Hopkins saw how bitter selfishness is: self-love is a chamber of torture wherein one hears the single monotonous sound of one's own small song, never the freeing, vast symphony of Beethoven:

> I am gall, I am heartburn. God's most deep decree,
> Bitter would have me taste: My taste was me;
> Bones built in me, flesh filled, blood brimmed the curse.
>
> Self-yeast of spirit a dull dough sours. I see
> The lost are like this, and their scourge to be
> As I am mine, their sweating selves; but worse.[92]

A symphony is the power of people rising above their small individual selves, becoming part of something big and beautiful. If over 400 men and women can play and sing Beethoven's creation, why may not 400,000 sing the symphony that God wrote and David sang? "Ah, what is man that you spare a thought for him, the Son of Man that you should care for him? You have made him a little less than a god."[93] Ah yes, maybe we can, but only if together we follow the Conductor.

ON SAYING "GOODBYE" AND "HELLO"

After much agonizing, she finally made the decision to move from the apartment where she had lived for almost 30 years to the retirement home. It was a painful decision, made within days of her 90th birthday; and she came to it only because there was really nothing else she could do. Thirty years before, she had made an even more wrenching decision when she gave up the home she had kept for 35 years, and where she had raised her family.

Arriving at that decision left her in a deep depression, for she now thought of all the things she would have to leave behind. Alone in the dimly lighted apartment, she successfully suppressed the sobs that welled within her, as she surveyed companions she had intimately known for years: the dining room table, a birthday gift from her children; the silver tray and pitchers, a gift from her wedding day; an incomplete set of English bone china from her husband, long deceased; the ancient, revered, many times recovered sofa; her special easy chair and floor lamp; the coffee table that her mother used and left to her; the stone nativity scene that her father carved when he was a young man, which must have been done shortly after the Civil War; pictures, photographs, and, of course, the blue vase that was already an heirloom in the family when she was a child.

I was picturing all this, and thinking of all the people who experience what she was now experiencing, as I flew back home, looking out on the cloud bank that covered most of the Midwest. The physical separation from earth that one feels in a plane at 37,000 feet seemed symbolic of her separation from those old, familiar friends, a separation that takes place in all lives that grow old.

There is irony in the life cycle. We come into the world helpless and empty handed, intellectually, emotionally and physically unadorned. We quickly reach out to others to survive — grasping people and things — and in time, embellish ourselves, often wondrously. At the university we study the transcendentals, how all things are good, true, and beautiful; and that if we contemplate them sufficiently, we will see them each in its own way as God's amazing reflection. But we see Him in them, as St. Paul said, dimly, so dimly that often we don't see Him at all. Time passes; and as we move toward the end, those things one by one fall away till we are stripped of the embellishment they once afforded us.

This cycle of things doesn't surprise or alarm us; we see it all the time and recognize it as simply the nature of things. It's in the passage of every life we've known.

It doesn't alarm us, that is, until it happens to us. Then we experience it as a most discomforting and painful personal separation. As I reflected on it at 37,000 feet, I thought that maybe in God's design it's also a rare opportunity. It's been said that life is a series of "hellos" and "goodbyes." If that's so, birth must be the first "hello," and death the last "goodbye."

I am bold now to say that as we move to the last "goodbye," — through painful days, and maybe years, of slow separations from familiar, earthly friends, — we have this unique, if fearful opportunity of a lifetime to set aside all the accumulated adornments and look with anticipation to that "hello," which is an indescribable reunion and which, except for faith, is unbelievable.

In God's design it must be meant as a unique opportunity, and if so, one would not choose to miss it. An opportunity to give the very last thing that one has, and to receive what one most longs for. St. Ignatius has a prayer that goes like this: "Take, Lord, and receive all that I am, and all that I have. Give me only your love and your peace."[94] Spoken with full meaning from the depths of one's mind and will, it is a prayer of profound faith.

A few years ago I visited Fr. Jake Spills in the hospital. I had seen him go down over several years, as his health deteriorated. He had been a robust, strapping man with a big, open laugh. He came from a farming family, and all his priestly life worked as an Alaskan missionary. He set his fat, rough hands as well as his witty mind to building churches and schools, and educating Native Eskimos. They loved and admired that big and blunt, but sensitive and compassionate man who traveled on dog sled back and forth across Western Alaska to serve his people. The years wore on, and he aged and wore out.

When his superior told him that he must leave Alaska, he literally limped to the infirmary at Gonzaga University, leaving behind every place and face that had been friend to him for 50 years. At Gonzaga he played bridge and pinochle, which he loved; but gradually even that was taken from him. One night in the community room alone, attempting to find his way to his room, he fell to the floor where he lay unable to garner sufficient strength to get to his feet. He was discovered on his back staring at the ceiling and muttering, maybe even complaining, with characteristic familiarity: "Well, God, what do you want from me now?"

Weeks later at Sacred Heart Medical Center, he took my hand. I felt he was reaching for something to hang onto as one might for a plank in the sea. "I have nothing left to fight with," he said, "He's taken it all away. I have left only faith." That was a familiar scriptural theme: It's futile to rely on earthly things; put your trust in God. Maybe he was thinking of Paul's analogy, as he urged the Ephesians to gird themselves for battle: "Put on the buckle of truth, seize the sword of the spirit, and take up the shield of faith."[95]

In this matter of separation, the saints are so graced as to do it with love and joy. Most of us go to it compelled, digging in our heels, hanging on to every earthly thing. Only when we're laid bare, faith alone remaining, we set our sights on God. Happily we may recognize that this is what we wanted all along, happily we may finally understand Paul's paradox: "When I am weak, then I am strong."[96] It takes most of us more than a lifetime to understand that having God, we have all.

As the plane landed, I thanked God for all the good years He had given that good woman, and for the painful years, too, for they had been years of her deepening faith. The earthly things had been taken away, but it now mattered not at all. She was ready to say "hello."

ON AUTUMN...AND THEN SPRING

Autumn leaves are falling, days are growing shorter, and colder, nights coming on more quickly, animals hibernate, and nature seems to die. And in November, the Church asks us to remember and pray for the dead.

Death is an unpleasant thought — even Christ cried at the death of his friend Lazarus, and agonized at the foresight of his own death — unpleasant because it is the beginning of that final and complete decay of the human body in which we take much pride and on which we lavish much care; unpleasant and horrifying, because we know almost nothing about it, except that it will come. But when, how, where, and then what? People of all religions have sought answers, only to find themselves looking into a black abyss that offers no answers. So unpleasant is it that some freeze the corpses of their dead loved ones, and instruct that their own corpses be likewise frozen, in the hope that someday, somehow, the autumn leaves will not fall.

Death has always been a preoccupation of all religions: Christians and Jews, Muslims and Hindus, Shiites and Naturalists. The thing that separates Christianity and Judaism from every other religion in history is this: that all religions are beliefs about and searches for God, men and women seeking to find Him in the world of nature, seeking to know Him, to declare their dependency upon Him, to worship Him in some way, and to seek union with Him as far as is possible. But the Judeo-Christian tradition, while it shares these characteristics, distinguishes itself from all other religions in this: Judaism and Christianity are not primarily religions in which we seek God but in which God seeks us, first by revealing Himself through nature, then by, special revelations and emissaries that carry His word to tell us of Himself, and then in the case of Christianity, by the ineffable Incarnation of His Son who, as St. John wrote "we have heard and seen with our own eyes, and whom we have watched and touched with our own hands."[97] And of Himself our Lord said: "Blessed are they who have not seen, but believe."[98] Faith is the first characteristic of Christianity: faith in God who speaks, in His word, and in His covenant. Faith is a kind of conversation with God in which we recognize, in the very conversation, that it is God who speaks. And here are some of the things that He tells us about that ending of our earthly life and beginning of our heavenly life:

> This is the will of my father, that everyone who sees the Son and believes in Him may have eternal life, and I will raise him on the last day.[99]

> I am the resurrection and the life; whoever believes in me, even if he dies, will live.[100]

Do not let your hearts be troubled. In my father's house there are many dwelling places. I am going to prepare a place for you. [101]

If we have died with Him, we shall live with Him; if we persevere, we shall also reign with Him. [102]

Our citizenship is in Heaven, and from it we also await a savior, the Lord Jesus Christ. He will change our lowly body to conform with His glorified body.... [103]

What faith tells us, then, about death is at least this: that human life is purposeful; that its purpose is not fulfilled during its earthly time; that our deaths, and what follows, are somehow bound up with Christ's death and resurrection; that we will continue to live beyond our deaths, and it will be in some way a glorified new kind of life; that our bodies, as well as our spirits, will participate in this new, glorified state; and that it will be a life in the company of Christ, the saints and the Eternal God.

St. Augustine has said so many memorable things. Perhaps the one we're most familiar with is: "You have made us for yourself, O God, and our hearts are restless till they rest in Thee." [104] That's from his *The Confessions*, the first real autobiography, and I'm told that literary critics agree that it has never been surpassed. Augustine pours out his soul; he writes with passion.

Buried in his *Confessions* is another bright saying of but five words: *Deum et animam scire cupio.* "*Deum*," of course, is God. "*Animam*" means soul, from which we have the word animate. "*Scire*" is to know, from which we have the word "Science." And "*Cupio*" is a strong verb meaning "desire," from which we have the word cupidity. Augustine could have used several other verbs such as "I want" or "I wish" to know God and my own soul. Instead he uses "*cupio*" to say: I don't simply want, but "I strongly desire and I long to know God and my own soul." *Deum et animam scire cupio.*

Deum, God. Of course, we expect: the desire to know God. But *animam* — what is this soul that is so restless? I long to know my own soul which is destined to rest in God. I long to know my soul, which belongs to God.

Death reminds me that I am possessed of this soul that departs this body. To know my own soul. I can't see it, or hear it or feel it. But I see what it can do, what it does, and makes me wonder and long to know what it must be. I've stood over the dead many times. I've seen and heard the last expiring breath of the dead, as the soul leaves. And then, it is like standing over a dead log. You touch it and it's like touching a piece of dried bark that soon grows cold. Speak to it and it's like speaking to a post. Listen for it to respond, and nothing but silence from a mouth that once talked, joked, reasoned, sang songs.

The human body held a spirit, we call it soul. No, it was the soul that held the body and animated it, not the other way around. The soul is the life-giving principle. It's by the power of the soul that that lifeless being in some cases can run 100 meters under ten seconds, performs the triple axle on ice, runs its fingers over a keyboard, sings arias, writes poetry and philosophy. The likes of dried bark? *Animam scire cupio.*

Our Lord said: *"It is the spirit that gives life."*[105] What is a human soul — to make the likes of a dead log do all these things? What a power! What intelligence! Language, sonatas, poetry, philosophy and symphonies! From dried bark? *Deum et animam scire cupio.*

"In the beginning God created....God said: Let there be light....God said: Let the waters come together, and let dry land appear....God said: Let the earth produce vegetation....God said: Let the waters team with living creatures....And God saw that it was good."[106]

Then God said: "Let us make man in our own image, in the likeness of ourselves." The writer of Genesis did not want that act of creation to be missed. He said: "God created man in the image of himself," then he repeated:

> "in the image of God he created him,
> male and female he created them."[107]

Deum et animam scire cupio. The soul — the image of God — the power to transform body — to think, to understand, to know and love — even God. "We will know Him; we shall be like Him, for we shall see Him face to face."[108]

What we are and what we shall be! The power of a soul! But going one step further: the power of the soul glorified. I think of Christ's dead body, lifeless and cold in the tomb.

Then on Easter morning Christ's now glorified soul reanimates that body so that even the body takes on spiritual qualities: it passed through closed doors, was elevated above the earth, and was transported in an instant over long distances.

This is the way it was and is now for Christ's glorified body. And this, we are told, is the way it will be for us. *"I make all things new."*[109] There will be *"a new heaven and a new earth."*[110] *"Our citizenship is in heaven, and from it we also await a Savior, the Lord Jesus Christ. He will change our lowly bodies to conform with His glorified body."*

> Behold, I tell you a mystery....we will all be changed, in an instant, in the blink of an eye,.... For the trumpet will sound, and the dead will be raised incorruptible and we shall all be changed...[111]

So however much we stand ignorant and fearful before the great mystery of life and death, and life after death, we are certain of a resurrection with Christ. It is the certainty that comes from faith; the certainty that comes from the Spirit of God, who is sent to our spirits so that we may say, "Abba, Father." The same Spirit gives us the certainty to say with St. Paul, "Eye has not seen, ear has not heard what God has prepared for those who love him."[112]

The autumn leaves fall, the earth grows cold and hard. But in the spring the earth will soften and warm, new buds will appear on the trees, and green leaves will cover the fields. Autumn is here, and winter will soon be; but there will be spring, of that we are certain. Even more certain are we of an eternal spring, when we will see "all things made new." When there will be "a new heaven and a new earth."

Then that young man who said, "Oh, I'm nobody," will be amazed at what he really is. Image of God will look at God, fulfilling that prophecy, "We shall be like Him, for we shall see Him face to face as He is."

Imagine, if you can: "We shall be like Him." That's God's plan for His children. Our Founding Fathers knew and declared to the world that God is our Creator and Father; we His children are created equal and our new nation is founded upon God. In Him they put their trust. And the little nun said: "....I have no new teaching for America. I seek only to call you to faithfulness to what you once taught the world...."

NOTES

1. Of Loyola Ignatius Saint and Louis J. Puhl, *The Spiritual Exercises of St. Ignatius: Based on Studies in the Language of the Autograph*, 1st ed. (New York: Vintage Books, 2000), 176, http://catdir.loc.gov/catdir/bios/random052/00034948.html.

2. Jones, *The Jerusalem Bible*, Rom. 6:12.

3. Ignatius and Puhl, *The Spiritual Exercises of St. Ignatius: Based on Studies in the Language of the Autograph*, 48.

4. Ibid., 49.

5. Philip Babcock Gove and Inc Merriam-Webster, *Webster's Third New International Dictionary of the English Language, Unabridged* (Springfield, Mass: Merriam-Webster, 1993).

6. Jones, *The Jerusalem Bible*, Luke 10:18.

7. Stephen L. Carter, *The Culture of Disbelief: How American Law and Politics Trivialize Religious Devotion* (New York, NY: Basic Books, 1993), 4.

8. Ibid., 8.

9. Ibid., 11-12.

10. Ibid., 25.

11. Ibid., 51-2.

12. Jones, *The Jerusalem Bible*, 1 Cor. 4:7.

13. Mother Teresa and Robert P. George, "Brief Amicus Curiae of Mother Teresa of Calcutta, in Support of Petitioners' Petitions for a Writ of Certiorari," *Human Life Review* 27, no. 2 (Spring 2001, 2001), 97-100, http://search.ebscohost.com/login.aspx?direct=true&db=a9h&AN=14913945&site=ehost-live.

14. Matthew Levering, *On Marriage and Family: Classic and Contemporary Texts* (Lanham, MD: Rowman & Littlefield, 2005), 116, http://catdir.loc.gov/catdir/toc/ecip051/2004023041.html.

15. Jones, *The Jerusalem Bible*, Matt. 12:34.

16. Levering, *On Marriage and Family: Classic and Contemporary Texts*, 119.

17. Ibid., 115.

18. Jacques Maritain, *Existence and the Existent* (Westport, Conn: Greenwood Press, 1975).

19. W. Somerset Maugham, *Mr. Maugham Himself.* (Garden City, NY: Doubleday, 1954), 544.

20. Jacques Maritain, Donald Arthur Gallagher and Idella J. Gallagher, *A Maritain Reader: Selected Writings.*, 1st ed. ed. (Garden City, NY: Image Books, 1966), 171.

21. Ibid., 171.

22. Jones, *The Jerusalem Bible*, Phil. 2:7.

23. Maritain, Gallagher and Gallagher, *A Maritain Reader: Selected Writings*, 172.

24. Jones, *The Jerusalem Bible*, Ps. 139.

25. Ibid., Gen. 1:27.

26. Ibid., Ps. 139.

27. Etienne Gilson, *The Spirit of Thomism* (New York: P.J. Kenedy, 1964), 71.

28. Jones, *The Jerusalem Bible*, Exod. 3:13-14.

29. Ibid., 1 Cor. 4:7.

30. Gilson, *The Spirit of Thomism*, 69.

31. Ibid., 69-70.

32. Ibid., 70.

33. Ibid., 70-1.

34. Gerard Manley Hopkins and W. H. Gardner, *Poems and Prose of Gerard Manley Hopkins* (Harmondworth, Middlesex, England; New York, NY: Penguin Books, 1985), 31.

35. Ibid., 30.

36. *United States v. Eichman*, Nos. 89-1433, 89-1434 *United States v. Eichman*, 496, 310 (SUPREME COURT OF THE UNITED STATES).

37. "Symbol" Gove and Merriam-Webster, *Webster's Third New International Dictionary of the English Language, Unabridged.*

38. Niemeyer, *The Recovery of 'the Sacred'?*, 10.

39. Ibid., 10.

40. Jones, *The Jerusalem Bible*, Rom. 1:19-20.

41. Francis J. Connell, *The New Confraternity Edition, Revised Baltimore*, The text of the official rev. ed., 1949, with summarizations of doctrine and study helps, by Rev. Francis J. Connell ed. (New York: Benziger Bros, 1949), no. 304.

42. Jones, *The Jerusalem Bible*, Rom. 1:20.

43. Ibid., John 1:36.

44. Ibid., Ps. 40:6-8.

45. Ibid., Isa. 53.

46. Ibid., John 1:29.

47. Ibid., 1 Cor. 5.

48. Ibid., John 6:35.

49. Ibid., Matt. 26:28.

50. Ibid., Mark 14:22-24.

51. Ibid., Luke 22:18-19.

52. Marie-Joseph Nicolas, *What is the Eucharist?*, 1st ed. ed. (New York: Hawthorn Books, 1960), 63.

53. Jones, *The Jerusalem Bible*, Heb. 7:25.

54. Ibid., Rev. 5:6-10.

55. Nicolas, *What is the Eucharist?*, 64.

56. Jones, *The Jerusalem Bible*, John 15:9, 13:34.

57. Ibid., 2 Pet. 1:4.

58. Ibid., Gal. 4:6.

59. Ibid., John 15:13.

60. Ibid., John 21:15.
61. Ibid., 1 John 4:16.
62. Ibid., Ps. 73:28.
63. Ibid., John 3:16.
64. Kenneth L. Woodward and Andrew Murr, "Hail, Mary. (Cover Story)," *Newsweek* 130, no. 8 (08/25, 1997), 48, http://search.ebscohost.com/login.aspx?direct=true&db=a9h& AN=9708210111&site=ehost-live.
65. Jones, *The Jerusalem Bible*, Luke 1:28.
66. Leo Donald Davis, *The First Seven Ecumenical Councils (325-787): Their History and Theology* (Collegeville, Minn: Liturgical Press, 1990), 140.
67. Ibid., 134.
68. Jones, *The Jerusalem Bible*, Luke 1:43.
69. Léon Joseph Suenens, *Mary the Mother of God*, 1st American ed. ed. (New York: Hawthorn Books, 1959), 49.
70. Jones, *The Jerusalem Bible*, Matt. 1:21.
71. Ibid., Isa. 52:10.
72. Ibid., Luke 2:34-35.
73. Ibid., John 19:25.
74. Pope Pius XII, "Munificentissimus Deus: Defining the Dogma of the Assumption," (1 Nov 1950, 1950), 38, http://www.vatican.va/holy_father/pius_xii/apost_constitutions/documents/hf_p-xii_apc_19501101_munificentissimus-deus_en.html (accessed 31 Dec 2010).
75. Jones, *The Jerusalem Bible*, John 19:26-27.
76. Ibid., Luke 1:48-49.
77. John Keats and Horace Elisha Scudder, *The Complete Poetical Works and Letters of John Keats*, Cambridge ed. (Boston: New York: Houghton, Mifflin and Company, 1899), 135, http://hdl.loc.gov/loc.gdc/scd0001.00088105011; http://hdl.loc.gov/loc.gdc/scd0001.00088105011.
78. Aleksandr Isaevich Solzhenitsyn, *Stories and Prose Poems* (London: Bodley Head, 1971), 229-30.
79. Edward E. Ericson and Aleksander Isaevich, *Solzhenitsyn, the Moral Vision* (Grand Rapids, Mich: Eerdmans, 1982), 10.
80. Jones, *The Jerusalem Bible*, Rom. 1:20.
81. Celestine Bohlen, "Pope Passes Twin Tests of Health, Popular Appeal," *The Patriot* Sep 28, 1996, http://proxy.foley.gonzaga.edu:2048/login?url=http://proquest.umi.com/pqdweb?did=33912049&Fmt=7&clientId=10553&RQT=309&VName=PQD.
82. Thomas C. Reeves, "Not so Christian America," *First Things*, no. 66 (10/01, 1996), 16-21, http://search.ebscohost.com/login.aspx?direct=true&db=rfh&AN=ATLA0001010881&site=ehost-live.
83. Jones, *The Jerusalem Bible*, Matt. 13:30.
84. Ibid., Rev. 1:8.
85. John W. O'Malley, *The First Jesuits* (Cambridge, Mass: Harvard University Press, 1993), 23.
86. Ibid., 23.
87. James Bowen, *A History of Western Education* (London: Methuen, 1972-1981), 25.
88. Pope Paul VI, "Papal Statement to the Society of Jesus," Society of Jesus, http://www.jesuit.org/index.php/sidebar/one-mission-many-ministries/serving-christ-and-the-pope/pope-speaks-to-congregation/ (accessed 12/31, 2010).
89. Jones, *The Jerusalem Bible*, Rom. 1.
90. Ibid., Ps. 8.
91. Ibid., Gen. 1:26-27.
92. Hopkins and Gardner, *Poems and Prose of Gerard Manley Hopkins*, 44-5.
93. Jones, *The Jerusalem Bible*, Ps. 8:4-5.
94. *Francis, Prayer of St.*, 538-539.
95. Jones, *The Jerusalem Bible*, Eph. 6:11-17.
96. Ibid., 2 Cor. 12:10.
97. Ibid., 1 John 1.

98. Ibid., John 20:29.
99. Ibid., John 6:40.
100. Ibid., John 11:25.
101. Ibid., John 14:2.
102. Ibid., 2 Tim. 2:11-12.
103. Ibid., Phil. 3:20.
104. Augustine and others, *The Confessions*, Book 1, Ch. 1, Lines 10-12.
105. Jones, *The Jerusalem Bible,* John 6:63.
106. Ibid., Gen. 1.
107. Ibid., Gen. 1:27.
108. Ibid., 1 John 3:2.
109. Ibid., Rev. 21:5.
110. Ibid., Rev. 21:1.
111. Ibid., 1 Cor. 15:51.
112. Ibid., 1 Cor. 2:9.

Bibliography

Action for Children's Television v. FCC, No. 93-1092, No. 93-1100 F.3d, 11, 170 (UNITED STATES COURT OF APPEALS FOR THE DISTRICT OF COLUMBIA CIRCUIT).

Action for Children's Television v. FCC, No. 88-1916 F.2d, 932, 1504 (UNITED STATES COURT OF APPEALS FOR THE DISTRICT OF COLUMBIA CIRCUIT).

Adams, John. "John Adams' Inaugural Address." *John Adam's Inaugural Address* (01/04, 2009): 1, http://search.ebscohost.com/login.aspx?direct=true&db=a9h&AN=21212438& site=ehost-live (accessed 12/13/2010).

Adams, John, Abigail Adams, and Charles Francis Adams. *Familiar Letters of John Adams and His Wife Abigail Adams, during the Revolution: With a Memoir of Mrs. Adams*. New York: Hurd and Houghton, 1876.

Ahmad, Bashiruddin Mahmud. *The Holy Quran: With English Translation and Commentary. Uniform Title: Tafsir-i Kabir. English*. Tilford, Surrey, U.K: Islam International Publications, 1988.

Anderson, Vinton R., Bp. "We Hold these Truths: A Statement of Christian Conscience and Citizenship." *First Things* no. 76 (10/01, 1997): 51-54, http://search.ebscohost.com.proxy.foley.gonzaga.edu:2048/login.aspx?direct=true&db=rfh& AN=ATLA0001004834&site=ehost-live (accessed 8/21/2010).

Anonymous. *Letter to the Author*, Edited by Fr. Bernard J. Coughlin, S.J., 1992.

Anselm, Saint, Archbishop of Canterbury and Thomas Williams. *Three Philosophical Dialogues*. Indianapolis, IN: Hackett Pub, 2002.

Ap. "Warnings for Cigarettes Go into Effect." *The New York Times,* October 13, 1985.

Aristotle and Hugh Lawson-Tancred. *Metaphysics*. Penguin Classics. London; New York: Penguin Books, 1998.

Aristotle and Martin Ostwald. *Nicomachean Ethics*. Library of Liberal Arts; 75. Indianapolis Ind: Bobbs-Merrill, 1962.

Aristotle and C. D. C. Reeve. *Politics*. Indianapolis, Ind: Hackett Pub, 1998.

Aristotle and W. Rhys Roberts. *Rhetoric*. Dover thrift eds ed. Mineola, NY: Dover Publications, 2004, http://catdir.loc.gov/catdir/enhancements/fy0618/2004052176-d.html.

Aristotle and J. E. C. Welldon. *The Politics of Aristotle*. London: Macmillan and Co, 1883.

Arkes, Hadley. "Abortion and Moral Reasoning." *Human Life Review* (Winter 1987).

Armario, Christine and Dorie Turner. "Nearly 1 in 4 Fails Army Entrance Test." *Journal - Gazette,* Dec 22, 2010, http://proxy.foley.gonzaga.edu:2048/login?url=http://pro-quest.umi.com/pqdweb?did=2219989841&Fmt=7&clientId=10553&RQT=309& VName=PQD.

Augustine, Saint,Bishop of Hippo, E. B. Pusey, Marcus Dods, and J. J. Shaw. *The Confessions*. Great Books of the Western World, v. 18. Chicago: Encyclopaedia Britannica, 1955.

Baer, Richard A. and Richard John Neuhaus. *Democracy and the Renewal of Public Education: Essays*. Encounter Series; 4; Variation: Encounter Series (Grand Rapids, Mich.); 4. Grand Rapids, Mich: W.B. Eerdmans Pub. Co, 1987.

Barfield, Owen. "Language, Evolution of Consciousness, and the Recovery of Human Meaning." *Teachers College Record* 82, no. 3 (03/01, 1981): 427-33, http://search.ebscohost.com/login.aspx?direct=true&db=eric&AN=EJ246370&site=ehost-live (accessed 12/10/2010).

Barth, Karl, Geoffrey William Bromiley, and Thomas F. Torrance. *Church Dogmatics*. 1st pbk. ed. London; New York: T. & T. Clark International, 2004.

Barton, Blanche and Anton Szandor La Vey. *The Secret Life of a Satanist: The Authorized Biography of Anton LaVey*. Los Angeles, CA: Feral House, 1992, http://catdir.loc.gov/catdir/toc/fy0903/98169959.html.

Bellah, Robert N. "The Church in Tension with a Lockean Culture." *New Oxford Review* 57, no. 10 (December 1990, 1990): 10-16.

Bennett, William J. "Quantifying America's Decline." *Wall Street Journal,* Mar 15, 1993, http://proxy.foley.gonzaga.edu:2048/login?url=http://proquest.umi.com/pqdweb?did=4321929&Fmt=7&clientId=10553&RQT=309&VName=PQD.

Bennett, William J. and of Education Department. *American Education: Making it Work. A Report to the President and the American People* 1988, http://search.ebscohost.com/login.aspx?direct=true&db=eric&AN=ED289959&site=ehost-live (accessed 1/14/2011).

Berger, Peter. "Religion in a Revolutionary Society." Christ Church, Alexandria, Virginia, American Enterprise Institute for Public Policy Research, 4 Feb 1974, 1974.

Beveridge, William Henry Beveridge, Baron. *Voluntary Action; a Report on Methods of Social Advance*. New York: Macmillan Co: 1948.

Bill of Rights, (1789): , http://www.archives.gov/exhibits/charters/bill_of_rights.html (accessed 28 Dec 2010).

Bishop, John and State Univ of New York, Ithaca School of Industrial and Labor Relations at Cornell Univ. *Is the Test Score Decline Responsible for the Productivity Growth Decline? Working Paper no. 87-05,* 1987, http://search.ebscohost.com/login.aspx?direct=true&db=eric&AN=ED299282&site=ehost-live (accessed 1/15/2011).

Bloom, Allan David. *The Closing of the American Mind*. 1st Touchstone ed. New York: Simon and Schuster, 1988.

Blumenfeld, Samuel L. *Is Public Education Necessary?*. Old Greenwich, Conn: Devin-Adair Co, 1981.

Board of Education v. Allen, No. 660 U.S., 392, 236 (SUPREME COURT OF THE UNITED STATES).

Boaz, David. "Libertarianism." *The Free Press* (1997).

Bohlen, Celestine. "Pope Passes Twin Tests of Health, Popular Appeal." *The Patriot,* Sep 28, 1996, http://proxy.foley.gonzaga.edu:2048/login?url=http://proquest.umi.com/pqdweb?did=33912049&Fmt=7&clientId=10553&RQT=309&VName=PQD.

Bok, Derek. "On the Purposes of Undergraduate Education." *Daedalus* 103, no. 4, American Higher Education: Toward an Uncertain Future, Volume I (Fall, 1974): pp. 159-172, http://www.jstor.org/stable/20024257.

Bork, Robert H. "Hard Truths about the Culture War." *First Things* no. 54 (06/01, 1995): 18-23, http://search.ebscohost.com/login.aspx?direct=true&db=rfh&AN=ATLA0000901089&site=ehost-live (accessed 12/13/2010).

Bottum, Joseph. "Facing Up to Infanticide." *First Things* no. 60 (02/01, 1996): 41-44, http://search.ebscohost.com/login.aspx?direct=true&db=rfh&AN=ATLA0001008636&site=ehost-live (accessed 8/21/2010).

Bowen, James. *A History of Western Education*. London: Methuen, 1972-1981.

Boyce, Mary. *Textual Sources for the Study of Zoroastrianism*. Variation: Textual Sources for the Study of Religion. Chicago: University of Chicago Press, 1990, http://catdir.loc.gov/catdir/enhancements/fy0609/90044072-b.html.

Boyer, Ernest L. and Arthur Levine. *Common Learning: A Carnegie Colloquium on General Education*. Washington, DC: Carnegie Foundation for the Advancement of Teaching, 1981.

Briggs, David. "Religion's Fading Role Leaves Many Adrift Morality: Increased Separation of Church and State has Silenced the `voice of Conscience' for Many, but some Groups Vow to Continue Battle Against the Nation's Social Ills." *Los Angeles Times (Pre-1997 Fulltext),* Jan 5, 1991, http://proxy.foley.gonzaga.edu:2048/login?url=http://proquest.umi.com/pqdweb?did=60991105&Fmt=7&clientId=10553&RQT=309&VName=PQD (accessed 9/11/2010).

Brookes, Warren T. "Public Education and the Global Failure of Socialism." *Imprimis* 19, no. 4 (April 1990, 1990), http://www.hillsdale.edu/news/imprimis/archive/issue.asp?year=1990&month=04 (accessed 15 Jan 2011).

Bryk, Anthony S. *Catholic Schools and the Common Good.* Cambridge: Harvard Univ Press, 1995.

Buckley, Madeline. "Protesters Line Entrance to Campus." *The Observer: The Independent Newspaper Serving Notre Dame and Saint Mary's,* 17 May 2009, 2009, sec. News, http://www.ndsmcobserver.com/2.2754/protesters-line-entrance-to-campus-1.254833 (accessed 28 Dec 2010).

Burke, Edmund and J. C. D. Clark. *Reflections on the Revolution in France.* Stanford, Calif: Stanford University Press, 2001, http://www.loc.gov/catdir/description/cam021/00063732.html.

Burnett, Victoria. "Jesuit Killings in El Salvador could Reach Trial in Spain." *The New York Times,* November 14, 2008, sec. A; Foreign Desk.

Butler, Ruth. *Rodin: The Shape of Genius.* New Haven: Yale University Press, 1993.

Byfield, T., Ross Amy, Society to Explore and Record Christian History, and Christian History Project. *A Glorious Disaster: A.D. 1100 to 1300: The Crusades: Blood, Valor, Iniquity, Reason, Faith.* The Christians: Their First Two Thousand Years; 7th v.; Variation: Christians, their First Two Thousand Years; 7. Edmonton: SEARCH, the Society to Explore and Record Christian History, 2008.

Calhoun, John C. and Hunter, R. M. T. "Life of John C. Calhoun Presenting a Condensed History of Political Events from 1811 to 1843." Harper & Brothers. http://www.gale.com/ModernLaw/; http://www.gale.com/ModernLaw/.

Calvin, Jean. *Commentaries on the Four Last Books of Moses: Arranged in the Form of a Harmony.* Calvin Translation Society. Edinburgh: Printed for the Calvin Translation Society, 1852-1855.

Camus, Albert. *The Rebel: An Essay on Man in Revolt.* New York: Knopf, 1956.

Carter, Stephen L. *The Culture of Disbelief: How American Law and Politics Trivialize Religious Devotion.* New York, NY: Basic Books, 1993.

Carus, Paul. *The History of the Devil and the Idea of Evil: From the Earliest Times to the Present Day.* New York: Land's End Press, 1969.

Chesterton, G. K. *Orthodoxy.* San Francisco: Ignatius, 1995.

Childs, John L. b. 1889. *Education and Morals; an Experimentalist Philosophy of Education.* American Education: Its Men, Ideas, and Institutions. Series II. New York: Arno Press, 1971.

Chubb, John. "Why the Current Wave of School Reform Will Fail." *Public Interest* no. 90 (Winter, 1988): 28, http://proxy.foley.gonzaga.edu:2048/login?url=http://proquest.umi.com/pqdweb?did=1439702&Fmt=7&clientId=10553&RQT=309&VName=PQD.

Cicero, Marcus Tullius, Marcus Tullius Cicero, De natura deorum, English, Marcus Tullius Cicero, De republica, English, and Charles Duke Yonge. *Tusculan Disputations: On the Nature of Gods, and the Commonwealth.* New York: Cosimo Classics, 2005.

Cochran v. Louisiana State Bd. of Education, No. 468 U.S., 281, 370 (SUPREME COURT OF THE UNITED STATES).

Coleman, James Samuel and Public and private schools. *Coleman Report on Public and Private Schools: The Draft Summary and Eight Critiques.* ERS School Research Forum; Variation: ERS School Research Forum. Arlington, Va: Educational Research Service, 1981.

Congdon, Lee. "Culture War." *Virginia Viewpoint* 2005-5, (September 2005, 2005), http://www.virginiainstitute.org/viewpoint/2005_09_5.html (accessed 14 January 2011).

Connell, Francis J. *The New Confraternity Edition, Revised Baltimore.* The text of the official rev. ed., 1949, with summarizations of doctrine and study helps, by Rev. Francis J. Connell ed. New York: Benziger Bros, 1949.

Corwin, Edward Samuel. *The "Higher Law" Background of American Constitutional Law.* Ithaca, N.Y: Great Seal Books, Div. of Cornell University Press, 1929.

Coughlin, Bernard J., S.J. "Commencement Address." Spokane, Washington.

———. *Report of the President.* Spokane, Washington: Gonzaga University, 1991-1992.

Crusius, Timothy W. and Carolyn E. Channell. *The Aims of Argument: A Rhetoric and Reader.* 2nd ed. Mountain View, Calif: Mayfield Pub. Co, 1998.

Curry, Dean C. "Written on the Heart: The Case for Natural Law." First Things no. 77 (11/01, 1997): 56-59, http://search.ebscohost.com.proxy.foley.gonzaga.edu:2048/login.aspx?direct= true&db=rfh&AN=ATLA0000335890&site=ehost-live (accessed 8/21/2010).

Dahrendorf, Ralf. *Essays in the Theory of Society.* Stanford: Calif, Stanford University Press, 1968.

Daniel-Rops, Henri. *Israel and the Ancient World: A History of the Israelites from the Time of Abraham to the Birth of Christ.* Garden City, NY: Image Books, 1964.

Davis, Leo Donald. *The First Seven Ecumenical Councils (325-787): Their History and Theology.* Theology and Life Series; 21; Variation: Theology and Life Series; v. 21. Collegeville, Minn: Liturgical Press, 1990.

"The Declaration of Independence." *Essential Documents: Declaration of Independence* (01/ 03, 2009): 1, http://search.ebscohost.com/login.aspx?direct=true&db=a9h&AN=21213404 &site=ehost-live (accessed 12/13/2010).

Dostoyevsky, Fyodor, Richard Pevear, and Larissa Volokhonsky. *The Brothers Karamazov: A Novel in Four Parts with Epilogue.* New York: Farrar, Straus and Giroux, 2002, http:// www.loc.gov/catdir/bios/hol051/2002022757.html.

Dulles, Avery. *The Prophetic Humanism of John Paul II.* McGinley Lecture Series; September 28, 1993. New York: Fordham University, 1994.

Eastland, Terry. *Religious Liberty in the Supreme Court: The Cases that Define the Debate Over Church and State.* Washington, DC: Ethics and Public Policy Center, 1993.

Eaton, William. *Who Killed the Constitution?: The Judges v. the Law.* Washington, D.C; New York, NY: Regnery Gateway; Distributed by Kampmann, 1988.

Ericson, Edward E. and Aleksander Isaevich. *Solzhenitsyn, the Moral Vision.* Grand Rapids, Mich: Eerdmans, 1982.

Etzioni, Amitai and Chamber of Commerce of the United States, Washington, DC National, Chamber Foundation. *Self-Discipline, Schools, and the Business Community,* 1984, http:// search.ebscohost.com/login.aspx?direct=true&db=eric&AN=ED249335&site=ehost-live (accessed 1/15/2011).

Evans, M. Stanton. *The Theme is Freedom: Religion, Politics, and the American Tradition.* Washington, DC; Lanham, MD: Regnery Pub; Distributed to the trade by National Book Network, 1994.

Everett, Carol and Jack Shaw. *Blood Money.* Sisters, OR: Multnomah, 1992.

Everson v. Bd. of Educ., No. 52 (SUPREME COURT OF THE UNITED STATES).

Faulkner, Raymond O., James Wasserman, Ogden Goelet, and Eva Von Dassow. *The Egyptian Book of the Dead: The Book of Going Forth by Day: Being the Papyrus of Ani (Royal Scribe of the Divine Offerings), Written and Illustrated Circa 1250 B.C.E., by Scribes and Artists Unknown, Including the Balance of Chapters of the Books of the Dead Known as the Theban Recension, Compiled from Ancient Texts, Dating Back to the Roots of Egyptian Civilization.* 2nd rev. ed. San Francisco: Chronicle Books, 2008.

Finn Jr., Chester E. "The Choice Backlash." *National Review* 41, no. 21 (11/10, 1989): 30-32, http://search.ebscohost.com/login.aspx?direct=true&db=a9h&AN=8911130305& site=ehost-live (accessed 1/14/2011).

"Five U.S. Supreme Court Justices just had their Say on Abortion. Now it's Your Turn. (Advertisement)." *Plain Dealer,* July 12, 1989.

Fluehr-Lobban, Carolyn. "Cultural Relativism and Universal Rights." *The Chronicle of Higher Education* 41, no. 39 (Jun 9, 1995): B1, http://proxy.foley.gonzaga.edu:2048/login?url=http: //proquest.umi.com/pqdweb?did=6659629&Fmt=7&clientId=10553&RQT=309& VName=PQD.

Foucault, Michel. *The Order of Things: An Archaeology of the Human Sciences.* Routledge Classics. London; New York: Routledge, 2002.

"Francis, Prayer of St." In *The HarperCollins Encyclopedia of Catholicism*, edited by Richard P. McBrien and Harold W. Attridge. 1st ed., 538-539. New York: HarperCollins, 1995.

Francisco, MELINDA BECK with TESSA NAMUTH in New York, MARK MILLER in Washington, LYNDA WRIGHT in San and Bureau Reports. 'A Nation Still at Risk'. *Newsweek*, May 2, 1988. 54.

Gardner, David P., National Commission on Excellence, in Education and Others. *A Nation at Risk: The Imperative for Educational Reform. an Open Letter to the American People. A Report to the Nation and the Secretary of Education*, 1983, http://search.ebscohost.com/ login.aspx?direct=true&db=eric&AN=ED226006&site=ehost-live (accessed 1/14/2011).

Gay, Peter. *The Enlightenment: An Interpretation.* New York: Norton, 1995.

George, Robert P. *The Clash of Orthodoxies: Law, Religion, and Morality in Crisis.* Wilmington, Del: ISI Books, 2001.

George, Robert P. "God and Gettysburg." *First Things: A Monthly Journal of Religion & Public Life* no. 205 (Aug, 2010): 15-17, http://search.ebscohost.com/login.aspx?direct= true&db=a9h&AN=52092771&site=ehost-live (accessed 12/27/2010).

Giannella, Donald A. *Religion and the Public Order: Number Five: An Annual Review of Church and State, and of Religion, Law and Society.* Ithica, NY: Cornell Univ, 1969.

———. *Religion and the Public Order. Number Four.* Ithaca, NY: Cornell University Press, 1968.

Gilson, Etienne. *The Spirit of Thomism.* A Wisdom and Discovery Book. New York: P.J. Kenedy, 1964.

Goldthwait, John. Philosophy Professor at State University of New York.

Gouldner, Alvin Ward. *The Future of Intellectuals and the Rise of the New Class: A Frame of Reference, Theses, Conjectures, Arguments, and an Historical Perspective on the Role of Intellectuals and Intelligentsia in the International Class Contest of the Modern Era.* His the Dark Side of the Dialectic; v. 2; A Galaxy Book; Variation: Gouldner, Alvin Ward; 1920-; Dark Side of the Dialectic; v. 2. New York: Oxford University Press, 1982.

Gove, Philip Babcock and Inc. Merriam-Webster. *Webster's Third New International Dictionary of the English Language, Unabridged.* Springfield, Mass: Merriam-Webster, 1993.

Graham, Billy. *A Biblical Standard for Evangelists.* Minneapolis, MN: World Wide Publications, 1984.

Graham, By Ellen. "Children — Coping with Change: 'Values' Lessons Return to the Classroom — Educators Say Kids Today are 'Rudderless'." *Wall Street Journal*, Sep 26, 1988, http://proxy.foley.gonzaga.edu:2048/login?url=http://proquest.umi.com/ pqdweb?did=27392891&Fmt=7&clientId=10553&RQT=309&VName=PQD.

Grossman, Ron. "Firing of Teacher for Flunking Students Offers a Lesson to American Teachers." *Chicago Tribune*, 2 Aug 1993.

Havel, Vaclav. "The Need for Transcendence in the Postmodern World." Independence Hall, Philadelphia, PA, Global MindShift, 4 July 1994, 1994, http://www.global-mindshift.com/ discover/Memebase/TheNeedforTranscendenceinthePostmodernWorld.pdf (accessed 19 Dec 2010).

Heilbroner, Robert L. *The Limits of American Capitalism.* 1st ed. New York: Harper & Row, 1966.

Heller, Scott. "'Radical Critique' Says Reform of Higher Education is Timid and Narrow." *The Chronicle of Higher Educationi* 34, no. 11 (11 Nov 1987, 1987): A13-A21.

Herberg, Will. "What is the Moral Crisis of our Time?" *Intercollegiate Review* 4, no. 2-3 (1968): 63-69.

Hodge, Archibald Alexander, Presbyterian Church in the U.S.A, and Board of Publication. *Popular Lectures on Theological Themes.* Philadelphia: Presbyterian board of publication, 1887.

Holmes, Oliver Wendell. "The Path of the Law." *Harvard Law Review* 10, no. 8 (Mar. 25, 1897): pp. 457-478, http://www.jstor.org.proxy.foley.gonzaga.edu/stable/1322028.

Hopkins, Gerard Manley. *Poems of Gerard Manley Hopkins.* Nevada City, Calif: H. Berliner, 1986.

Hopkins, Gerard Manley and W. H. Gardner. *Poems and Prose of Gerard Manley Hopkins.* Penguin Classics. Harmondworth, Middlesex, England; New York, NY: Penguin Books, 1985.

Howe, Mark De Wolfe and Frank L. Weil Institute for Studies in Religion and the Humanities. *The Garden and the Wilderness; Religion and Government in American Constitutional History.* Chicago: University of Chicago Press, 1965.

HRH The Prince of Wales. "An Address by HRH the Prince of Wales Tercentenary Celebrations of the College of William and Mary, Williamsburg, Virginia USA." Williamsburg, Virginia, 13 Feb 1993, 1993 (accessed 13 Dec 2010).

"Humanist Manifesto I." American Humanist Association. http://www.americanhumanist.org/Who_We_Are/About_Humanism/Humanist_Manifesto_I (accessed 12/10, 2010).

"Humanist Manifesto II." American Humanist Association. http://www.americanhumanist.org/Who_We_Are/About_Humanism/Humanist_Manifesto_II (accessed 12/10, 2010).

Ignatius, of Loyola, Saint and Louis J. Puhl. *The Spiritual Exercises of St. Ignatius: Based on Studies in the Language of the Autograph.* Vintage Spiritual Classics. 1st ed. New York: Vintage Books, 2000, http://catdir.loc.gov/catdir/bios/random052/00034948.html.

Illinois ex rel. McCollum v. Bd. of Educ., No. 90 (SUPREME COURT OF THE UNITED STATES).

Ioannes Paulus PP. II. . *Address of His Holiness Pope John Paul II to H.E. Mrs. Corinne (Lindy) Claiborne Boggs, New Ambassador of the United States of America to the Holy See .* The Vatican, Rome, Italy: Libreria Editrice Vaticana, 1997, http://www.vatican.va/holy_father/john_paul_ii/speeches/1997/december/documents/hf_jp-ii_spe_19971216_ambassador-usa_en.html (accessed 27 Dec 2010).

———. *Evangelium Vitae.* The Vatican, Rome, Italy: Libreria Editrice Vaticana, 1995, http://www.vatican.va/holy_father/john_paul_ii/encyclicals/documents/hf_jp-ii_enc_25031995_evangelium-vitae_en.html (accessed 28 Dec 2010).

———. *Redemptoris Missio: On the Permanent Validity of the Church's Missionary Mandate.* The Vatican, Rome, Italy: Libreria Editrice Vaticana, 1990, http://www.vatican.va/holy_father/john_paul_ii/encyclicals/documents/hf_jp-ii_enc_07121990_redemptoris-missio_en.html (accessed 19 Dec 2010).

———. *Veritatis Splendor.* The Vatican, Rome, Italy: Libreria Editrice Vaticana, 1993, http://www.vatican.va/holy_father/john_paul_ii/encyclicals/documents/hf_jp-ii_enc_06081993_veritatis-splendor_en.html (accessed 19 Dec 2010).

Jameson, Frederic. "Marxism and Teaching." *New Political Science* 1, no. 2/3 (1979/1980): 31-36.

Jefferson, Thomas and Eric S. Petersen. *Light and Liberty: Reflections on the Pursuit of Happiness.* Modern Library ed. New York: Modern Library, 2004, http://catdir.loc.gov/catdir/toc/fy0606/2003044283.html.

Jefferson, Thomas and Merrill D. Peterson. *The Political Writings of Thomas Jefferson.* Monticello Monograph Series. Charlottesville, VA: Thomas Jefferson Memorial Foundation, 1993, http://catdir.loc.gov/catdir/description/unc041/94112063.html.

Jencks, Christopher. *Inequality; a Reassessment of the Effect of Family and Schooling in America.* New York: Basic Books, 1972.

John Paul II, Pope and Joseph Durepos. *Go in Peace: A Gift of Enduring Love.* Chicago, Ill: Loyola Press, 2003.

John Paul II, Pope and Vittorio Messori. *Crossing the Threshold of Hope.* New York: Knopf, 1995.

Jones, Alexander. *The Jerusalem Bible;* London: Darton, Longman & Todd, 1966.

Josephson, Michael S. and Wes Hanson. *The Power of Character: Prominent Americans Talk about Life, Family, Work, Values, and More.* 2nd ed. Bloomington, Ind; Los Angeles: Unlimited Pub; Josephson Institute of Ethics, 2004.

Jugoslavia; the Virgin and the Commissars. *The Economist,* September 12, 1981. 60 (U.S. Edition Pg. 50).

Kagan, D. "An Address to the Class of 1994." *Commentary* 91, no. 1 (01, 1991): 47, http://search.ebscohost.com/login.aspx?direct=true&db=a9h&AN=9104221850&site=ehost-live (accessed 12/13/2010).

Kammeyer, Kenneth C. W. *Marriage and Family: A Foundation for Personal Decisions.* Boston: Allyn and Bacon, 1987.

Kane, Jeffrey. *In Fear of Freedom: Public Education and Democracy in America.* Proceedings / Myrin Institute; no. 38; Variation: Proceedings (Myrin Institute); no. 38. New York, NY: Myrin Institute, 1984.

Kauper, Schempp, and Sherbert. "Studies in Neutrality and Accommodation." *Religion and the Public Order* 3, no. 14 (1963).

Kaylin, Jennifer. Bass, Yale, and Western Civ. *Yale Alumni Magazine,* Summer 1995, 1995. , http://www.yalealumnimagazine.com/issues/95_07/bass.html (accessed 13 Dec 2010).

Keats, John and Horace Elisha Scudder. *The Complete Poetical Works and Letters of John Keats.* The Cambridge Poets; Variation: Cambridge Edition of the Poets. Cambridge ed. Boston: New York, Houghton, Mifflin and Company, 1899, http://hdl.loc.gov/loc.gdc/scd0001.00088105011.

Kevorkian v. Thompson, No. 96-CV-73777-DT F. Supp., 947, 1152 (UNITED STATES DISTRICT COURT FOR THE EASTERN DISTRICT OF MICHIGAN, SOUTHERN DIVISION).

Kidder, Rushworth M. "Tuition Vouchers: Should Parents Set School Policy?" *Christian Science Monitor (Boston, MA),* April 8, 1985.

Kimball, Roger. "'Heterotextuality' and Other Literary Matters." *Wall Street Journal,* Dec 31, 1992, http://proxy.foley.gonzaga.edu:2048/login?url=http://proquest.umi.com/pqdweb?did=4314261&Fmt=7&clientId=10553&RQT=309&VName=PQD.

King, Martin Luther, Jr. and Jesse Jackson. *Why we can't Wait.* New York: Signet Classic, 2000.

Knox, Ronald Arbuthnott. *Enthusiasm.* A Galaxy Book, GB59. New York, Oxford University Press: 1961.

Koring, Paul. "100,000 in Prague Demand Reform." *The Globe and Mail (Canada),* November 21, 1989.

Kristol, Irving. *Neoconservatism: The Autobiography of an Idea.* New York: Free Press, 1995.

Lannie, Vincent P. *Public Money and Parochial Education; Bishop Hughes, Governor Seward, and the New York School Controversy.* Cleveland: Press of Case Western Reserve University, 1968.

Lemon v. Kurtzman, No. 71-1470 U.S., 411, 192 (SUPREME COURT OF THE UNITED STATES).

Levering, Matthew. *On Marriage and Family: Classic and Contemporary Texts.* Lanham, MD: Rowman & Littlefield, 2005, http://catdir.loc.gov/catdir/toc/ecip051/2004023041.html.

Lincoln, Abraham and Joseph R. Fornieri. *The Language of Liberty: The Political Speeches and Writings of Abraham Lincoln.* Rev. bicentennial ed. Washington, DC: Regnery Pub, 2009.

Little, Joyce A. "Naming Good and Evil." *First Things* no. 23 (05/01, 1992): 23-30, http://search.ebscohost.com/login.aspx?direct=true&db=rfh&AN=ATLA0000851033&site=ehost-live (accessed 12/20/2010).

Mann, Horace and Edward A. Newton. *The Common School Controversy: Consisting of Three Letters of the Secretary of the Board of Education of the State of Massachusetts, in Reply to Charges Preferred Against the Board by the Editor of the Christian Witness and by Edward A. Newton, Esq., of Pittsfield, Once a Member of the Board; to which are Added Extracts from the Daily Press, in Regard to the Controversy.* Boston: J.N. Bradley, 1844.

Maritain, Jacques. *Existence and the Existent.* Westport, Conn: Greenwood Press, 1975.

Maritain, Jacques, Donald Arthur Gallagher, and Idella J. Gallagher. *A Maritain Reader: Selected Writings.* 1st ed. ed. Garden City, NY: Image Books, 1966.

Marsden, George M. *The Soul of the American University: From Protestant Establishment to Established Nonbelief.* New York: Oxford University Press, 1994, http://www.loc.gov/catdir/enhancements/fy0639/93025486-d.html.

Martin, Lynn, Deloitte, Lynn Martin , who was Secretary of Labor in the Bush Administration, advises the accounting firm, and Touche on women's issues. "For Children Who have Children." *The New York Times,* September 8, 1993.

Marx, Karl, Friedrich Engels, Selections, English, and 1972. *Critique of the Gotha Programme. Uniform Title: Randglossen Zum Programm Der Deutschen Arbeiterpartei. English.* 1st ed. ed. Peking: Foreign Languages Press, 1972.

Maugham, W. Somerset. *Mr. Maugham Himself.* Garden City, NY: Doubleday, 1954.

Mayflower Compact, 1620, http://avalon.law.yale.edu/17th_century/mayflower.asp (accessed 20 Dec 2010).

McGowan v. Maryland, No. 8 (SUPREME COURT OF THE UNITED STATES).

Medved, Michael. *Hollywood Vs. America: Popular Culture and the War on Traditional Values.* 1st ed. New York, NY; Grand Rapids, Mich: HarperCollins; Zondervan, 1992.

Miller, Henry, Frank L. Kersnowski, and Alice Hughes. *Conversations with Henry Miller.* Literary Conversations Series. Jackson: University Press of Mississippi, 1994.

Moberly, W. H. Sir, b.1881. *The Crisis in the University.* London: SCM Press, 1949.

Moss, Robert. "Anglocommunism?" *Commentary* February, (1977).

Muggeridge, Malcolm. *Confessions of a Twentieth-Century Pilgrim.* 1st U.S. ed. San Francisco: Harper & Row, 1988.

Muncy, Mitchell S., Richard John Neuhaus, and Anatomy of a controversy. *The End of Democracy?: The Celebrated First Things Debate, with Arguments Pro and Con: And, the Anatomy of a Controversy, by Richard John Neuhaus.* Dallas: Spence Pub. Co, 1997.

Murchison, William. "The Straight '90s." *Human Life Review* (Summer 1993, 1993): 15.

Murray, John Courtney. *We Hold these Truths; Catholic Reflections on the American Proposition.* New York: Sheed and Ward, 1960.

Nechaev, Sergei Gennadievich, Mikhail Aleksandrovich Bakunin, and Black Panther Party. *The Revolutionary Catechism.* Red Pamphlet; no. 1; Variation: Red Pamphlet; no. 1. United States: Black Panther Party, 1970-1979.

Neuhaus, Richard John. "Dignity, Death and Dependence." *The Religion and Society Report* 5, no. 8 (August 1988, 1988).

Neuhaus, Richard John. "The Innovationist Edge." *First Things* no. 27 (11/01, 1992): 64-66, http://search.ebscohost.com/login.aspx?direct=true&db=rfh&AN=ATLA0000856918& site=ehost-live.

———. *The Naked Public Square: Religion and Democracy in America.* Grand Rapids, Mich: W.B. Eerdmans Pub. Co, 1984.

———. "The Splendor of Truth: A Symposium." *First Things* no. 39 (01/01, 1994): 14-29, http://search.ebscohost.com/login.aspx?direct=true&db=rfh&AN=ATLA0000875901& site=ehost-live (accessed 9/11/2010).

Newport, Frank. . *Americans More Likely to Believe in God than the Devil , Heaven More than Hell; Belief in the Devil has Increased since 2000.* RELIGION AND SOCIAL TRENDS, 2007.

Nicolas, Marie-Joseph. *What is the Eucharist?.* Twentieth Century Encyclopedia of Catholicism,; 52. 1st ed. ed. New York: Hawthorn Books, 1960.

Niemeyer, Gerhart. "The Eternal Meaning of Solzhenitsyn." *National Review* 25, (19 January 1973, 1973): 83-86.

———. "The Recovery of 'the Sacred'?" *The Intercollegiate Review* 24, no. 2 (Spring 1989, 1989): 3-12.

Nietzsche, Friedrich Wilhelm and Walter Arnold Kaufmann. *The Gay Science; with a Prelude in Rhymes and an Appendix of Songs. Uniform Title: Fröhliche Wissenschaft. English.* 1st ed. ed. New York: Vintage Books, 1974, http://catdir.loc.gov/catdir/description/random045/73010479.html.

Nisbet, Robert A. *Twilight of Authority.* Indianapolis: Liberty Fund, 2000.

Novak, Michael. "Awakening from Nihilism: The Templeton Prize Address." *First Things* no. 45 (08/01, 1994): 18-22, http://search.ebscohost.com/login.aspx?direct=true&db=rfh& AN=ATLA0000881609&site=ehost-live (accessed 9/11/2010).

Obama, Barack. "Text of President Obama's Address to Graduates." *The Observer: The Independent Newspaper Serving Notre Dame and Saint Mary's,* 17 May 2009, 2009, sec. News, http://www.ndsmcobserver.com/2.2754/text-of-president-obama-s-address-to-graduates-1.254844 (accessed 28 Dec 2010).

O'Malley, John W. *The First Jesuits.* Cambridge, Mass: Harvard University Press, 1993.

"The Oregon Death with Dignity Act." *Issues in Law & Medicine* 11, no. 3 (Winter95, 1995): 333, http://search.ebscohost.com/login.aspx?direct=true&db=a9h&AN=9602261647&site= ehost-live (accessed 4/3/2011).

Patterson, James and Peter Kim. *The Day America Told the Truth: What People really Believe about Everything that really Matters.* New York, NY, U.S.A: Plume, 1992.

Patton, John M., Conway Robinson, and Virginia. *The Code of Virginia: With the Declaration of Independence and Constitution of the United States; and the Declaration of Rights and Constitution of Virginia.* Richmond: Printed by W.F. Ritchie, 1849.

Peck, M. Scott. *People of the Lie: The Hope for Healing Human Evil.* New York: Simon and Schuster, 1983.

Phenix, Philip Henry. *Education and the Common Good; a Moral Philosophy of the Curriculum.* 1st ed. ed. New York: Harper, 1961.

Pierce v. Soc'y of Sisters, Nos. 583, 584 U.S., 268, 510 (SUPREME COURT OF THE UNITED STATES).

Planned Parenthood v. Casey, No. 91-744 (SUPREME COURT OF THE UNITED STATES).

Plutarch and John Langhorne. *Plutarch's Lives.* Philadelphia: Crissy, 1828.

Pope Paul VI. "Papal Statement to the Society of Jesus." Society of Jesus. http:// www.jesuit.org/index.php/sidebar/one-mission-many-ministries/serving-christ-and-the-pope/pope-speaks-to-congregation/ (accessed 12/31, 2010).

Pope Pius XII. "Munificentissimus Deus: Defining the Dogma of the Assumption." (1 Nov 1950, 1950).

Popper, Karl Raimund, Sir. *The Open Society and its Enemies. V. 1, the Spell of Plato.* 5th ed., rev. ed. Princeton, NJ: Princeton University Press, 1966.

Reeves, Thomas C. "Not so Christian America." *First Things* no. 66 (10/01, 1996): 16-21, http://search.ebscohost.com/login.aspx?direct=true&db=rfh&AN=ATLA0001010881& site=ehost-live.

Reich, Bernard. *A Brief History of Israel.* 2nd ed. New York, NY: Facts On File/Checkmark Books, 2008, http://catdir.loc.gov/catdir/toc/ecip089/2008003838.html.

Rhee, Michelle. "What I've Learned. (Cover Story)." *Newsweek* 156, no. 24 (12/13, 2010): 36-41, http://search.ebscohost.com/login.aspx?direct=true&db=a9h&AN=55695685&site= ehost-live (accessed 1/13/2011).

Richards, Mary Caroline. *Toward Wholeness: Rudolf Steiner Education in America.* 1st ed. Middletown, Conn; Irvington, NY: Wesleyan University Press; distributed by Columbia University Press, 1980.

Riesman, David, Nathan Glazer, and Reuel Denney. *The Lonely Crowd: A Study of the Changing American Character.* Yale Nota Bene. Abridged and rev. ed. / with a foreword by Todd Gitlin ed. New Haven, CT: Yale University Press, 2001.

Rodkinson, Michael Levi, Isaac Mayer Wise, and Godfrey Taubenhaus. *New Edition of the Babylonian Talmud.* New York: New Talmud Pub. Co, 1896-1903.

Rodriguez, Junius P. *Slavery in the United States: A Social, Political, and Historical Encyclopedia.* Santa Barbara, Calif: ABC-CLIO, 2007, http://catdir.loc.gov/catdir/toc/ecip077/ 2006101351.html.

Roemer v. Bd. of Public Works, No. 74-730 U.S., 426, 736 (SUPREME COURT OF THE UNITED STATES).

Roof, Wade Clark and William McKinney. *American Mainline Religion: Its Changing Shape and Future.* New Brunswick, NJ: Rutgers University Press, 1987.

Roszak, Theodore. "On the Contemporary Hunger for Wonders." *Michigan Quarterly Review* XIX, no. 3 (1980): 303-321 (accessed 10 Dec 2010).

Schall, James V., S.J. "Intelligence and Academia." *International Journal of Social Economics* 15, no. 10 (1988): 63-71.

Sch. Dist. of Abington Twp. v. Schempp, No. 142 U.S., 374, 203 (SUPREME COURT OF THE UNITED STATES).

Seuffert, Virginia. "Home Remedy." *Policy Review* no. 52 (Spring90, 1990): 70, http://search.ebscohost.com/login.aspx?direct=true&db=a9h&AN=9608140357&site=ehost-live (accessed 9/30/2010).

Shakespeare, William. *Hamlet*. A Bantam Classic., edited by David M. Bevington. Toronto; New York: Bantam Books, 1988, http://www.loc.gov/catdir/bios/random051/87024096.html.

———. *Julius Caesar*. English Classics. NY: Harper, 1895.

Shakespeare, William and Nick De Somogyi. *Macbeth: The Tragedie of Macbeth*. The Shakespeare Folios; Variation: Shakespeare, William; 1564-1616.; Plays (Nick Hern Books). London: Nick Hern Books, 2003.

Simpson, George Gaylord. *The Meaning of Evolution: A Study of the History of Life and of its Significance for Man*. Yale Paperbound. Rev. ed. New Haven: Yale University Press, 1974.

Singer, Peter. *Practical Ethics*. 2nd ed. Cambridge; New York: Cambridge University Press, 1993, http://catdir.loc.gov/catdir/description/cam025/92023819.html.

———. *Rethinking Life and Death: The Collapse of our Traditional Ethics*. New York: St. Martin's Griffin, Projected Date: 1111, 1996, http://catdir.loc.gov/catdir/bios/hol056/96003653.html.

———. *Writings on an Ethical Life*. 1st ed. New York: Ecco Press, 2000.

Sisk, Gregory C. "The Moral Incompetence of the Judiciary." *First Things* no. 57 (11/01, 1995): 34-39, http://search.ebscohost.com.proxy.foley.gonzaga.edu:2048/login.aspx?direct=true&db=rfh&AN=ATLA0000902481&site=ehost-live (accessed 8/21/2010).

Smith, John and Edward Arber. *Works; 1608-1631*. The English Scholar's Library; no. 16. Birmingham: English Scholar's Library, 1884.

Solzhenitsyn, Aleksandr Isaevich. *Cancer Ward*. New York: Farrar, Straus and Giroux, 1969.

———. *Stories and Prose Poems*. London: Bodley Head, 1971.

———. *Warning to the West*. 1st ed. New York: Farrar, Straus and Giroux, 1976.

Sommers, Christina Hoff. "Ethics without Virtue: Moral Education in America." *American Scholar* 53, no. 3 (Summer84, 1984): 381, http://search.ebscohost.com/login.aspx?direct=true&db=a9h&AN=5317528&site=ehost-live (accessed 9/11/2010).

———. "Teaching the Virtues." *Public Interest* no. 111 (Spring93, 1993): 3-13, http://search.ebscohost.com/login.aspx?direct=true&db=a9h&AN=9306015516&site=ehost-live (accessed 9/11/2010).

Sommers, Christina Hoff and Frederic Tamler Sommers. *Vice & Virtue in Everyday Life: Introductory Readings in Ethics*. 5th ed. Fort Worth, TX: Harcourt College Publishers, 2000.

Sophocles, David Grene, and Richmond Alexander Lattimore. *Sophocles I*. The Complete Greek Tragedies / Edited by David Grene and Richmond Lattimore. Chicago: University of Chicago Press, 1954.

Spero, Arayeh. "Therefore Choose Life: How the Great Religions View abortion." *Policy Review* 48, (Spring 1989, 1989): 38-44.

The Spokesman Review, 14 June 1995, 1995.

State v. Cooper, [NO NUMBER IN ORIGINAL] N.J.L., 22, 52 (NEW JERSEY SUPREME COURT).

Stedman, Edmund Clarence, Ellen Mackay Hutchinson Cortissoz, Mrs., Joint, and Arthur Stedman. *A Library of American Literature from the Earliest Settlement to the Present Time*. New York: C.L. Webster, 1888.

Suenens, Léon Joseph. *Mary the Mother of God*. Twentieth Century Encyclopedia of Catholicism, v. 44. Section 4: The Means of Redemption; 44; Variation: Twentieth Century Encyclopedia of Catholicism; 44; Twentieth Century Encyclopedia of Catholicism.; Section 4; Means of Redemption. 1st American ed. ed. New York: Hawthorn Books, 1959.

Tancock, John L. and Rodin Museum. *The Sculpture of Auguste Rodin: The Collection of the Rodin Museum, Philadelphia*. Philadelphia: Philadelphia Museum of Art, 1976.

Teresa, Mother and Robert P. George. "Brief Amicus Curiae of Mother Teresa of Calcutta, in Support of Petitioners' Petitions for a Writ of Certiorari." *Human Life Review* 27, no. 2 (Spring2001, 2001): 97-100, http://search.ebscohost.com/login.aspx?direct=true&db=a9h& AN=14913945&site=ehost-live.

Thielicke, Helmut and John W. Doberstein. *Theological Ethics. Volume 3, Sex.* Variation: Thielicke, Helmut; Theological Ethics; v. 3. Grand Rapids, Mich: Eerdmans, 1979.

Thomas, Aquinas, Saint, Josef Pieper, and Drostan MacLaren. *The Human Wisdom of St. Thomas: A Breviary of Philosophy from the Works of St. Thomas Aquinas.* San Francisco: Ignatius Press, 2002.

Thomas, Cal. *Things that Matter most.* New York: Harperperennial, 1995.

Thomas v. Collins, No. 14 U.S., 323, 516 (SUPREME COURT OF THE UNITED STATES).

Tilton v. Richardson, No. 153 (SUPREME COURT OF THE UNITED STATES a).

Torcaso v. Watkins, No. 373 (SUPREME COURT OF THE UNITED STATES b).

Trace, Arther S. *Christianity and the Intellectuals.* 1st ed. La Salle, Ill: Sherwood Sugden, 1983.

United States Congress. "Congressional Record Containing the Proceedings and Debates of the 108th Congress, First Session." 149, pt. 20, (5 November 2003 to 11 November 2003, 2003), http://www.bibliothek.uni-regensburg.de/ezeit/?2139924.

United States. Congress. House. Committee on the Judiciary. Subcommittee on the Constitution. *Origins and Scope of Roe v. Wade: Hearing before the Subcommittee on the Constitution of the Committee on the Judiciary, House of Representatives, One Hundred Fourth Congress, Second Session, April 22, 1996.* Serial no. 80 (United States. Congress. House. Committee on the Judiciary) ed. Washington: U.S. G.P.O.: For sale by the U.S. G.P.O., Supt. of Docs., Congressional Sales Office, 1996.

United States v. Butler, No. 401 (SUPREME COURT OF THE UNITED STATES c).

United States v. Eichman, Nos. 89-1433, 89-1434 U.S., 496, 310 (SUPREME COURT OF THE UNITED STATES).

United States v. Macintosh, No. 504 U.S., 283, 605 (SUPREME COURT OF THE UNITED STATES).

Vatican Council II. . *Declaration on Religious Freedom* [Dignitatis Humanae]. The Vatican, Rome, Italy: Libreria Editrice Vaticana, 1965, http://www.vatican.va/archive/hist_councils/ ii_vatican_council/documents/vat-ii_decl_19651207_dignitatis-humanae_en.html (accessed 28 Dec 2010).

Vitz, Paul C. and New York Univ, NY Dept. of Psychology. *Religion and Traditional Values in Public School Textbooks: An Empirical Study*, 1985, http://search.ebscohost.com/lo-gin.aspx?direct=true&db=eric&AN=ED260019&site=ehost-live (accessed 1/14/2011).

von, der Heydt. "Russia's Spiritual Wilderness." *Policy Review* no. 70 (Fall94, 1994): 12, http:/ /search.ebscohost.com/login.aspx?direct=true&db=a9h&AN=9411046135&site=ehost-live (accessed 12/19/2010).

Wallace, Scott. "Six Salvador Jesuits Tortured and Killed: Gangland-Style Murders Recall Days of Death Squads." *The Guardian (London),* November 17, 1989.

Wasiolek, Edward. *Dostoevsky: The Major Fiction.* Cambridge: Mass, M.I.T. Press, 1964.

Whatever Happened to Ethics? *Time Magazine,* 25 May 1987, 1987. 14.

Wilkerson, Isabel. "AT HOME WITH: Ann Landers; She could Sign Herself 'Open-Minded in Chicago'." *The New York Times,* June 10, 1993.

Wills, Garry. *Head and Heart: American Christianities.* New York: Penguin Press, 2007, http:/ /catdir.loc.gov/catdir/toc/ecip0714/2007012631.html.

Wolf, Naomi. "Our Bodies, our Souls." *The New Republic* 213, no. 16 (Oct 16, 1995): 26, http:/ /proxy.foley.gonzaga.edu:2048/login?url=http://proquest.umi.com/pqdweb?did=7722286& Fmt=7&clientId=10553&RQT=309&VName=PQD.

Woodward, Kenneth L. and Andrew Murr. "Hail, Mary. (Cover Story)." *Newsweek* 130, no. 8 (08/25, 1997): 48, http://search.ebscohost.com/login.aspx?direct=true&db=a9h&AN= 9708210111&site=ehost-live.

Zieba, Maciej. "The Liberalism that we Need." *First Things* no. 40 (02/01, 1994): 23-27, http:// search.ebscohost.com/login.aspx?direct=true&db=rfh&AN=ATLA0000876080& site=ehost-live (accessed 9/11/2010).

Zitner, Aaron. "Many Look Back, Recall Satanism." *Boston Globe,* 16 Oct 1992, 1992.
Zorach v. Clauson, No. 431 U.S., 343, 306 (SUPREME COURT OF THE UNITED STATES).

Index